Cloud Security Automation

Get to grips with automating your cloud security on AWS
and OpenStack

Prashant Priyam

BIRMINGHAM - MUMBAI

Cloud Security Automation

Commissioning Editor: Gebin George
Acquisition Editor: Rohit Rajkumar
Content Development Editor: Nithin Varghese
Technical Editor: Khushbu Sutar
Copy Editors: Safis Editing, Laxmi Subramanian
Project Coordinator: Virginia Dias
Proofreader: Safis Editing
Indexer: Aishwarya Gangawane
Graphics: Tom Scaria
Production Coordinator: Shraddha Falebhai

First published: March 2018

Production reference: 1270318

Published by Packt Publishing Ltd.
Livery Place
35 Livery Street
Birmingham
B3 2PB, UK.

ISBN 978-1-78862-786-3

www.packtpub.com

`mapt.io`

Mapt is an online digital library that gives you full access to over 5,000 books and videos, as well as industry leading tools to help you plan your personal development and advance your career. For more information, please visit our website.

Why subscribe?

- Spend less time learning and more time coding with practical eBooks and Videos from over 4,000 industry professionals

- Improve your learning with Skill Plans built especially for you

- Get a free eBook or video every month

- Mapt is fully searchable

- Copy and paste, print, and bookmark content

PacktPub.com

Did you know that Packt offers eBook versions of every book published, with PDF and ePub files available? You can upgrade to the eBook version at `www.PacktPub.com` and as a print book customer, you are entitled to a discount on the eBook copy. Get in touch with us at `service@packtpub.com` for more details.

At `www.PacktPub.com`, you can also read a collection of free technical articles, sign up for a range of free newsletters, and receive exclusive discounts and offers on Packt books and eBooks.

Contributors

About the author

Prashant Priyam is an astute professional with a great deal of experience in cloud technologies, specifically requirement analysis, solution architecture, design, and delivery. He also has experience in cloud services and solutions, cloud consultancy and deployment, and data center services.

This book is dedicated to my mom, papa, and Prasun bhaiya, for their endless love and support. Thanks to Shivani, Gajanan, and my colleagues at Velocis for their comments, feedback, and support.

To all my friends, who always forced me to look beyond boundaries and go the extra mile.

About the reviewers

Fabio Alessandro Locati, commonly known as **Fale**—is the director of Otelia, a public speaker, author, and open source contributor. His main areas of expertise are Linux, automation, security, and cloud technologies. Fale has over 12 years, working experience in IT; many of those years were spent consulting for many companies, including dozens of Fortune 500 companies. This has allowed him to consider technologies from different points of view and to develop critical thinking about them.

Deep Mehta is currently working as a DevOps engineer in the San Francisco Bay Area. He is currently working with different clients to help them to improve their CI/CD and DevOps cycles. He helps them to follow the microservices pattern and create resilient and fault tolerant infrastructure. Deep is mainly interested in distributed systems, containers, data science, and the cloud. He also worked as a reviewer on the book, *Learning Continuous Integration with Jenkins*.

Packt is searching for authors like you

If you're interested in becoming an author for Packt, please visit authors.packtpub.com and apply today. We have worked with thousands of developers and tech professionals, just like you, to help them share their insight with the global tech community. You can make a general application, apply for a specific hot topic that we are recruiting an author for, or submit your own idea.

Table of Contents

Preface

Security is critical for organizations when they are planning to run, or are already running, their workload on the cloud. On the cloud, security also comes under the sharing responsibility model, where the cloud provider and cloud consumer have defined boundaries for their security responsibilities based on cloud services (IaaS, PaaS, or SaaS).

On a private cloud, one has to take complete responsibility for security, from physical components to the application itself.

In addition to security, organizations also have to meet compliance requirements if they are applicable.

Although there are different sets of security tools and services available on AWS, it's always the customers'/users' responsibility to use these tools and services effectively to ensure the security of their data and applications and to meet compliance requirements.

This book is a comprehensive learning guide to securing your cloud account's structure in AWS and the OpenStack environment. It also gives you insight on how DevOps processes can help you to automate the security processes.

Who this book is for

This book is targeted at DevOps engineers, security professionals, and any stakeholders responsible for securing cloud workloads. Prior experience with AWS or OpenStack will be an advantage.

What this book covers

Chapter 1, *Introduction to Cloud Security*, helps you understand cloud security models for the public cloud (AWS) and OpenStack at different levels for different services.

Chapter 2, *Understanding the World of Cloud Automation*, introduces the basics of automation, the automation process, tools and requirements, and the benefits of cloud automation.

Chapter 3, *Identity and Access Management in the Cloud*, gives you an in-depth understanding of IAM and other AWS services, such as Inspector, WAF, HSM, and Certificate Manager, in order to improve security.

Chapter 4, *Cloud Network Security*, talks about different components, such as NACL, security groups, and VPN, that help us to ensure the security of data in transit.

Chapter 5, *Cloud Storage and Data Security*, gives you an in-depth understanding of how to secure storage and data accessibility using data encryption and IAM roles and policies.

Chapter 6, *Cloud Platform Security*, discusses how to ensure security for PaaS services, such as database and analytics services.

Chapter 7, *Private Cloud Security*, explains how to secure your private cloud on the compute, network, and storage and application levels.

Chapter 8, *Automating Cloud Security*, helps you understand automation and the role of automation in securing cloud infrastructure.

Chapter 9, *Cloud Compliance*, introduces you to different aspects of security compliance for the cloud and how to make a solution compliant with ISMS and PCI DSS.

To get the most out of this book

Readers should have a basic understanding of AWS, OpenStack, and CentOS.

An AWS user account is required. If you don't have a user account, ensure that you have your credit card ready in order to open a free account. (While we have taken care to use the free-tier systems in AWS, make sure that you use the appropriate instance sizes and AMI IDs if you are creating an environment in a different region.)

Download the example code files

You can download the example code files for this book from your account at www.packtpub.com. If you purchased this book elsewhere, you can visit www.packtpub.com/support and register to have the files emailed directly to you.

You can download the code files by following these steps:

1. Log in or register at www.packtpub.com.
2. Select the **SUPPORT** tab.
3. Click on **Code Downloads & Errata**.
4. Enter the name of the book in the **Search** box and follow the onscreen instructions.

Once the file is downloaded, please make sure that you unzip or extract the folder using the latest version of:

- WinRAR/7-Zip for Windows
- Zipeg/iZip/UnRarX for Mac
- 7-Zip/PeaZip for Linux

The code bundle for the book is also hosted on GitHub at `https://github.com/PacktPublishing/Cloud-Security-Automation`. We also have other code bundles from our rich catalog of books and videos available at `https://github.com/PacktPublishing/`. Check them out!

Download the color images

We also provide a PDF file that has color images of the screenshots/diagrams used in this book. You can download it here: `https://www.packtpub.com/sites/default/files/downloads/CloudSecurityAutomation_ColorImages.pdf`.

Conventions used

There are a number of text conventions used throughout this book.

`CodeInText`: Indicates code words in text, database table names, folder names, filenames, file extensions, pathnames, dummy URLs, user input, and Twitter handles. Here is an example: "We have selected the bucket called `velocis-manali-trip-112017`."

A block of code is set as follows:

```
{
    "Sid": "AllowCreationOfServiceLinkedRoles",
    "Effect": "Allow",
    "Action": [
        "iam:CreateServiceLinkedRole"
    ],
    "Resource": "*"
}
```

When we wish to draw your attention to a particular part of a code block, the relevant lines or items are set in bold:

```
{
    "Sid": "AllowCreationOfServiceLinkedRoles",
    "Effect": "Allow",
    "Action": [
        "iam:CreateServiceLinkedRole"
    ],
    "Resource": "*"
}
```

Any command-line input or output is written as follows:

```
wget https://d1wk0tztpsntt1.cloudfront.net/linux/latest/install
sudo bash install
```

Bold: Indicates a new term, an important word, or words that you see onscreen. For example, words in menus or dialog boxes appear in the text like this. Here is an example: "On the wizard, select **Choose or create role**, tag your instance, and install the AWS agent."

Warnings or important notes appear like this.

Tips and tricks appear like this.

Get in touch

Feedback from our readers is always welcome.

General feedback: Email `feedback@packtpub.com` and mention the book title in the subject of your message. If you have questions about any aspect of this book, please email us at `questions@packtpub.com`.

Errata: Although we have taken every care to ensure the accuracy of our content, mistakes do happen. If you have found a mistake in this book, we would be grateful if you would report this to us. Please visit www.packtpub.com/submit-errata, selecting your book, clicking on the Errata Submission Form link, and entering the details.

Piracy: If you come across any illegal copies of our works in any form on the Internet, we would be grateful if you would provide us with the location address or website name. Please contact us at copyright@packtpub.com with a link to the material.

If you are interested in becoming an author: If there is a topic that you have expertise in and you are interested in either writing or contributing to a book, please visit authors.packtpub.com.

Reviews

Please leave a review. Once you have read and used this book, why not leave a review on the site that you purchased it from? Potential readers can then see and use your unbiased opinion to make purchase decisions, we at Packt can understand what you think about our products, and our authors can see your feedback on their book. Thank you!

For more information about Packt, please visit packtpub.com.

Disclaimer

The information within this book is intended to be used only in an ethical manner. Do not use any information from the book if you do not have written permission from the owner of the equipment. If you perform illegal actions, you are likely to be arrested and prosecuted to the full extent of the law. Packt Publishing does not take any responsibility if you misuse any of the information contained within the book. The information herein must only be used while testing environments with proper written authorizations from appropriate persons responsible.

Introduction to Cloud Security 1

In this chapter, we will learn the basics of the cloud and cloud security.

To understand cloud security, we first need to understand the types of clouds and their architecture. There are many global standard organizations such as NIST and CSA who are defining the different aspects of clouds.

As per the NIST definition of cloud computing (`https://www.nist.gov/programs-projects/nist-cloud-computing-program-nccp`), in simple terms we can say that the cloud offers on-demand accessibility of computing, networking, storage, databases, and applications. Here you do not have to worry about the purchase of physical boxes (CapEx) to run your application. You pay the cost of the resource based on the usage (OpEx).

CapEx stands for **capital expenditures** and denotes one-time cost investment to purchase any resource, for example, the purchase of a physical server.

OpEx stands for **operating expenditures** and denotes expenses to make the resource operational, for example, the purchase of manpower, power, OS, and so on to make the server operational.

We can say that the cloud provides abstraction of the underlying infrastructure using hypervisors and orchestrates to allocate resources to multiple tenants from the aggregated resource pool on demand.

The cloud offers *multitenancy*, *agility*, *scalability*, *availability*, and *security*. Let's understand what all these terms mean.

We will cover the following topics in this chapter:

- Types of cloud
- Cloud security
- Shared responsibility model
- Key concern areas of cloud security

Types of cloud

There are different models of the cloud. We broadly categorize them on the basis of deployment and service.

If we look at the cloud from a deployment perspective, there are three models.

Public cloud

This model of cloud is open to the public. This means that anyone can sign up and subscribe to set up their infrastructure to host their solution. For example, we have AWS, Microsoft Azure, Google Cloud Platform , IBM Cloud (SoftLayer), Alibaba Cloud, and so on.

Private cloud

This model of cloud is specific to an organization that wants to run their workload in a self-provisioned, secure way, internal to the organization. Organizations deploy private clouds using OpenStack, Apache CloudStack, Eucalyptus, OpenNebula, and so on as orchestration, and for hypervisors they are using VMware ESXi, XenServer, Hyper-V, KVM, and so on.

Hybrid cloud

This model of cloud combines the features of both private and public cloud, or you can say it integrates the public cloud and the on-premise hosted cloud. For example, suppose we have an internally deployed OpenStack cloud platform and now we want it to integrate with any of the public clouds. For this, there are multiple tools available that enable you to integrate both clouds and also facilitate you to lift and shift the workload to and fro. Recently, Cisco came up with a product called Cisco CloudCenter (formerly known as CliQr) providing the same facility.

On the basis of service, we categorize clouds into three parts, which we call the SPI model.

In the SPI model, **S** represents **Software as a Service**, **P** represents **Platform as a Service**, and **I** represents **Infrastructure as a Service**.

Software as a Service

In this model, an application running on the cloud is offered directly to the end consumer as a service. Being the end consumer, we subscribe the service and start using it. You do not have access to control and manage the infrastructure layer and platform. Here, you do not need to worry about the IT infrastructure, application, and security. In this model, the **Software as a Service** (**SaaS**) provider is responsible for managing the underlying infrastructure.

Platform as a Service

In this model, the cloud provider sets up a platform to develop your application or run your application. For example, AWS provides the **relational database service** (**RDS**) service, which is a DBMS service wherein you just need to subscribe the RDS service and dump your database and start using it. You need not worry about infrastructure, OS, and other operational stuff. **Platform as a Service** (**PaaS**) services can be accessed using the API too.

Infrastructure as a Service

IaaS stands for **Infrastructure as a Service**. In this model of cloud, you can subscribe to the complete infrastructure (networking, computing, and storage) that is required to run your application. Here, you will get the building blocks that you need to assemble to run your application as per your requirement. Suppose you want to run one web application that is developed in PHP and MySQL. To run this on the IaaS platform you need to subscribe to computing, networking, and storage. Now, you will configure each of them to run your application.

As we have now got a fair understanding of the cloud and cloud models, let's see the architecture so that we can correlate it when we start learning about the security aspects:

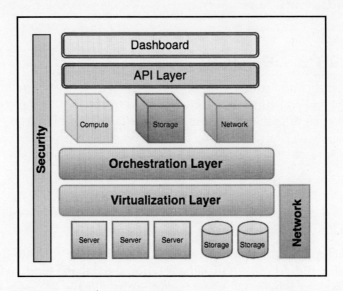

In the aforementioned architecture, we can see that the base layer of every cloud is a physical server, storage, and network. On top of it, we have installed the **Virtualization Layer** (hypervisor), which abstracts all the resources.

Before the hypervisor, we have the **Orchestration Layer**, which communicates with the **Virtualization Layer** and makes available resource chunks (computing, storage, and network) to be shared among the multiple tenants on demand.

The user logs in to the cloud dashboard to subscribe the resource and starts running their service or application on it.

One thing we can see here is that the **Security** layer starts from base and goes up until the top. This means that we need to focus on the security aspect at each layer (from the physical layer to the user layer).

Cloud security

Organizations started shifting their workload from on-premise physical infrastructures to the public cloud, or started to deploy their own private clouds to get all the benefits of the cloud. But security is a major concern, mostly in the case of the public cloud where we do not have control of the physical infrastructure. Also, there are compliance requirements that organizations need to match for example, ISO/IEC, NIST, FedRAMP, PCI DSS, HIPAA, and so on.

In this section, we will learn the basics of security and the security options available in the public cloud.

In any environment for security, we always start with the following models:

- CIA
- AAA

The **CIA** model focuses on **Confidentiality**, **Integrity**, and **Availability**. We also call it the CIA triad:

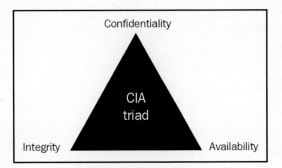

Confidentiality

Confidentiality denotes protecting the data from unauthorized access. We cannot disclose our data to everyone if it is critical, such as the bank statement, which includes all our financial transactions. We must ensure that a bank statement is disclosed only to our banker or the accountant who works on it. Similarly, this applies for an organization as well. In an organization, we have multiple departments and different roles. Here we define the roles for each user to access the information. Alternatively, you can say we define rules to decide who will access what.

Integrity

Integrity means protecting the data from unauthorized modification. All the data that we have in our organization is valuable. If it's modified this could be a huge loss for the organization. Let's take a financial statement as an example, which includes all the financial information of the organization. If it is tampered with or modified it can cause huge business losses. We must ensure that the data we are storing and that is being accessed by users is secure enough to maintain its integrity.

Availability

Availability denotes that the information is available to authorized users. If it isn't available to authorized users, again it will incur a loss. Information has value if the right people can access it at the right time. Almost every week you can find news about high profile websites being taken down by **distributed denial of service** (**DDoS**) attacks. The main aim of a DDoS attack is not to allow users with any website access to the resources of the website. Such downtime can be very costly.

Now coming onto the next model, the **AAA** model focuses on **Authentication**, **Authorization**, and **Auditing**.

Authentication

Only authenticated users should be able to access the data. The focus is on user validation, or authenticity of users. User validation is done with the user login credentials, or access keys, which are matched with the user database, LDAP, Active Directory, or key stores.

Authorization

Once the user is authenticated, there must be some authority defined for the user to access the data so that he can perform the required action. Basically, here we define the access policies and roles for users. Users with read permission should not be able to modify the data.

Auditing

Auditing does the accounting of user activity on data. Here, we log all the activity of users including login time, session duration, and all the activities that they perform.

The cloud offers multiple options to implement the security, but it solely depends upon the security requirement and our expertise to implement it.

One thing we need to understand is that implementing security in the cloud is a bit different from what we have been practicing with on-premise or traditional infrastructures.

We learned previously that the cloud runs on top of physical boxes, such as storage, servers, and networking equipment. All these resources are controlled by a layer of abstraction that we call a hypervisor or virtualization layer. Further, all the aggregated resources are being controlled and managed by an orchestration. Internally, all these layers communicate with each other through an **application program interface** (**API**).

In the cloud we can also start implementing security with CIA and AAA models. Here, we have the following services in the cloud to implement CIA and AAA models:

- **Confidentiality**: Here, we use **Identity and Access Management** (**IAM**) to define the resource accessibility permissions. In IAM, we can define users, groups, roles, and policies. IAM also helps to manage the API access using access keys and secret keys. Similarly, we have a keystone in OpenStack to define users, groups, roles, and policies. You can define policies to access the other OpenStack services and APIs.
- **Integrity**: For integrity, we have multiple types of encryption for the storage where data is stored and for data in transit we can use SSL. If we want to implement an additional layer of security, we can use the AWS CloudHSM module as well. In OpenStack, we have the following process to manage integrity. It starts from the bootstrap level and goes up until the file level. (We've studied this process in detail in the *Private cloud* section.)
- **Availability**: For availability, AWS offers you many services that ensure the service availability at different layers. We have Route 53 as DNS, **Elastic Load Balancing** (**ELB**), and autoscaling. All three services ensure that you have the service available in case of DDoS attacks as well. Availability of the application or solution also depends on how it is designed and deployed. Let's take an example of a web application; here, in order to ensure maximum availability of the application, we should always design the solution in such a way that there is no single point of failure. For this, we must consider **high availability** (**HA**), autoscaling, and also try to decouple the resources (using message queuing) so that it can be fault tolerant as well.

Now, let's map the AAA model in the cloud:

- **Authentication**: In AWS, we have IAM for user identity. Here, we can define users and groups. IAM enables you to define the password-based authentication and key-based authentication for users. Apart from this, for the application, we can use the AWS Directory Service and Cognito (token-based authentication) for user authentication. For console users, we can also enable **multi-factor authentication** (**MFA**) as well. In OpenStack, we have a keystone, which provides user and service authentication. Here, we also create users and groups and define password-based and key-based authentication for users. Apart from this, we can use SAML-based authentication, OAuth, and OpenID-based authentication.

 It's always advisable to access the public cloud service using access keys. Do not access the console using root account credentials, and also make sure that you have enabled MFA for user accounts.

- **Authorization**: For authorization, AWS uses IAM roles and policies. There are many predefined user roles for different services. Apart from this, we can define custom roles. For example, suppose we have an EC2 instance, that needs to access the **Simple Storage Service** (**S3**) resource and CloudWatch Logs. Here we can also define a custom role of an EC2 instance which grants access to the S3 bucket and CloudWatch Logs and binds that role with the EC2 instances. There is no need to store the access keys in text format on EC2 instances, but you will find that people are not practicing this. In the same way, if you need to manage multiple or linked accounts then you should define the role for cross-account access and use it instead of logging in using the root account. Similarly, in OpenStack, we have a keystone where we can define different roles and policies for users and groups. For each service, there is an associated access policy file defined in JSON format.

 In OpenStack, it is always advisable to use TLS-based authentication and also define formal access control policies.

- **Auditing**: AWS provides CloudTrail to log all the action or activity for AWS services. Apart from this, we have **Virtual Private Cloud** (**VPC**) logs and ELB logs, which can be stored in the S3 bucket or can be transferred to CloudWatch Logs. For analysis, we can use the Elasticsearch service or query it using Athena. For solution auditing, you can use AWS Config and Trusted Advisor. Now we are moving toward machine learning and **Internet of Things** (**IoT**). For this, AWS started a new service called Macie, which uses machine learning to identify the accessibility of data and services. In OpenStack, we have a telemetry service called **Ceilometer** to store and manage logs. Apart from this, you can use custom monitoring solutions called **New Relic**.

Shared responsibility model

In the cloud, we can define stakeholders in two categories:

- **Cloud provider**: This is the one who provides cloud services
- **Cloud consumer**: This is the one who consumes cloud services

In cloud security, compliance is defined on the shared responsibility model. Here, the cloud provider is responsible for managing security and compliance at the physical infrastructure level, hypervisor level, physical network level, storage level, and orchestration layer.

The cloud consumer assumes responsibility for managing security and compliance from the virtual machine level to the application level.

In AWS it's a bit more clarified, and here the security responsibility model is defined in three different categories:

- A shared responsibility model for infrastructure
- A shared responsibility model for container service
- A shared responsibility model for abstract service

Let's see the broad shared responsibility models of AWS:

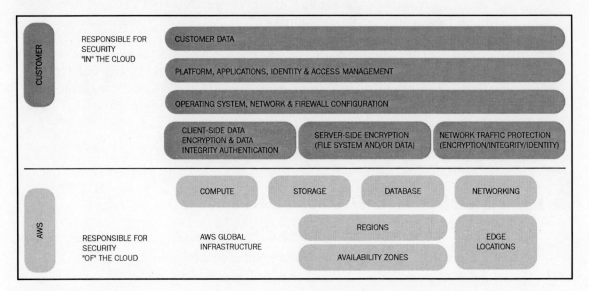

In the shared responsibility model, the cloud provider (AWS) is responsible for managing security and compliance at the data center level or the physical infrastructure level, such as server, storage, and physical network.

The cloud consumers (end users) will be responsible for managing security and compliance from the guest OS level (security patches and updates); VPC security, such as configuration of security groups, network **access control lists** (**ACLs**); and other software configuration, as well as the integration of other services (for example, RDS, S3, **Simple Queue Service** (**SQS**), **Simple Email Service** (**SES**), and more).

In the shared security model, AWS is responsible for the security of infrastructure where all the AWS cloud service offering is running. Here, the infrastructure consists of all the hardware, software, and the physical perimeters.

The customer's responsibility is determined on the basis of the services they subscribe. For example, if the customer subscribed the EC2 instance, they need to ensure security of the guest OS and configuration. For S3, they need to define the ACL and roles. Similarly, for the RDS, they need to define passwords, security group policy, encryption, and backup policy.

For the customers to ensure the security at each level, there are many services that are already available, such as AWS Config, Trusted Advisor, IAM, X-Ray, and Macie, which helps to make your security work easier.

Now, let's look at the previously mentioned categories of the shared responsibility model.

Shared responsibility model for infrastructure

In this model, AWS is responsible for securing its virtualization, server, storage, physical network, and data center. The customer who has subscribed to the infrastructure service is responsible for defining security from the guest OS, application level, virtual network (VPC) level, data level, and finally, the user access level.

Shared responsibility model for container service

In AWS, we have container-based services. In computing, we have ECS, for databases, we have RDS, and so on. Here, AWS security responsibility goes higher up to the guest OS and platform level. Similar to RDS, AWS is responsible for managing security from the physical level to the database application level. Customers are only responsible for defining security at a subnet level, security group, encryption and password policy, and IAM roles.

Shared responsibility model for abstract services

AWS also provides abstract services such as SQS, SES, **Simple Notification Service (SNS)**, and S3. For all these services, AWS is responsible for the complete security of the physical layer, virtualization layer, network level, storage, OS, software, and so on. Users or consumers need to define only the user-level permission and encryption if it is applicable for the service.

Now, let's understand the shared responsibility model in the cloud from the service perspective.

In IaaS, the cloud provider is responsible for only managing the physical infrastructure and security at the physical level. Being a user, we are responsible for the following:

- VM level security
- Application and data security
- User management
- Virtual network level security

In the case of IaaS, the API plays a significant role, as all the internal components talk to each other using the API via HTTP methods: GET, PUT, and DELETE. The API enables cloud consumers to access the service using the REST API (available in all the clouds). We will look at the use of APIs in the automation section and also learn about how automation uses APIs to speed up deployment and enhance security.

In the cloud, we have multiple options to apply security on all the aforementioned levels but it completely depends on us as to how we are utilizing it.

In the PaaS model, the cloud provider responsibility increases; it is responsible for managing the platform too. Here, the platform denotes the environment on which our application will run. For example, most of the cloud providers have Database as a Service. Here, the cloud provider is responsible for managing the physical infrastructure, compute, and OS level security. Being a user, we will focus on user management, virtual networks, and data security.

In the SaaS model, the cloud provider is responsible for providing end-to-end security until the application levels. We are only responsible for ensuring user management and data security. In AWS, there is no SaaS service, which is a part of the AWS cloud offering, but there are many partners who provide SaaS services. AWS equips you to ensure maximum security for your SaaS offering as well.

Key concern areas of cloud security

There are many agencies who are continuously working to define the global standards and also publish their recommendations for cloud computing.

Cloud Security Alliance (CSA) is one of them. It continuously works to address the security options of the cloud. CSA has identified key areas where we need to focus on cloud security:

- Infrastructure level
- User access level
- Storage and data level
- Application access level
- Network level
- Logging and monitoring level

Infrastructure level

Infrastructure level security is of the utmost importance. In a public cloud, the physical infrastructure is the cloud provider's responsibility. But in a private cloud, we must ensure the security at the infrastructure level as well. In OpenStack, all the components are separate services and they communicate with each other via APIs. It's very complex to ensure security at each level.

In OpenStack, we have services such as keystone, nova, and neutron, which have dependencies on their underlying databases. Here, it is always advisable that each database has its unique access credentials. This will help when any particular component gets compromised as it will not affect the other components.

Hypervisor in OpenStack must be enabled with SELinux or AppArmor. Most of the time, people disable it during configuration, but it's not recommended as it gives you a virtual boundary to protect your VMs. Apart from this, all the security patches must be deployed on the hypervisor.

There should always be an isolation between networks responsible for management, guest, and storage traffic. It's always preferred to have a separate VLAN for internal users so that users with infected or compromised machines cannot affect the cloud infrastructure.

There must be use of internal and external firewalls with OpenStack to control external and internal traffic.

In OpenStack, each service communicates with each other on specific ports; so, on the firewall, only these ports should be open.

 Do not open all the ports for all the services.

You must watch the activity performed by users, such as successful versus failed logins, and unique transactional behavior, such as users trying to download all the images at once.

In AWS, to secure the infrastructure, you can use IAM, Trusted Advisor, and AWS Config. All these services help you identify the loopholes in the configuration. Enabling logs, monitoring, and alerts using CloudWatch helps you to strengthen security.

For the instance level, we must update the guest OS for updated security patches. VPC logs must be enabled to monitor network-level activity. Using custom alerts on the AWS service, you can proactively manage the security aspects. For example, we can create alerts on NIC of EC2 instances. If the same instance broadcasts traffic massively, we can easily identify the issue by going through the logs.

User access level

In the cloud, it is critical to define users and user access. In this section, we define the users, groups, roles, and policies. **Users** are entities who will access the cloud infrastructure using the console or APIs. A **group** defines the collection of users who will perform a similar set of actions. **Roles** define the nature of the job the user will perform, while a **policy** defines the rules for resource access. It also describes how the users will access the services or applications, and how one service will securely communicate with another service. In the public cloud, communication or integration of different services is usually the user's responsibility, where the consumer defines the secure way for communication. But most of the time, we make a mistake in this process and leave this part vulnerable to security breaches.

For example, we have a solution where EC2 instances need to store the static files on S3 storage. In this case, ideally we should create an EC2 role that has permissions to access specific S3 buckets, but most people put the access key and secret key into the test file in EC2 instances, which is not recommended. This is because if the VM gets compromised, then the whole account is at a risk if the stored key has root account access keys.

Similarly, we must use MFA for console access and should not use the root account to access the console. However, in real life, most of the users do this—they access the console using the root credentials and they also do not use MFA.

For audit purposes, we must use IAM events and we should be logged in to CloudTrail.

In OpenStack we also have identity management to define user access. As in the case of the AWS service, here also we define users, groups, and roles. Identity management in OpenStack provides you with the **Role-Based Access Control** (**RBAC**) and ACLs.

 OpenStack identity management does not provide a method to control an unsuccessful login attempt. If a brute force attack happens, it won't be able to control it. So here, for prevention, you can use external authentication services, which can control the number of failed attempts to log in.

Storage and data level

Storage and data level security is very important. Recently, we have heard about many cases of security breaches, such as Verizon, which suffered with a data leak on S3 due to it being publicly open. This also happened with Accenture, where the server was exposing the data to the public. These cases happened due to not implementing the security policy at the storage and data level. In the cloud, we have the following types of storage:

- **Volume storage**: This type of storage is used as a block storage, which can be mapped with VM as a partition. To ensure security, we can use OS-based encryption or HSM to ensure the security of data. For data protection, we can define RAID as well. For example, in AWS we have **Elastic Block Store** (**EBS**), which provides an encryption facility and also provides the feature to create RAID.
- **Object storage**: This type of storage is used to store static content, such as images and documents. Here, we can define encryption and ACLs to ensure the security of data. There are many cloud providers who already keep multiple copies of object storage data to ensure safety. For example, in AWS we have S3, which keeps six copies of data for redundancy.
- **Database storage**: This is the type of storage that we use to store our database. In AWS, we have RDS. To ensure data security, we must ensure that encryption is enabled and also that only authorized users have access.

In general terms, we define data security in storage in two parts:

- **Data at rest**: For data at rest security, we enable encryption using **Key Management Service** (**KMS**) or HSM. Here, we can enable encryption at the storage level. All the aforementioned examples of security for storage are for data at rest encryption.
- **Data in transit**: For data in transit, we must define the secure channel to maintain the integrity of data. For this, we use SSL/TLS while communicating with the external service or users. From a management perspective, we always prefer to use a secure VPN tunnel.

Application access level

Application access is one of the most important areas of concern in terms of security. Here, we have our data and information in transit. We must secure this transferring data using a secure channel, such as SSL. Apart from this, if our application is a web application, we must ensure availability. We have heard about cases of DDoS attacks, SQL injections, and so on. There are always bad guys who work in the dark to steal your important data. To disable this, we must ensure that we have defined preventive parameters such as the use of the **web application firewall** (**WAF**), and that our infrastructure should be deployed in such a way that it can handle the DDoS attack. Security groups should allow the traffic on specific ports and from specific sources only. For example, we have a web application that runs with SSL on port 443, so make sure that only port 443 is open for public access. Network ACLs should also be configured to allow only legitimate traffic.

We can also use WAF to stop malicious traffic and prevent DDoS attacks. WAF also helps to apply rules on your websites for accessibility. You can also manage the traffic on the basis of geographical locations.

If your application uses a **Content Delivery Network** (**CDN**) to make your site perform faster, you must define security at the CDN level. The CDN keeps the local copy of all static content locally, which is transferred from one origin. So you must define security at the origin level and the CDN level regarding file access.

For APIs, security must ensure that the API is accessible only to authorized users with key-based authentication and the API should be accessible over SSL only.

Internet-based applications are more prone to DDoS and brute force attacks where there will be large amount of illegitimate traffic on your application, which results in the unavailability of your application. For online businesses, a DDoS can be critical, as the application's unavailability will essentially halt the revenue stream.

To tackle these situations, we can use a global DNS service such as Route 53, which can handle a traffic burst. The application must be deployed in HA with autoscaling running under the load balancer so that, if the peak comes, it should autoscale the resource to handle the traffic.

There is also a chance that your VM gets compromised and starts broadcasting the packet. To eliminate this situation, we must do the security hardening of the virtual machine and enable monitoring so that, if any such adverse situation comes about, you will get an alert to take appropriate action.

Most of the time, we secure our environment externally, but what about the internal users? This case is very common in a private cloud or hybrid cloud environment. So, we must watch the user activity, the number of sessions, and the kind of transactions taking place. For this you can check the load balancer logs, application server logs, and user access, or you can use any monitoring tool that can display real-time logs in a meaningful way. Here we can utilize the **Elasticsearch, Logstash, and Kibana (ELK)** stack, which gives very interactive dashboards and graphs.

Network level

When we are moving to the cloud or opting for the cloud, network security is of the utmost importance. On the cloud, we can define the policy at our firewall level to allow and deny the traffic. In AWS, we use VPC to define the network. In VPC, we must create subnets to define the public, private, and management subnets. For SSH or RDP access, we must have either a jump server or bastion host. This will add one additional layer of security. The route table should be properly defined. We must define and configure network ACL to control the incoming and outgoing packets. In security, we only require the ports to be open and the source should be clearly specified. Do not open all the ports to the public.

For private subnet VMs, we can use the NAT service to enable internet access.

If you need to meet a specific compliance, you can use IPS and IDS to make the environment more secure.

To access resources from a management perspective, we should use a VPN connection. There are different types of VPN connections offered by AWS.

For a private and secure connection, we can use the Direct Connect connection between the customer site to AWS.

In OpenStack, we must understand how the workflow process for the tenant instance creation needs to be mapped to security domains. There are a few services that directly communicate with neutron and these services must be mapped to security domains, as follows:

- **OpenStack dashboard**: Public and management
- **OpenStack identity**: Management
- **OpenStack compute node**: Management and guest
- **OpenStack network node**: Management, guest, and possibly public, depending upon the neutron plugin in use

- **SDN services node**: Management, guest, and possibly public, depending upon the product used

To isolate sensitive data communication between neutron and other OpenStack core services, we configure communication channels to only allow communication over an isolated management network.

We must restrict the neutron API connection to a specific interface using specifying details in the neutron configuration file.

Likewise, we must define the incoming and outgoing traffic using security groups.

When using flat networking, we cannot assume that projects that share the same layer 2 network (or broadcast domain) are fully isolated from each other. These projects may be vulnerable to ARP spoofing, risking the possibility of man-in-the-middle attacks.

To prevent this, we must enable `prevent_arp_spoofing` in the Open vSwitch configuration file.

Logging and monitoring level

Logging and monitoring is a very important aspect of any IT infrastructure. Here we get granular details about all the events performed in the infrastructure at each level. Logging and monitoring is a bit complex in the cloud. In logs, we cannot always filter on the basis of IP due to dynamic allocation of IP. There can arise a situation where one IP was earlier representing the *x* virtual machine, but is now representing the *y* virtual machine.

Apart from this, the cloud comprises different services. We must ensure the activity logging at each service.

In AWS, we can use CloudTrail to log all the activity for each service and we can either store these logs to an S3 bucket or we can forward them to CloudTrail logs.

Recently, CloudTrail logs enabled at the load balancer helped us to identify the illegitimate traffic. Let's consider, we are running one financial application in HA and an autoscaling environment. Over the last few days, we have seen a peak in resource utilization. As it's configured in autoscaling, it could not affect the application's performance. But, when we tried to investigate the issue, we found that there was a bad guy who was attacking our application:

```
2017-10-23T00:12:54.164535Z ASP-SaaS-Prod-ELB 90.63.223.128:46838
172.31.2.240:80 0.000038 0.001246 0.000057 404 404 0 0 "HEAD
http://X.X.X.X:80/mysql/admin/ HTTP/1.1" "Mozilla/5.0 Jorgee" - -
```

```
2017-10-23T00:12:54.294395Z ASP-SaaS-Prod-ELB 90.63.223.128:46838
172.31.1.37:80 0.000069 0.000936 0.000051 404 404 0 0 "HEAD
http://X.X.X.X:80/mysql/dbadmin/ HTTP/1.1" "Mozilla/5.0 Jorgee" - -
2017-10-23T00:12:54.423798Z ASP-SaaS-Prod-ELB 90.63.223.128:46838
172.31.2.240:80 0.000051 0.001275 0.000052 404 404 0 0 "HEAD
http://X.X.X.X:80/mysql/sqlmanager/ HTTP/1.1" "Mozilla/5.0 Jorgee" - -
2017-10-23T00:12:54.553557Z ASP-SaaS-Prod-ELB 90.63.223.128:46838
172.31.1.37:80 0.000047 0.000982 0.000062 404 404 0 0 "HEAD
http://X.X.X.X:80/mysql/mysqlmanager/ HTTP/1.1" "Mozilla/5.0 Jorgee" - -
2017-10-23T00:12:54.682829Z ASP-SaaS-Prod-ELB 90.63.223.128:46838
172.31.2.240:80 0.000076 0.00103 0.000065 404 404 0 0 "HEAD
http://X.X.X.X:80/phpmyadmin/ HTTP/1.1" "Mozilla/5.0 Jorgee" - -
```

In the aforementioned logs, you can see how the bad guy is sitting on IP `90.63.223.128`.

He is trying to hack the application using different URLs or passing different headers.

To prevent this, we enabled WAF and blocked all the traffic from the outside world. Also, you can make WAF learn about this malicious traffic so that whenever such a request comes, WAF will reject the packet. It won't let the packet pass through WAF.

In the monitoring, you must define the metrics and alarm. It helps us to take preventive action. If anything goes against your expectation, you get an alarm and can take appropriate action to mitigate the risk:

```
Alarm Details:
- Name:                     awsrds-dspdb-CPU-Utilization
- Description:
- State Change:             OK -> ALARM
- Reason for State Change:  Threshold Crossed: 1 datapoint [51.605
(24/10/17 07:02:00)] was greater than or equal to the threshold (50.0).
- Timestamp:                Tuesday 24 October, 2017 07:07:55 UTC
- AWS Account:              XXXXXXX
Threshold:
- The alarm is in the ALARM state when the metric is
GreaterThanOrEqualToThreshold 50.0 for 300 seconds.
Monitored Metric:
- MetricNamespace:          AWS/RDS
- MetricName:               CPUUtilization
- Dimensions:               [DBInstanceIdentifier = aspdb]
- Period:                   300 seconds
- Statistic:                Average
- Unit:                     not specified
```

In the preceding example, we have defined an alarm on CPU utilization at the RDS level. We got this alert when there was CPU utilization of more than 50% but less than 70%. As soon as we got the alert, we started investigating, which caused the CPU utilization.

Now, let's see the summarized security risk and preventive action at different levels in the cloud:

- **Hypervisor level**: In the cloud, we have our VMs running on shared resources. There could be a chance that there is a host, which runs x and y VMs. In case the x VM got compromised or hacked, there can be a risk of the y VM getting compromised as well. Luckily, it's not possible due to isolation of resources, but what if the attacker gets access to the host? So, we must update the required security patches on the hypervisor. We must ensure that all the security parameters are configured at the VM level. Most of the time, it happens when we disable the underlying security parameters. This happens mostly with the private cloud. At the hypervisor level, we also segregate the traffic at the vSwitch level where we must have at least management, guest, and storage traffic running on different VLANs.
- **Network level**: The network is the backbone of the cloud. If the network is compromised, it can completely break down the cloud. The most common attacks on the network are DDoS, network eavesdropping, illegal invasion, and so on. To secure the network, we must define the following:
  - Isolation of traffic (management, storage, and guest)
  - ACL for network traffic
  - Ingress and egress rules must be clearly defined
  - IDS and IPS must be enabled to control the intrusion
  - Antivirus and antispam engines should be enabled to scan the packets
  - Network monitoring must be configured to track the traffic
- **Storage level**: Storage is also a critical component of the cloud where we store our critical data. Here, we can have risk of data loss, data tampering, and data theft. At the storage level, we must ensure the following to maintain security and integrity of data:
  - All the data at rest must be encrypted
  - Backup must be provisioned
  - If possible, enable data replication to mitigate the risk of hardware failure
  - User roles and data access policy must be defined
  - A DLP mechanism should be enabled
  - All the data transaction should happen using encrypted channels
  - Access logs should be enabled

- **VM level**: At the VM level, we can have the risk of password compromise, virus infection, and exploited vulnerabilities. To mitigate this, we must ensure the following:
  - OS-level security patches must be deployed from time to time
  - Compromised VMs must be stopped instantly
  - Backup should be provisioned using **continuous data protection (CDP)** or using a snapshot
  - Antivirus and antispam agents should be installed
  - User access should be clearly defined
  - If possible, define key-based authentication instead of passwords
  - The OS must be hardened and the OS-level firewall and security rule should also be enabled
  - Logs management and monitoring must be enabled

- **User level**: User identity and access is critical for every cloud. We must clearly define the users, groups, roles, and access policy. This is the basis of cloud security. This is the portion where we authorize them to play with the infrastructure and service. And, if the identity and access is not clearly defined, it can lead to a disaster at any time. To ensure security, we must define the following:
  - Users, groups, roles, and access policies
  - Enable MFA for user authentication
  - The password policy and access key must be defined
  - Make sure that the users are not accessing the cloud using the root account
  - Logs must be enabled for audit purposes

- **Application level**: Once your application is hosted and open for public access, then actual risks arise to maintain the availability and accessibility of the service. Here, you will face DDoS, SQL injection, man-in-the-middle attack, cross-site scripting, and so on. To prevent all such attacks, we must use the following:
  - Scalable DNS
  - Load balancer
  - Provision autoscaling
  - SSL
  - WAF
  - User IAM policies and roles

- **Compliance**: If you have to match some compliance, such as ISO 27001, PCI, and HIPAA, then you must follow the guidelines of all these compliances and design the solutions accordingly. We will read about compliances in the last chapter and learn how to meet them.

 While designing the solution, always think that you are designing for failure. Identify all the single points of failure and find appropriate solutions for them. Also, while designing the solution for the cloud, always consider security, reliability, performance, and cost efficiency, as these factors have a huge impact on your solution as well as organization.

Summary

Now that we have a fair idea about cloud computing concepts and the basics of cloud security, in the next chapter, we will study automation and discuss how it helps to implement security in the cloud.

Understanding the World of Cloud Automation

2

First, we must understand what automation means. In layman's terms, we can say that automation is to automate or process something without requiring any human intervention.

Once we have automated the process, it will perform all the activity automatically as per the flow or sequence.

We all know that manual activity is prone to errors and mistakes. To eliminate this, we automate the process using different tools. Automation not only eliminates errors and mistakes, but also saves time and costs.

We are in the era of the cloud, where automation is the utmost requirement everywhere. Organizations are now focused toward automation for improving quality of service while at the same time saving on costs and time.

DevOps is a combination of the following two words:

- **Development**: This denotes the development of applications
- **Operations**: This denotes the management of applications

Earlier, we had different employees who performed different sets of activities, as we had separate employees for each workload, and everyone worked in sync to deliver the optimum performance.

There are many organizations who have an operations team to manage and support their application because the software development team does not have experience with infrastructure.

However, in the cloud, every service is API based, which means they can be accessed using programming language or can be embedded into code. So here, the word **DevOps** is coined, where one person can play the role of **developer** as well as managing **operations**.

For automation, DevOps people use automation tools and the automation process. Here, popular DevOps tools are Chef, Puppet, Jenkins, GitHub, Selenium, and so on.

The following topics will be covered in this chapter:

- DevOps
- The need of automation
- Infrastructure as a Code
- Configuration management
- Automate deployment—AWS OpsWorks

Now, let's understand DevOps in depth.

What is DevOps?

DevOps is a combination of culture, practice, and tools that increase the ability to deploy and deliver applications and services. It also helps us improve the product and service delivery faster in comparison to a traditional development model.

DevOps, as we read earlier, merges two teams into one to manage the complete development life cycle. Alternatively, there can be multiple teams responsible for each activity. As well as, the DevOps process is also tightly coupled with the security and quality teams in a full cycle.

We say DevOps is a practice because here we practice how to automate the process that was defined in history and was manual, complex, and slow.

"DevOps isn't any single person's job. It's everyone's job."

– Christophe Capel, Principal Product Manager, JIRA Service Desk

To automate the process, we use different tools and technology that equip us to transform the process quickly and reliably. Here, one person can complete the task without being dependent on other teams.

In DevOps, we have multiple processes. We could say that we have a process chain, as each activity is dependent on another. The following are the activities or processes that we have in DevOps:

- **Code**: At this stage, we plan to define infrastructure. Here, we must have a platform where we can let people work on the same application in a collaborative environment. For this, we have tools such as GitHub, Jira, and SVN.
- **Build**: In the build process, we actually fetch the code from the source repository and organize it into builds and then perform testing. Here, you could say that builds are prereleased packages. For a build, we use *MAKE* and *ANT*. To test the builds, we need infrastructure where we can run the code. For this, we can consider *Docker* and *Vagrant*, which help us provision instant infrastructure.
- **Package**: Once builds are tested, we organize them into packages. Packages are collections of builds that are ready for release. Basically, here all modules are combined together to form a release for testing. For packaging, we use a universal package manager such as Nexus or artifactory, and system-level packaging tools such as Git.
- **Release**: Once a package is tested, it is transferred as a release. This includes schedule and deployment into a production environment. We have tools such as Puppet and XebiaLabs for this.
- **Configure**: Once the release is complete, it goes into the configuration stage, where we need to perform some steps to do the required configurations for infrastructure deployment and application deployment. We have the Ansible, Chef, Puppet, and Salt tools for configuration management.
- **Monitor**: Now, when a configuration is done to run the application or release, it goes into the monitoring stage, where all the components should be monitored very minutely, and alerts/alarms on anomalies are sent. For this, we have New Relic, Zabbix, Cacti, Wireshark, and so on.

Why do we need automation?

Let's think now why we need to automate processes. One instant point that comes to my mind is to save time or hasten processes.

Actually, when we were working on the waterfall model, we had to iterate with development life cycle stages one by one, and modules were tightly coupled. Due to this, the development was a very long-term, complex process.

 In 1970, Winston Royce introduced the waterfall model for software development, which actually defined software development and different phases. Each phase is a specified set of operations that need to be performed during SDLC.

Now we move on to the agile development process, where each iteration between phases is very fast. It works in **continuous integration** (**CI**) and continuous development mode.

During this mode, we have a repeated set of tasks to complete. If we do all of these manually, it will take more time and there will also be a chance of human error. So, we automate the repetitive set of tasks to hasten the process and save some time.

As well as repetitive tasks, we also have a few critical and complex tasks that do not occur frequently, but need more man hours to be completed. As it is manual, there is a higher chance of getting errors. For example, data migration—we need consistency to perform migration work.

Here, if we automate the process, we will be able to remove the human dependencies and manual errors, which will result in improved consistency. Likewise, if we use a Cisco CloudCenter type tool where we model the app once, we can deploy and migrate it anywhere without human intervention.

With automation, we gain speed and momentum in our delivery process. For example, an infrastructure team is given the responsibility of creating a thousand VMs, which all need an operation system to be installed, security patching, and other configuration to be done. If we do manual provisioning, this task will probably take weeks to complete, and there will be at least a 10% chance of error unless we have a team of perfectionists.

Now, suppose that I am using Ansible to perform this task; it will take just a few hours to complete all these tasks and deliver the VMs. In Ansible, we just need to write a playbook to create a VM with all the configuration details along with security patches. Whenever we need a VM, we just need to run the Ansible playbook and it will create a complete infrastructure, ready for delivery.

Automation also helps us perform scheduled tasks; for example, we have to make a backup of all the VMs, applications, and databases. For the sake of minimal interference with application performance, we mostly schedule backup for odd hours.

If it is a manual job, we need a human who will be working these odd hours. Again, here, there is a chance for errors or mistakes. There is also the possibility that we might miss the backup for a few apps.

However, if we have automated the backup task using bash, or some other automation tool, it will start the process on time and complete it with positive results. If there are any errors, you will get a notification, and then you can take appropriate action.

Automation makes life easier for system administrators.

Let's summarize the benefits of automation:

- Time and cost saving
- Faster deployment and delivery
- Elimination of the chance of human error
- Improved collaboration
- Easy to implement security

To adopt the DevOps process, we have to complete a few prerequisites. As said earlier, DevOps is a practice, and to adopt it, we have to adhere to the process of DevOps.

So, to adopt the DevOps culture, we need to have the following things:

- **CI**: In CI, process development teams store their code in a central repository from which automatic build and test processes run. CI processing helps us find bugs quickly and also lets you validate updates and deliver them fast. For example, we use *Jenkins*, which provides a complete CI/CD process.
- **Continuous delivery (CD)**: In this process, all the developed code is automatically built, tested, and ready for release and production. Once CD is successfully implemented, a developer will get all the production-ready artifacts/packages available for rollout.

- **Microservices**: Its process is to build an application into a set of small services. Each service runs its own processes and communicates with other services using a well-defined framework or API. For example, we either use Docker Swarm or Kubernetes, which run microservices in containers.

- **Infrastructure as Code**: The best part of DevOps is that we defined Infrastructure as Code, and it is idempotent in nature. Infrastructure is coded and also stored similarly to the applications that have version control and a CI process. We know that clouds give us API-level access to all the components and services. We use APIs to code the infrastructure instead of provisioning it manually. In the AWS environment, we have CloudFormation to code complete infrastructure into a simple JSON code. Infrastructure as Code also has the following two subprocesses:

  - **Configuration management**: In the configuration management process, we code all the configuration-level activity such as patch management, OS update and upgrade, and the security hardening process. Because configuration management is a repetitive process, it consumes too much time for system or operation teams. For this, we use tools such as Ansible, Chef, and Puppet, where we code configuration management stuff once and run it when it is required. In the following code, its Ansible playbook code snippet installs the IIS service on Windows. It's easy and simple. We write it once and can run it on Windows Server:

```
---
- name: Install IIS
  hosts: all
  gather_facts: false
  tasks:
    - name: Install IIS
      win_feature:
        name: "Web-Server"
        state: present
        restart: yes
        include_sub_features: yes
        include_management_tools: yes
```

- **Policy as code**: Once we have coded our infrastructure, it's time to code our policy as well, which will include security and compliance. There are different cloud vendor-specific tools that let you manage the security and compliance, and also send you alerts and notifications. In AWS, we have AWS configuration service. We will study AWS configuration in more detail in the next chapter.

- **Monitoring and logging**: This is an important section for the whole organization. Here, we get the details of what is happening in the backend infrastructure and application and, at the same time, we also get to know the status using events and alarms. Here, we use monitoring and logging tools to automate the monitoring and log management. We have the **Elasticsearch, Logstash, and Kibana (ELK)** stack, New Relic, Nagios, and so on, which perform monitoring processes and send you alerts on an event basis.
- **Collaboration and communication**: As we know, DevOps is a practice where the development and operation teams work in collaboration. Here, we define the workflow for top to bottom-level communication. We also use tools that can be used for code tracking; communication between the team using chat also can give detail about bugs.

Infrastructure as Code

Now, as you have already learned about the basic fundamentals of DevOps, let's start to understand it by example. As an example, I will use the CloudFormation template to describe how easy and fast it is to deploy solutions in AWS.

CloudFormation is an AWS service that is used to provision your IT Infrastructure as Code. Once it's coded, you can deploy it in any region, and it also gives you facility to customize it as per your own wishes.

As we can see in the following screenshot, CloudFormation gives you a very rich GUI where you can drag and drop the required components and establish relations between them, and in backend code is automatically generated in the JSON and YAML formats. Once you are done drawing using drag and drop, you save this as a template and start deployment:

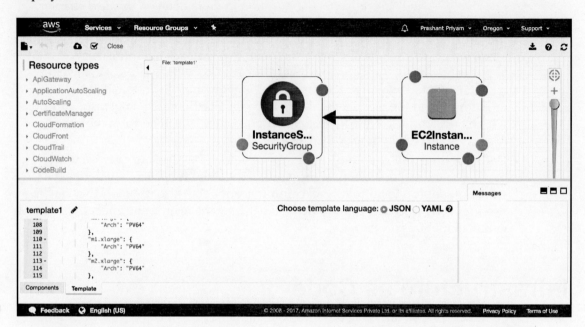

In CloudFormation, we generate code in the JSON or YAML formats. **JSON** stands for **JavaScript Object Notation**, and **YAML** stands for **Yet Another Markup Language**. Both are very easy to understand and work on key-value form.

In the CloudFormation template, we have the following section:

- `Description`: It describes the purpose of the template, and that is what it will do.
- `Metadata`: It is defined as data about data. It's an optional section where we define some custom values.
- `Parameters`: It is also an optional section in the CloudFormation template where we define the runtime parameters for the template. We use it in the `Resources` and `Output` section of code.
- `Mapping`: Here, we map a key with associated values for conditional parameters.

- Conditions: It defines how certain resources are created or assigned a value during the creation process or the update process.
- Resources: The only mandatory component of the CloudFormation template; it defines what resource needs to be created.
- Output: It also displays output about specified resources whenever you view your stack.

Now we understand the sections of the CloudFormation template and their functionality, it's time to see the example. In the preceding screenshot, we created a CloudFormation template using CloudFormation designer. Now, let's look at the anatomy of the code:

```
{
    "Description": "AWS CloudFormation Template
    EC2InstanceWithSecurityGroup",
```

In the preceding code, we have defined the description of this template, that is, what exactly it will do:

```
"Parameters": {
    "KeyName": {
        "Description": "Name of an existing EC2 KeyPair",
        "Type": "AWS::EC2::KeyPair::KeyName"
    },
    "InstanceType": {
        "Description": "WebServer EC2 instance type",
        "Type": "String",
        "Default": "t2.medium",
        "AllowedValues": [
            "t1.micro",
            "t2.nano",
            "t2.micro",
            "t2.small",
            "t2.medium",
            "t2.large",
            "m1.small",
            "m1.medium",
            " List of all the compute "
        ],
        "ConstraintDescription": "must be a valid EC2 instance type."
    },
    "SSHLocation": {
        "Description": "SSH Open for Public Network",
        "Type": "String",
        "Default": "0.0.0.0/0"
    }
},
```

In the preceding code block, we have passed the parameter to the template.

In the parameter, we have passed the key-value pair for the instance, which is required for SSH-access (for Linux instances) and RDP access (for Windows instances).

Then, we have passed the parameter to specify the instance type and default instance type. The allowed values for compute type specify that we can use any of the listed values for the InstanceType, but if we do not choose it will use the default value.

Now, as it's going to be a Linux instance, we have passed the SSHLocation parameter, which says by default SSH access is enabled from 0.0.0.0/0 (public internet).

Once we have completed the Parameters section, we will map the AMI to create the VMs. In the following code snippet, we have mapped the compute with AMI type and AMI types mapped with AMI ID in the AWS regions:

```
"Mappings": {
    "AWSInstanceType2Arch": {
        "t1.micro": {
            "Arch": "PV64"
        },
        "t2.nano": {
            "Arch": "HVM64"
        },
        "t2.micro": {
            "Arch": "HVM64"
        },
        "t2.small": {
            "Arch": "HVM64"
        },
        "t2.medium": {
            "Arch": "HVM64"
        },
        "t2.large": {
            "Arch": "HVM64"
        },
        "m1.small": {
            "Arch": "PV64"
        },
        "m1.medium": {
            "Arch": "PV64"
        },
        "m1.large": {
            "Arch": "PV64"
        },
        "m1.xlarge": {
```

```
                "Arch": "PV64"
            },
            "m2.xlarge": {
                "Arch": "PV64"
            },
            "m2.2xlarge": {
                "Arch": "PV64"
            },
            "m2.4xlarge": {
                "Arch": "PV64"
            },
            "m3.medium": {
                "Arch": "HVM64"
            },
            "m3.large": {
                "Arch": "HVM64"
            },
            "m3.xlarge": {
                "Arch": "HVM64"
            },
            "m3.2xlarge": {
                "Arch": "HVM64"
            },
            "m4.large": {
                "Arch": "HVM64"
            },
            "m4.xlarge": {
                "Arch": "HVM64"
            }
        },
        "AWSRegionArch2AMI": {
            "ap-southeast-1": {
                "PV64": "ami-df9e4cbc",
                "HVM64": "ami-a59b49c6",
                "HVMG2": "ami-3e91ed5d"
            },
            "ap-southeast-2": {
                "PV64": "ami-63351d00",
                "HVM64":"ami-dc361ebf",
                "HVMG2": "ami-84a142e6"
            },
            "ap-south-1": {
                "PV64": "NOT_SUPPORTED",
                "HVM64": "ami-ffbdd790",
                "HVMG2": "ami-25ffbe4a"
            }
        }
    },
```

In the following code snippet, the deployed resource is defined. In the `Resources` section, we have specified the `InstanceType` and referred to it with the `InstanceType` defined in the `Parameters` section. Instance is defined with all of its properties `InstanceType`, `SecurityGroups`, `KeyName`, and `ImageId`. Then, we have specified the security group and referred to it as `InstanceSecurityGroup`. `KeyName` is referred to with the SSH `KeyName` section.

The SSH port and ingress rules are also defined in the `InstanceSecurityGroup` section:

```json
"Resources": {
    "EC2Instance": {
        "Type": "AWS::EC2::Instance",
        "Properties": {
            "InstanceType": {
                "Ref": "InstanceType"
            },
            "SecurityGroups": [
                {
                    "Ref": "InstanceSecurityGroup"
                }
            ],
            "KeyName": {
                "Ref": "KeyName"
            },
            "ImageId": {
                "Fn::FindInMap": [
                    "AWSRegionArch2AMI",
                    {
                        "Ref": "AWS::Region"
                    },
                    {
                        "Fn::FindInMap": [
                            "AWSInstanceType2Arch",
                            {
                                "Ref": "InstanceType"
                            },
                            "Arch"
                        ]
                    }
                ]
            }
        }
    },
    "InstanceSecurityGroup": {
        "Type": "AWS::EC2::SecurityGroup",
        "Properties": {
```

```
                "GroupDescription": "Enable SSH access on port 22",
                "SecurityGroupIngress": [
                    {
                        "IpProtocol": "tcp",
                        "FromPort": "22",
                        "ToPort": "22",
                        "CidrIp": {
                            "Ref": "SSHLocation"
                        }
                    }
                ]
            }
        }
    },
}
```

Finally, we have defined the output values in the `Outputs` section:

```
"Outputs": {
    "InstanceId": {
        "Description": "InstanceId of the EC2 instance",
        "Value": {
            "Ref": "EC2Instance"
        }
    },
    "AZ": {
        "Description": "Availability Zone of EC2 instance",
        "Value": {
            "Fn::GetAtt": [
                "EC2Instance",
                "AvailabilityZone"
            ]
        }
    },
    "PublicDNS": {
        "Description": "Public DNSName of EC2 instance",
        "Value": {
            "Fn::GetAtt": [
                "EC2Instance",
                "PublicDnsName"
            ]
        }
    },
    "PublicIP": {
        "Description": "Public IP address of EC2 instance",
        "Value": {
            "Fn::GetAtt": [
                "EC2Instance",
```

```
                    "PublicIp"
              ]
          }
      }
  }
```

Here, we have specified all the details that we require as output in `Fn:GetAtt`. Once the CloudFormation template is executed, it will return `InstanceID`, `AZ`, `PublicDNS`, and `PublicIP`.

You can save the same JSON code and deploy it whenever you want, and it can also be updated whenever required.

This summarizes our examples for Infrastructure as Code.

Configuration management

In the previous section, we have seen how we can automate the infrastructure deployment in AWS Cloud using CloudFormation. Now we will automate the configuration management task using Ansible.

Here, we will see how automation helps with configuration management. In both OpenStack and AWS, we have the option to pass the custom script in the user data section to automate the package installation task.

In AWS, we use the following steps to pass to user data:

1. Log in to AWS Management Console.
2. Search for **EC2** services.
3. Click on **Create Instance** | **Choose AMI** | **Choose Instance Type** and click on **Configure Instance**:

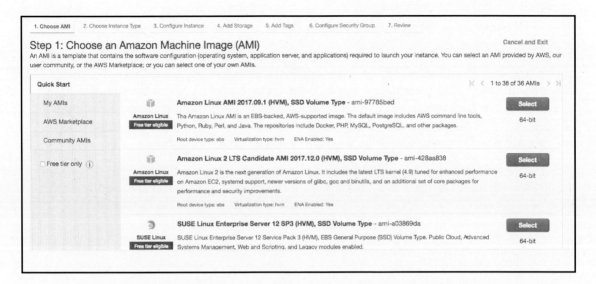

4. Here, pass all the required details, such as number of instances, network, subnet, IAM role, and monitoring, and then click on the **Advanced Details** tab where, you will get the **User data** section, as depicted in the following screenshot:

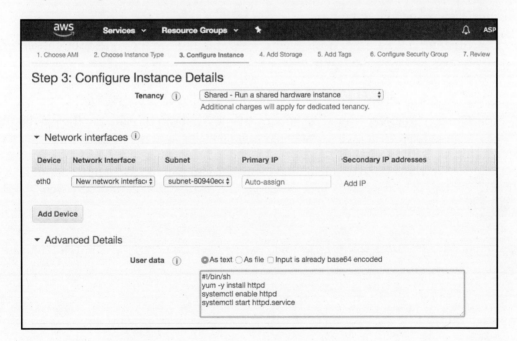

In the preceding screenshot, you can see that we have passed a bash script to install the Apache web server.

Let's understand how this happens. Once this instance boots up, it will start executing the script mentioned in the **User data** section. In the code, you can see that we are installing `httpd` (which is the Apache package for RPM-based Linux), starting it, and enabling this service. So it will automatically install the Apache and start and enable it. Here, we can additionally specify other tasks that we want to install on the instance.

However, the limitation with the **User data** section is that you need to pass the user data while creating the instance, or you need to shut down the instance if it is already running, then pass the user data script and start the instance. So it's not always useful for automation.

We can do the same work with the configuration management tool. Now, we will see an example that will help us deploy a WordPress application on a server using Ansible.

The best part of Ansible is that it's agentless, whereas Chef and Puppet are agent-based. To run the Ansible code, you just need to define the environment variables for the cloud where you want to run the Ansible code (which we call a playbook).

In Ansible, we use the following terms:

- **Inventory**: It's a list of hosts where we wanted to run the code or target servers. It can be both static and dynamic.
- **Playbook**: It's YAML code that plays to-do actions on target servers.
- **Role**: It's a category of task, such as common task and web server.
- **Group variables**: These are global variables that can be called in the playbook.
- **Task**: This is the list of actions that will be performed by a role.

 We won't go in depth about Ansible. If you want to learn more about it, please visit `http://docs.ansible.com`. Here you will find very rich documentation.

In the following code, we have defined that specified `roles` will be configured by hosts defined in the inventory:

```
---
- name: Install Packages
  hosts: all
  remote_user: root
```

```
roles:
  - common
  - mysql
  - nginx
  - php-fpm
  - wordpress
```

Now we have common roles where we have defined all the common packages and the repository required to install the required packages:

```
---
- name: Install libselinux-python
  yum: name=libselinux-python state=present

- name: Reload ansible_facts
  setup:

- name: Copy the EPEL repository
  copy: src=epel.repo dest=/etc/yum.repos.d/epel.repo

- name: Copy GPG key for EPEL
  copy: src=RPM-GPG-KEY-EPEL-6 dest=/etc/pki/rpm-gpg

- name: Define Iptables Rules
  copy: src=iptables-save dest=/etc/sysconfig/iptables
  notify: restart iptables
```

In the aforementioned code, we have given the instruction to install the required packages, configured the required repository, and also defined the firewall (named `iptables`).

In the `copy` section, we have given the instruction to copy the content stored in files to destination files, and the `notify` section is calling handler (which is also a YAML code) to restart `iptables`:

```
---
- name: restart iptables
  service: name=iptables state=restarted
```

Now we will see the MySQL roles, where we have defined the code to install MySQL service and also used a template to copy the configuration files for MySQL:

```
---
- name: Install Mysql
  yum: name={{ item }} state=present
  with_items:
    - mysql-server
    - MySQL-python
```

```
          - libselinux-python
          - libsemanage-python

      - name: Configure SELinux for mysql
        seboolean: name=mysql_connect_any state=true persistent=yes
        when: ansible_selinux.status == "enabled"

      - name: Making MySql Configuration entry
        template: src=my.cnf.j2 dest=/etc/my.cnf
        notify:
        - restart mysql

      - name: Start Mysql Service
        service: name=mysqld state=started enabled=yes
```

Here we can see that initially it starts all the services related to MySQL and then it also enables SELinux to allow MySQL service. In the template section, we copy the MySQL configuration file to /etc/my.cnf.

Let's see what is defined in the template file called my.cnf.j2. j2 is a jinja2 script file, which is used by Ansible:

```
[mysqld]
datadir=/var/lib/mysql
socket=/var/lib/mysql/mysql.sock
user=mysql
security risks
symbolic-links=0
port={{ mysql_port }}

[mysqld_safe]
log-error=/var/log/mysqld.log
pid-file=/var/run/mysqld/mysqld.pid
```

If you have worked on MySQL, you are very well versed in this code. It's just the my.cnf file content.

Like the template, we also have a handler that gives the instruction to start the MySQL service:

```
      ---
      - name: restart mysql
        service: name=mysqld state=restarted
```

So, now we have prepared a server with common roles and installed MySQL server.

Now let's see the NGINX configuration:

```
---
- name: Install nginx
  yum: name=nginx state=present

- name: Nginx Configuration of Wordpress
  template: src=default.conf dest=/etc/nginx/conf.d/default.conf
  notify: restart nginx
```

Similar to other roles, we have defined code to install NGINX and also a template from which the NGINX configuration is being copied, and instructed the handler to restart the NGINX:

```
---
- name: restart nginx
  service: name=nginx state=restarted enabled=yes
```

In the `php-fpm` role, we have defined code that installs and configures `php-fpm` for the WordPress application. Here, too we have a template from where the configuration will be copied and a handler to restart the service:

```
---
- name: Install php
  yum: name={{ item }} state=present
  with_items:
    - php
    - php-fpm
    - php-enchant
    - php-mbstring
    - php-mysql
    - php-process
    - php-xml

- name: Disable default pool
  command: mv /etc/php-fpm.d/www.conf /etc/php-fpm.d/www.disabled
creates=/etc/php-fpm.d/www.disabled
  notify: restart php-fpm

- name: php-fpm configuration
  template: src=wordpress.conf dest=/etc/php-fpm.d/
  notify: restart php-fpm
```

Finally, we will work on the WordPress role, where we will install the WordPress service and configure it:

```
---
- name: WordPress Download
  get_url: url=http://wordpress.org/wordpress-{{ wp_version }}.tar.gz
dest=/srv/wordpress-{{ wp_version }}.tar.gz

- name: Extract Wordpress Package

  command: chdir=/srv/ /bin/tar xvf wordpress-{{ wp_version }}.tar.gz
creates=/srv/wordpress

- name: Create group "wordpress"
  group: name=wordpress

- name: Create user "wordpress"
  user: name=wordpress group=wordpress home=/srv/wordpress/

- name: Create WordPress database
  mysql_db: name={{ wp_db_name }} state=present

- name: Create WordPress database user
  mysql_user: name={{ wp_db_user }} password={{ wp_db_password }} priv={{
wp_db_name }}.*:ALL host='localhost' state=present

- name: Copy WordPress config file
  template: src=wp-config.php dest=/srv/wordpress/

- name: Change ownership of WordPress installation
  file: path=/srv/wordpress/ owner=wordpress group=wordpress
state=directory recurse=yes setype=httpd_sys_content_t

- name: Start php-fpm Service
  service: name=php-fpm state=started enabled=yes
```

In the preceding code, we can see the {{ }} notation, which is a global variable. It's being called for facts. Here, we are downloading the WordPress package version (defined in global variable), installing it on the server, configuring the database, defining ownership of the WordPress site, and finally starting the service.

If things go correctly, you will get the page in the following screenshot:

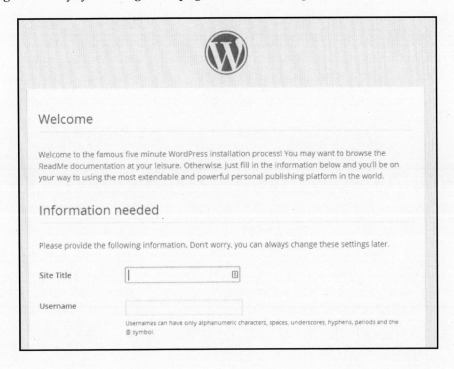

Now, let's see the global variable files that contain all the variables that have been called throughout the application in all the roles:

```
---

wp_version: 4.9.2
wp_db_name: wordpress
wp_db_user: wordpress
wp_db_password: secret

mysql_port: 3306
server_hostname: mysite.local
automatic updates
auto_up_disable: false
core_update_level: true
```

This code can be modified at any point in time and can also be rolled out without even touching the server.

If we had planned to do the same work manually, it would take a minimum of 3 to 4 hours, that's if it is a single server. Let's assume that we have to deploy a WordPress package of a thousand VMs—how much time would that take?

But, using Ansible, we automated and we can do the same deployment for a thousand servers in a few minutes.

Automate deployment – AWS OpsWorks

AWS OpsWorks provides configuration management using managed Chef and Puppet instances. This helps you automate your deployment, configuration, and management processes.

In AWS OpsWorks, we create a stack that is a collection of resources such as your web server, load balancer, and database servers. After that, we have a layer where we define the configuration of components. As per AWS:

> *"A layer is a blueprint for a set of Amazon EC2 instances. It specifies the instance's settings, associated resources, installed packages, profiles, and security groups."*

After adding the layer, we have a list of the instances that will be running our workload, and then the application will be deployed on the infrastructure. Finally, there is monitoring, which monitors the infrastructure.

The only limitation with OpsWorks is that you cannot do the SSH into instances or do any custom configuration manually.

Let's see how easy it is to deploy a sample Node.js application using AWS OpsWorks.

To complete the deployment, first log in to AWS Management Console and search for the OpsWorks service. Here, you will get the following screenshot:

Now we will choose **Go to OpsWorks Stacks**. Here, you will get options to choose the stack as per your requirement. I will go for sample application:

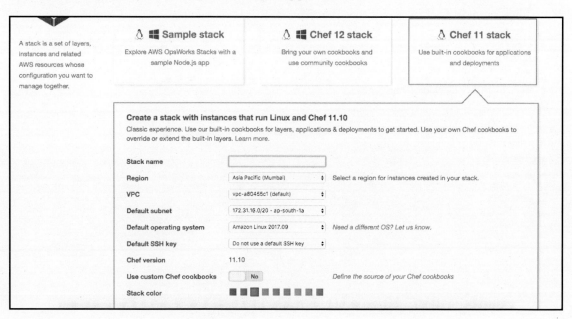

Now you can choose your environment, fill in all the details, and click on **Add Stack**. After that, you will have to add layers:

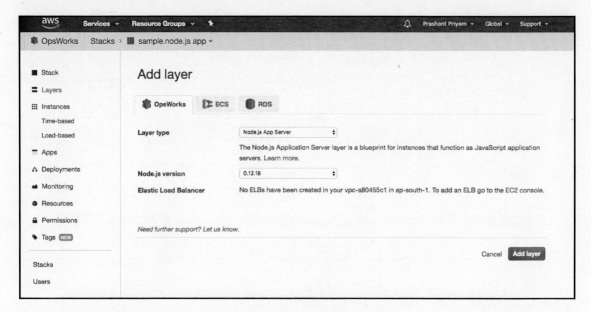

Now click on **Add Instance** with the required compute capacity:

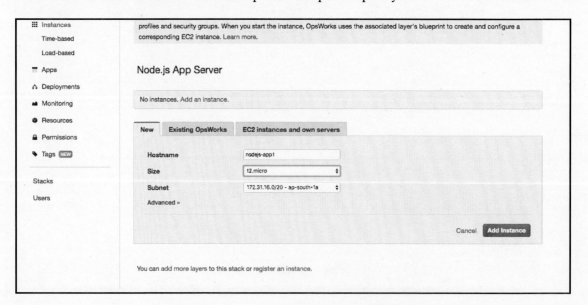

Once the instance is added, start the instance and add your application:

Once the instance is booted up successfully, click on **Deploy app**, choose the instance, and click on **Deploy**.

This will deploy the application. Once the application is successfully deployed, and after accessing the `http://<your instance ip>` URL, you will get the following page:

Once the application is deployed, you can see the monitoring of the infrastructure from the Console itself:

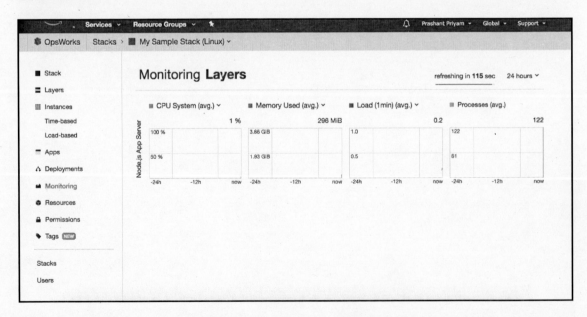

This is how easy it is to deploy an application using OpsWorks.

Quick recap

DevOps is a combination of culture, practice, and tools, which increases the ability to deploy and deliver applications and services. It helps to hasten the development and delivery process using automation.

The traditional way, when we were doing things manually, made the process slower, which delayed delivery. In contrast, using DevOps, things become faster.

The benefits of automation are:

- Time and cost saving
- Faster deployment and delivery
- Elimination of human error
- Improved collaboration
- Easy security implementation

In AWS we have seen that there are many services available to help you in automating the process too, such as Elastic Beanstalk, OpsWorks, and CloudFormation.

AWS Elastic Beanstalk helps us deploy our code developed in few clicks using Elastic Beanstalk, and it also helps us set up a blue-green deployment model, which is also known as a testing and production model. Elastic Beanstalk automatically handles the details of capacity provisioning, load balancing, scaling, and application health monitoring.

AWS OpsWorks provides configuration management using managed Chef and Puppet instances, which helps you automate your deployment, configuration, and management processes.

CloudFormation is a tool that helps you create Infrastructure as Code. You can deploy complete infrastructures using simple JSON code.

Apart from this, we have also seen that there are multiple tools, such as Jenkins, Git, Ansible, Docker, Vagrant, Chef, and Puppet, that can help you in different DevOps processes.

However, you will still hear many myths about DevOps, as follows:

- **DevOps is meant for startups**: In reality, many internet giants, such as Amazon, Netflix, and Google, are using DevOps. They understood the complexity and pain of manual deployment and delivery, and successfully adopted and implemented DevOps.
- **DevOps replaces agile**: In fact, DevOps principles are compatible with agile, and agile turned out to be an enabler of DevOps because of its focus on continuous delivery of high-quality services to customers.
- **DevOps is incompatible with ITIL**: In real life, DevOps can be made compatible with ITIL. In fact, it has automated many areas of ITIL for faster delivery. As far as incident and problem management is concerned, it's always relevant in the case of DevOps.
- **DevOps is incompatible with ISMS**: Many have concern that the absence of traditional control can eliminate the information security and compliance professional, which is also not true. Because you have control of a project since the early stages and at each stage, it ensures better quality, security, and compliance.
- **DevOps means removing IT operations**: Many people think that DevOps will remove IT operational jobs or it will be a no ops job, which is also not correct. We have seen in this chapter that DevOps strengthens the responsibility of operations people. It's a fact that there is a bit of modification to their role. DevOps always makes life easier for operations people by automating their repetitive jobs.
- **DevOps is only Infrastructure as Code**: Many people think that DevOps is just defining Infrastructure as Code, which is also not correct; we have seen in this chapter that DevOps takes care of the overall responsibility of infrastructure deployment, management, and monitoring, as well as applications.
- **The biggest myth—DevOps is only for open source technology**: This myth was true until Microsoft adopted open source. Now you can do all of its activities on a Windows platform with the same ease as a Linux platform.

Summary

This chapter was all about automation, the automation process, and the tools, needs, and benefits of cloud automation. In the next chapter, we will have a look at Identity and Access Management in the cloud.

3
Identity and Access Management in the Cloud

In Chapter 1, *Introduction to Cloud Security*, we read about the AAA model of security, where we saw that authentication and authorization are very critical points. In cloud, we defined the two parts, authentication and authorization, using IAM.

IAM stands for **Identity and Access Management**. It plays a critical role in security implementation in the cloud. Here, we define users, groups, roles, and policies.

In AWS, when we subscribe the services, we actually create a root account, which is single sign in for all the services.

In single sign in, we enter our user credentials once and we can move through all the connected applications without being prompted for user credentials.

It's always advisable to not access the AWS Console using the root account, and also make sure that you have enabled **multi-factor authentication (MFA)**.

In this chapter, we will look at the following topics:

- Users and groups
- Roles and policies
- WAF and Shield
- Certificate manager
- Amazon Macie
- Case study

IAM features

In AWS, IAM is available as a service that is global in scope. Here, global means the usage scope of IAM is global; it is defined once and can be used across all the AWS regions. It's not a region-specific service.

IAM provides the following features:

- **Shared or cross-account access**: Using IAM, you can permit other users to administer your AWS services and can also allow users in other AWS accounts to manage your AWS services without passwords or access keys.
- **Component level permission**: In IAM, you can define access policies on a component level. Suppose that if you have allowed a user to access only one S3 bucket, he/she won't be able to access other services and other S3 buckets.
- **Secure access of services to an application that runs on EC2 or ECS**: Let's assume that we have a web server running on an AWS EC2 instance and the static content is stored on a S3 bucket. One method is to provide access keys- and secret keys-based access to S3 bucket, which will be hardcoded with web application code. However, it's a security risk because if EC2 gets compromised, there is a chance that the access keys will be revealed. Here, the best practice is to define the EC2 role, which includes policies to grant access to specific buckets.
- **MFA**: IAM also facilitates to have MFA for Console access using a configured device's code-based authentication. It's additional security for accessing the services apart from using passwords and access keys. Let's assume that your account is enabled with MFA using Google Authenticator. Now, to log in to your account, you need to provide a user ID, password, and the random code generated with Google Authenticator on your registered device.
- **Identity information audit**: If you have enabled CloudTrail, you can see the real-time logs regarding who has accessed what. If users are facing any issues accessing the Console, you can get detailed information.
- **No cost component**: In AWS, IAM comes for free; there is no cost associated with it.
- **Eventual consistent**: IAM is an eventual consistent service in AWS. So, any modification in role and policies takes time to propagate across all the regions.
- **PCI DSS compliant**: IAM supports the processing, storage, and transmission of credit card data by a merchant, and it has been validated as being compliant with **Payment Card Industry (PCI) Data Security Standard (DSS)**.

How does AWS work in IAM?

Now we will look at the anatomy of IAM and see how it works. In AWS, IAM consists of six elements:

- Principal
- Request
- Authentication
- Authorization
- Actions
- Resources

Let's understand what all these six elements are:

- **Principal**: Principal is an entity that performs some action on AWS resources. It is basically an **Amazon Resource Name (ARN)** such as `Principal": { "AWS": "arn:aws:iam:: 202785070987:root" }`. It means that all the users, roles, groups, and federated applications are principals, as they all are responsible for performing an action on AWS resources.

- **Request**: When principal wants to perform an action, it actually sends a request to AWS. Here, a request consists of the following:
  - Who is going to perform an action (that is, information about principal)
  - Which action will be performed (that is, action detail)
  - Where the action will be performed (that is, resources)
  - So, request data includes the following:
    - Principal information
    - Environment variables such as IP, user agent, and SSL status
    - Data related to the resources that will be created

- **Authentication**: All the principals need to access AWS services for which they must be authenticated. Authentication happens with:
  - User ID and password for principal with ID and password
  - User ID, password, and MFA token when principal is enabled with MFA authentication
  - Access keys and secret keys for API-based access

- **Authorization**: In the authorization phase, all the principal request data is evaluated against the defined JSON-based policies to allow or deny action. During the evaluation process, if a single policy includes a denied action, IAM denies the entire request and stops evaluating. This is called an **explicit deny**. Let's take an example; say we have a policy that allows access to an S3 bucket called image, and we have defined a policy to deny an object access. In that case, any request for object access will override the S3 bucket's allow rule. Because requests are denied by default, IAM authorizes your request only if every part of your request is allowed by the matching policies.

- **Actions**: Once the authentication and authorization process completes, now principal actions are being approved for execution. Actions are defined by the resources. You cannot create the same actions for all the resources; each resource has its own specific set of actions. For example, S3 services can have the following actions for a bucket:

```
s3:CreateBucket
s3:DeleteBucket
s3:ListBucket
s3:ListBucketVersions
s3:ListAllMyBuckets
s3:ListBucketMultipartUploads
```

- **Resources**: After AWS approves the actions, it is performed on resources (meaning AWS services). A resource is an entity that exists within a service, such as an Amazon EC2 instance, an IAM user, or an Amazon S3 bucket. The service defines a set of actions that can be performed on each resource. If you create a request to perform an unrelated action on a resource, that request is denied.

Anatomy of IAM users, groups, roles, and policies

In this section, we will look at IAM users, groups, roles, and policies in depth.

IAM users

To access the AWS Management Console, we need IAM users who can log in and access the Console in secure way.

For this, we have the following three major types of users:

- **First time users (root account)**: This is the account with which we subscribed to the AWS services. It is also named the root account, and will have super admin privileges on all the services. You can access all the services without a prompt for user credentials once you are signed in to the Console. There are a few best practices associated with a root account:
    - Do not allow the user root account to access AWS Console
    - You must enable MFA for the root account
    - Do not create access keys for root account
    - Have a complex password for the root account
- **Normal IAM users**: These are the users that we have defined purposefully and assigned the required sets of permission to perform some actions on AWS resources or services. We can have the following different sets of users:
    - **System administrator**: This is the user who will have administrator roles assigned.
    - **Network administrator**: This is the user who will manage the VPC aspects.
    - **S3 administrator**: This is the user who will manage the S3 object storage and so on. For all the normal users, we must ensure the following:
        - Users are assigned only the required sets of policies and roles
        - They must have a complex password
        - They are enabled with MFA for additional layer of security
        - Access keys must be rotated on a specific schedule
        - All the users' activity gets recorded on a CloudTrail for audit purposes

- **Federated users**: There are a few sets of users who already have a way to be authenticated. For example, by signing in to your corporate network, you can federate those user identities into AWS. A user who has already logged in replaces his or her existing identity with a temporary identity in your AWS account. This user can work in the AWS Management Console. Similarly, an application that the user is working with can make programmatic requests using permissions that you define. Federated users are useful in the following cases:
  - You already have an **Active Directory** (**AD**) kind of setup running on premise, and you want all the users who are a part of AD to get authenticated. In this scenario, you can use federated authentication of users using AD connector or SAML-based SSO.
  - Mobile application users who already have an internet authentication mechanism, such as authentication with Google and Facebook:

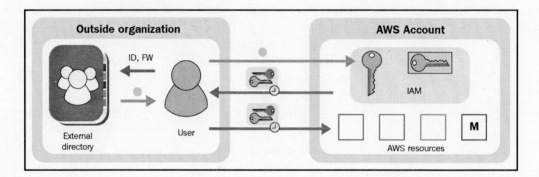

IAM groups

IAM groups are collections of similar sets of users. They help you easily create users and assign specific sets of roles and access policies by associating them with a specific group.

In the following screenshot, you can see that there is a group named `SysAdmin` that has administrative access. There is a user who is a part of this group; this means that users associated with this group will have administrator privileges:

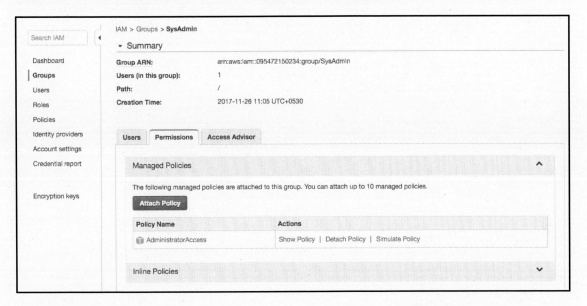

IAM roles

IAM roles are the most secure way to assign access permission to the entity you trust. It generates a short-term token to provide authentication. There are many roles already predefined in AWS IAM, and it also enables us to create custom roles.

In the following screenshot, we can see that there are already a few service-specific roles defined:

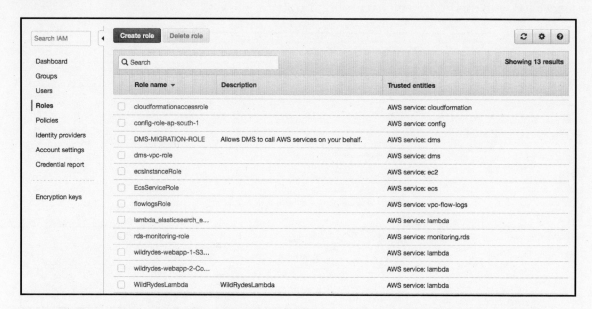

Now, let's see the **Database Migration Service (DMS)** migration roles, which are custom roles that I have created for the DMS. Here, you can see that there are seven policies associated with this role, and required for the DMS:

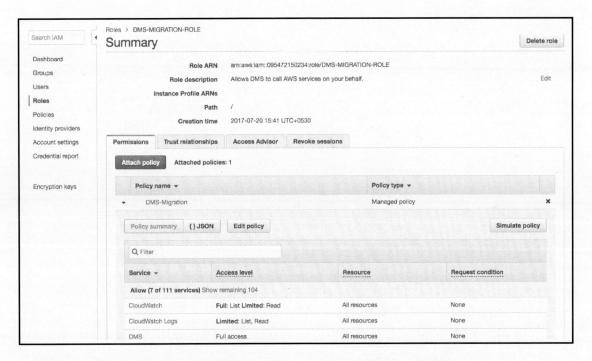

Now, let's see the policies associated with this role, which are JSON code.

In the following policy, we have permitted users to access the following resource.

The first section of the code allows users to perform all the operations of the DMS:

```
{
    "Version": "2012-10-17",
    "Statement": [
        {
            "Effect": "Allow",
            "Action": "dms:*",
            "Resource": "*"
        },
```

The second section of the code allows users read-only access to the **Key Management Service** (**KMS**) where a user can list the keys and get all the attributes of keys:

```
        {
            "Effect": "Allow",
            "Action": [
                "kms:ListAliases",
                "kms:DescribeKey"
            ],
```

```
        "Resource": "*"
    },
```

The third section of the code allows users to get the list of IAM roles, create new roles, and attach the roles to another AWS service:

```
    {
        "Effect": "Allow",
        "Action": [
            "iam:GetRole",
            "iam:PassRole",
            "iam:CreateRole",
            "iam:AttachRolePolicy"
        ],
        "Resource": "*"
    },
```

The fourth section of the code allows users read-only access to VPC details and the ability to perform create and delete operations on the network interface:

```
    {
        "Effect": "Allow",
        "Action": [
            "ec2:DescribeVpcs",
            "ec2:DescribeInternetGateways",
            "ec2:DescribeAvailabilityZones",
            "ec2:DescribeSubnets",
            "ec2:DescribeSecurityGroups",
            "ec2:ModifyNetworkInterfaceAttribute",
            "ec2:CreateNetworkInterface",
            "ec2:DeleteNetworkInterface"
        ],
        "Resource": "*"
    },
```

The fifth section of the code allows users read-only access to CloudWatch resources so that they can see the monitoring metrics:

```
    {
        "Effect": "Allow",
        "Action": [
            "cloudwatch:Get*",
            "cloudwatch:List*"
        ],
        "Resource": "*"
    },
```

The sixth section of the code allows users read-only access to CloudTrail logs where they can search and filter for logs, and view them:

```
{
    "Effect": "Allow",
    "Action": [
        "logs:DescribeLogGroups",
        "logs:DescribeLogStreams",
        "logs:FilterLogEvents",
        "logs:GetLogEvents"
    ],
    "Resource": "*"
},
```

The last section of the code allows users to get the details of Redshift cluster and associate IAM policies that are already existing or newly created:

```
{
    "Effect": "Allow",
    "Action": [
        "redshift:Describe*",
        "redshift:ModifyClusterIamRoles"
    ],
    "Resource": "*"
    }
  ]
}
```

Now, let's dive deep into IAM policies.

IAM policies

IAM policies are sets of JSON code that are based on allow and deny. Here, we define actions associated with a specific service, which will be either allowed or denied.

Let's take an example. My group went on a trip where we took lots of photographs and videos. We wanted to store them in an S3 bucket (named `manali-trip-2017`) and give access to IAM users so that all other members can access this bucket to download and upload the pictures and videos. And, later on, we want to create a web application that can display all these pictures to users.

For this, I created an S3 bucket, and created an IAM user who has permission to access the specific bucket:

```
{
    "Version": "2012-10-17",
    "Statement": [
        {
            "Sid": "Stmt1511326932281",
            "Action": "s3:*",
            "Effect": "Allow",
            "Resource": "arn:AWS:s3:::manali-trip-112017"
        },
        {
            "Sid": "Stmt1511326945574",
            "Action": "s3:*",
            "Effect": "Allow",
            "Resource": "arn:AWS:s3:::manali-trip-112017/*"
        },
        {
            "Sid": "Stmt1511327364570",
            "Action": [
                "s3:ListAllMyBuckets"
            ],
            "Effect": "Allow",
            "Resource": "arn:AWS:s3:::*"
        }
    ]
}
```

In the preceding code snippet, we have an S3 bucket named `manali-trip-112017`. One more thing; in AWS, all the resources have their ARN, which is required in the policy.

In the preceding policy, you can see that we have permitted the user to perform all the action on the bucket and underlying folders.

In the last block, we are just giving permission to see the list of buckets so that he can browse the `manali-trip-112017` bucket and perform actions.

Access right delegation using IAM

In IAM, you can give access to delegate rights to users or services that do not have access to AWS services. For this, IAM provides you with the following tools:

- Temporary credentials
- Cross-account access
- Identity federation

Temporary credentials

Let's create a scenario where we have an application running on an EC2 instance and want to access a few objects stored in an S3 bucket in a secure way. For this, we define the IAM role and associate it with an EC2 instance. Whenever an application running on an EC2 instance needs to access the S3 object, it calls for metadata and gets the temporary credential to access the S3 bucket. This enables you to not pass the credential or access keys to an application to access the S3 bucket and is also more secure, as passing permanent access or long duration access can be a security risk.

Cross-account access

Here, we will take the example of an enterprise that has multiple accounts for different kinds of workloads, and where the administration needs to access all the environment to do management and maintenance activities. So, creating an IAM user per account is a very time-consuming process, and there will always be a chance of forgetting the credentials and access keys. To get rid of this situation, IAM enables you to have a cross-account access policy. Here, we create an account and create a policy that allows users to get access to services in other accounts. To do this, users just need to switch the account using the defined role and account ID.

Let's see an example of a cross-account access policy:

```
{
    "Version": "2012-10-17",
    "Statement": [
        {
            "Sid": "AllowDeletionOfServiceLinkedRoleForOrganizations",
            "Effect": "Allow",
            "Action": [
                "iam:DeleteRole"
            ],
            "Resource": [
```

```
        "arn:AWS:iam::*:role/AWS-service-role/
        organizations.amazonaws.com/*"
    ]
},
{
    "Sid": "AllowCreationOfServiceLinkedRoles",
    "Effect": "Allow",
    "Action": [
        "iam:CreateServiceLinkedRole"
    ],
    "Resource": "*"
}
    ]
}
```

Identity federation

Here, we create an identity broker that works as an intermediary between corporate users and AWS services to grant the authentication and authorization process without creating the users in IAM.

Here, our corporate users log in to the identity broker application, which authenticates users with a local identity store. The identity broker application has access to the AWS **Security Token Service (STS)**, which is used to request temporary security credentials. Then, it directs users to a temporary URL to access the AWS Management Console. Microsoft Active Directory is an example of an identity broker application.

Let's understand the flow of identity federation. Assume we have an application run-in on premise infrastructure, but it needs to access the DynamoDB database service. For this application, first make an authentication request with the identity broker application, which will let it get authenticated with the local identity service, and then make a request to get temporary credentials from the STS API; using the temporary credential application will access DynamoDB services.

IAM best practices

As you have learned a lot about IAM, it's time to know the best practices for the AWS IAM service:

- **Do not use the root account to access AWS Console**: As we read earlier, the root account is automatically created during AWS service. It is a super admin account with all the privileges and permissions. So, it's always advisable to not log in to AWS Console using the root account.

- **Do not enable access keys for the root account**: We need access keys to access the AWS Console and services programmatically. It's always advised to not enable access keys for root users who have super admin rights, and also use a single sign-on account for all the AWS services. If your root account access keys or credentials are compromised, all of the data could be breached.

- **Regularly rotate the access keys**: To access AWS service, we need access keys. Best practice says that you must rotate the access keys frequently. To do this, AWS enables you to have two access keys at once to make the key rotation process easier.

- **Enable MFA access for root account**: We must enable MFA for the root account to improve security. If MFA is enabled and you have compromised credentials, it won't let bad guys access your AWS Console as a registered mobile gets the MFA code for login.

- **Create individual users**: It's always advised to create individual AWS IAM users and also enable CloudTrail to audit user activity.

- **Use AWS IAM policies to assign permissions**: It's always advised to have separate AWS accounts for all the users who need to access AWS Console, and so on.

- **Create user groups to define permissions**: We all know that a group is a set of entities. So, instead of defining user-based permissions, we must create a group and apply the required policies. So, whenever you are going to create new user, map it with a group. This helps you save time.

- **Grant the least required privileges**: AWS also recommends that you grant specific permissions. This also enables users to perform only a specific set of tasks.

- **Use access levels to review IAM permissions**: It's always advised to review the CloudTrail to see the events performed by a user.
- **Define a complex password policy for users**: It's always advised to have a complex password policy for users so that their passwords cannot be guessed easily.
- **Use IAM roles for applications**: It's advised to use IAM roles for applications that run on Amazon EC2 instances and want to access other AWS services, such as S3, CloudWatch Logs, and RDS services.
- **Delegate by using roles instead of by sharing credentials**: Cross-account access.
- **Remove unnecessary credentials**: Remove credentials that are not in use from IAM.

Other security options in AWS

Apart from IAM, AWS provides other services to harden security and match the security compliances.

Let's see what services are available in AWS Console, in the security section. In the following screenshot, we can see the list of security services:

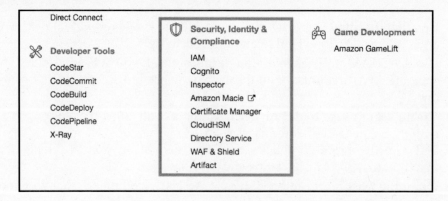

Let's understand all these one by one.

AWS Certificate Manager

AWS Certificate Manager (**ACM**) helps you create and manage the TLS and SSL certificates for websites and applications that run on AWS. ACM makes the SSL certificate procurement, deployment, and renewal processes easy.

SSL certificates obtained from ACM are available for free:

ACM facilitates the importing of commercial CA-signed SSLs, which can be easily offloaded to ELB, EC2, API Gateway, and CloudFront. You can offload SSLs on ELB during or after creation.

Let's see how we offload one during the creation process:

1. First, log in to AWS Console and go to **EC2**. In **EC2**, select **Load Balancers** and click on **Create Load Balancer**. Here, you need to specify a few details, such as name, VPC, internal or external load balancer, and subnet, as specified in the following screenshot:

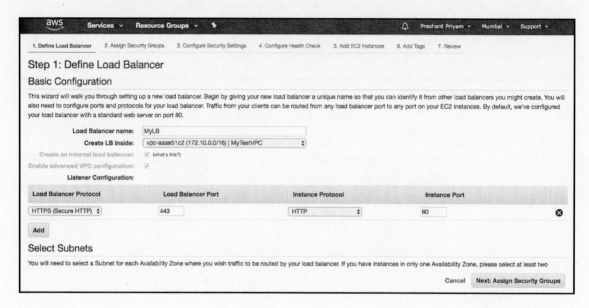

2. After that, you will choose to assign security groups, and then, under **Configure Security Settings**, you will be prompted for a mapping certificate; here, we select **Choose a certificate from ACM (recommended)**:

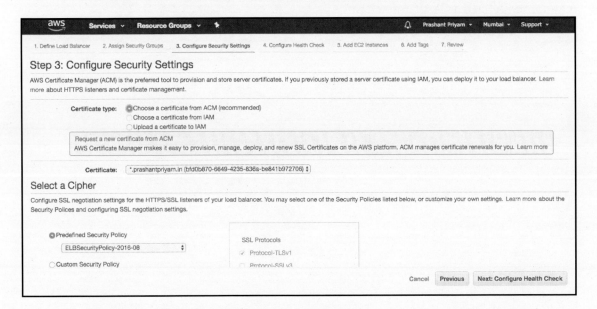

3. After that, we define health check and select EC2 instances, which will be registered under this load balancer.

While procuring the SSL from ACM, it validates the email and domain. It also creates a key pair while procuring the certificate.

ACM also enables you to store a commercial CA-signed certificate. You can import the certificate simply by logging in to AWS Console and selecting **Import a certificate**. For this, you must have a PEM-encoded certificate. For a commercial signed certificate, it's mandatory to have a **Certificate chain**:

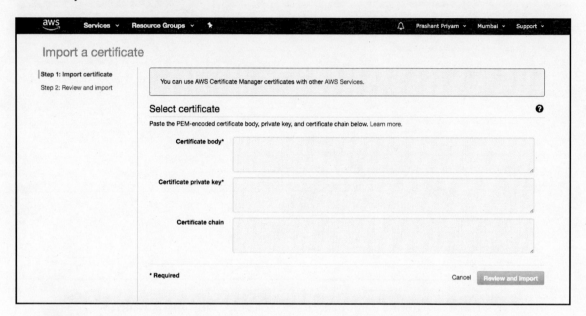

 ACM is specifically designed to protect the private keys of generated SSLs. It uses strong encryption while securing the private keys.

WAF and Shield

WAF stands for **web application firewall**. It is used to secure the application and Layer 7 traffic. WAF helps you secure your application from bad guys on the internet who always try to hijack your application and database using malicious scripts or headers.

It monitors the content delivered through CloudFront or an application load balancer, whereas the Shield service is used to protect from a DDoS attack on applications at the content delivery platform (CloudFront), DNS (Route 53) level, and load balancer (ELB).

You can enable WAF's role with AWS **Application Load Balancer** (**ALB**) or CloudFront.

To enable WAF, log in to AWS Management Console and, in the security section, select **WAF & Shield**. Now click on **Go to AWS WAF**:

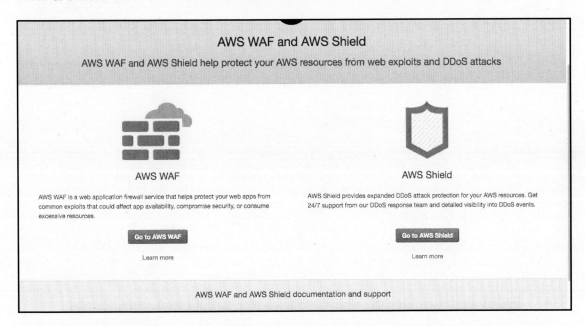

Now click on **Configure web ACL** (here, **ACL** stands for **access control list**) and then click on **Next**:

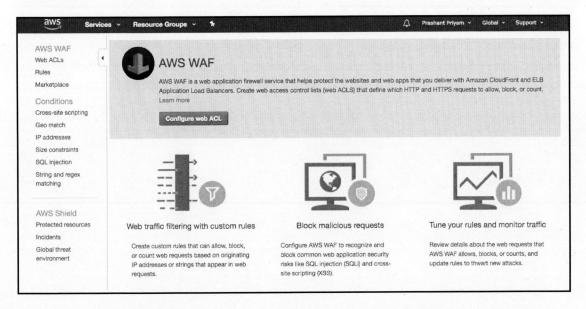

Here, you need to specify the name of ACL and AWS resources. We have set the name as
MYACL:

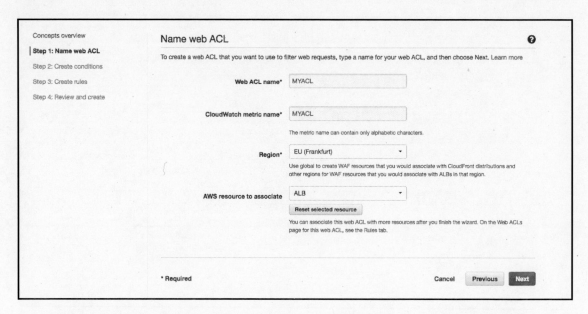

This is where we define WAF to use for ALB or CloudFront. Here, we have ALB as a
resource.

Click on **Next**; this is where you can define all the conditions to allow and deny the traffic:

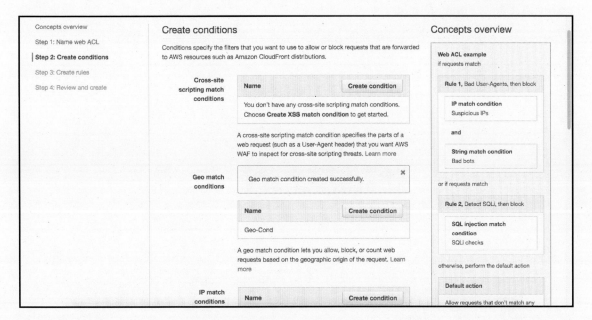

Now, we define the **Geo match conditions**, create the `IP-rule` for India, and add this rule to `MYACL`:

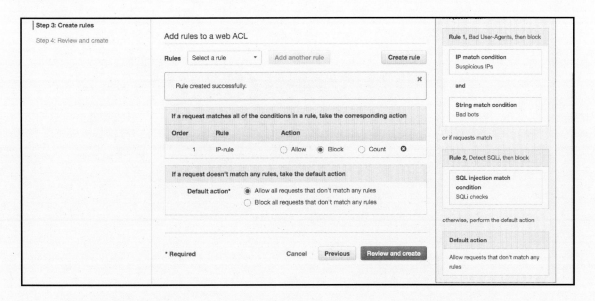

Now, in the rule, I have blocked all the traffic that matches the rule and process only the traffic that does not match the rule.

After creating this ACL, we will not be able to access ALB URL from India:

Now, we modify the ACL:

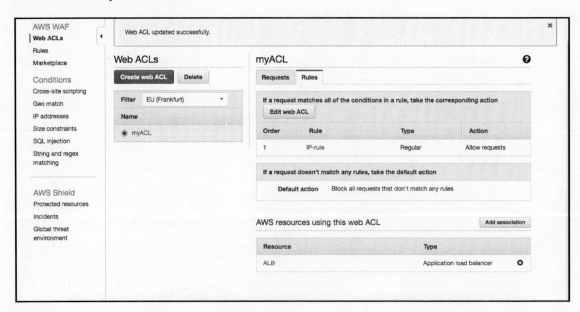

After modifying the ACL, we should access the ALB URL from India:

Here, we have seen how to use WAF. Now, let's see how WAF works.

AWS WAF enables you to choose:

- **Allow all the traffic except the one you specify**: This is applicable when CloudFront and ALB delivers content on the public internet and you want to block the malicious traffic.
- **Block all except the one you specify**: This is applicable when you want to serve content for a restricted website where application users can be identified in web requests, such as using IP information.
- **Count the request that matches the traffic you specify**: In this mode, AWS WAF counts the traffic on the basis of the match parameters defined, instead of allow or deny.

The basic securities that WAF provides are:

- Control SQL injections and cross-site scripting
- Geolocation-based traffic filtering
- Request header values-based filtering
- Filtering traffic not the basis of request length
- Real-time metrics

Apart from AWS WAF, you can use some third-party WAF solutions such as Barracuda WAF, available on AWS Marketplace, which includes many other facilities such as DDoS, file upload control, response control, and JSON payload inspection.

WAF actually works on conditions and rules:

- **Conditions**: Conditions are the characteristics that WAF monitors. All the preceding points such as SQL injections, IP details, and cross-site scripts can be specified as conditions.
- **Rules**: Here, we define the allow and deny policy on the basis of condition match. AWS WAF provides the following two types of rules:
    - **Regular rule**: It uses conditions to target only specific requests as follows:
        - IP address
        - Keywords in header
        - Query string, and so on
    - **Rate-based rule**: It's similar to the regular rule with one additional option named rate. A rate-based rule counts traffic every 5 minutes coming from an IP. If the count exceeds the limit, it starts blocking the traffic. For example, we have defined traffic from an IP on the application as 1500. WAF will count the traffic every 5 minutes; when it exceeds the limits it triggers an event to allow/deny the traffic as specified in ACL.

After defining conditions and rules, we merge them in web ACL where we exactly define the action, such as allow, block, or count.

AWS Shield provides extended DDoS protection for CloudFront and load balancer, Route 53-hosted zone, and Elastic IP-mapped EC2 instances.

If we try to secure Elastic IP using AWS Shield, it automatically deploys the network ACL to the AWS network border to control DDoS attacks on a large scale. In regular practice, NACL works at VPC level only.

Shield protects against multiple types of DDoS attack as follows:

- **UDP reflection attack**: In this process, the attacker spoofs the IP of the server and, using **User Datagram Protocol** (UDP), it requests a large chunk of data from the server, as a result of which the server network will be congested. This can prevent legitimate users from accessing the server.
- **SYN flood**: In this attack, an attacker leaves the TCP connection in a half open state that results in a heavy load on the server. Here, the TCP connection's half open state denotes that TCP three ways handshaking started but acknowledgment never returned.

- **DNS query flood**: In this process, an attacker attacks the DNS server with tons of queries, which results in the DNS failing to respond.
- **HTTP flood**: In this attack, an attacker sends simultaneous HTTP GET and PUT requests to the web application like normal users.

AWS Shield with WAF helps us control Layer 7 attacks on applications. If you are a Premium Support user, you can also get the help of AWS **DDoS response team (DRT)**.

 All the WAF and Shield events can be logged using CloudTrail. AWS Shield is an expensive service; it asks you to pay $3,000 plus additional data transfer charges, with a minimum 1 year contract.

Cloud hardware security module

Cloud **hardware security module (HSM)** is a device that processes encryption operation and stores the encryption keys.

With HSM, you can perform the following operations:

- Generating, storing, importing, exporting, and managing the encryption keys, and also storing symmetric and asymmetric keys
- The encryption of data using symmetric and asymmetric keys
- Cryptographic hash functions to compute message digests and **hash-based message authentication codes (HMACs)**
- Generating random data for cryptography using a pseudo-random number generator

It also helps you meet the compliance requirement of your organization, like PCI DSS.

In CloudHSM, we always create clusters to enable the high availability of HSM. Here, we use one HSM and all the events as updated are getting synced to another HSM:

1. To create a cluster, log in to AWS Console and then search for CloudHSM:

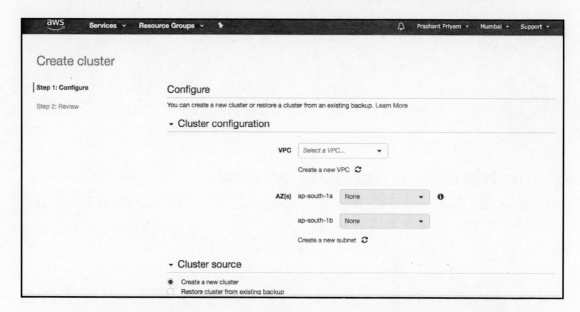

2. Now, you specify the VPC and subnets and click on **Create cluster**:

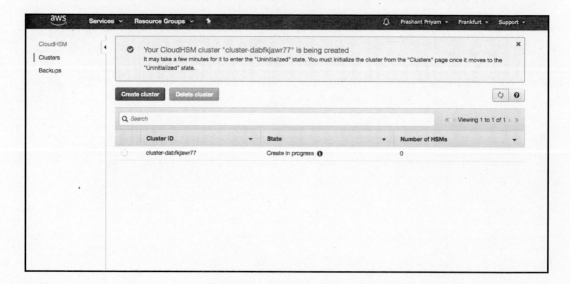

3. Once the cluster is created, now you have to initialize it:

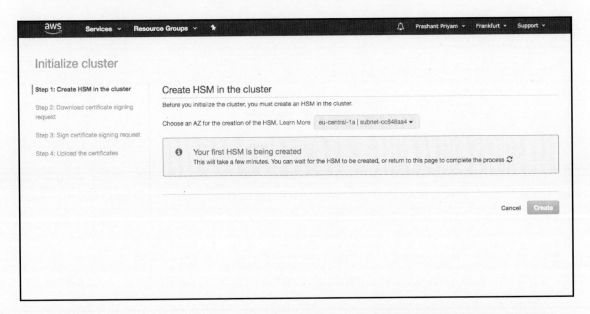

4. After the cluster is initialized, download the **certificate signing request** (CSR):

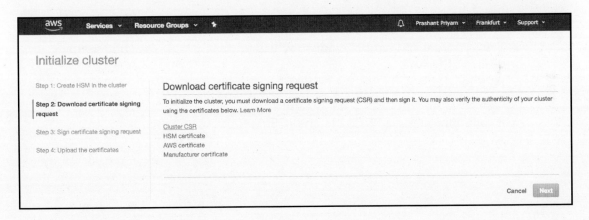

5. Finally, sign the CSR and upload the certificates:

CloudHSM is a client-side encryption method where you encrypt the data and store your keys to HSM. Master keys always reside in CloudHSM cluster.

It helps you encrypt data at S3, EBS, Redshift, and so on.

CloudHSM is a physical device that is:

- Tamper proof and tamper evident, which means that if it goes under attack, it destroys the keys
- FIPS 140-2 certified
- Enables you to timestamp the document
- It communicates via PKCS #11 and JCE

FIPS 140-1 was developed by a government and industry-based group composed of both operators and vendors. The working group identified requirements for four security levels for cryptographic modules to provide for a wide spectrum of data sensitivity (such as low-value administrative data, million dollar funds transfers, and life protecting data) and a diversity of application environments (for example, a guarded facility, an office, and a completely unprotected location). Four security levels are specified for each of the 11 requirement areas. Each security level offers an increase in security over the preceding level. These four increasing levels of security allow cost-effective solutions that are appropriate for different degrees of data sensitivity and different application environments. FIPS 140-2 incorporates changes in applicable standards and technology since the development of FIPS 140-1, as well as changes that are based on comments received from the vendor, laboratory, and user communities. (Source: https://csrc.nist.gov/publications/fips.)

Cognito

AWS Cognito provides a sign in and application authentication process using web identity providers such as Google, Facebook, Amazon for mobile, and web applications. It can handle getting millions of users authenticated with an application at once using web identity, along with a temporary token service, and it also lets users get authenticated using enterprise identity providers using SAML 2.0.

Cognito enables users to synchronize data across the devices to give them a seamless experience even when they upgrade the device or switch to a new device.

Let me give a personal example. I am a user of an online banking application. Recently, I upgraded my Android version to Oreo from Nougat. After the upgrade, when I tried to log in to the application, it did not let me sign in, giving an authentication failure error.

I tried resetting the password, but it still stopped me from logging in to the application. I registered a complaint, but also thought about why it did not allow me to log in to the application.

After trying for multiple hours, I uninstalled the application, reinstalled it, and configured my account, and then it registered my device as a new device, after which I signed in.

Ideally, it should not happen. AWS Cognito resolves this problem. Once you upgrade the device, or even if your device is offline, it stores the data location and later on syncs with Cognito to give a seamless experience. AWS Cognito lets you think about the web application while it takes care of the authentication process.

It provides the following:

- A scalable and secure user directory
- Identity federation for web identity providers and Enterprise identity providers (SAML2.0)
- IAM using OAuth 2.0, SAML 2.0, and OpenID Connect
- Security for application and users
- Easy integration with applications

Amazon Macie

We are in the era of machine learning, where we need everything to work on self-intelligence. AWS provides a machine learning-based security component named **Amazon Macie**.

To enable Amazon Macie, we need to log in to AWS Console and search for the Macie service:

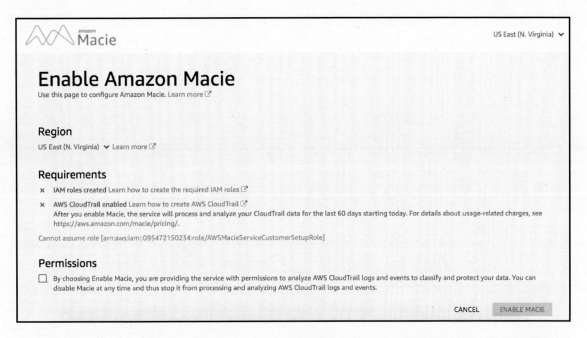

Now we have to define IAM roles and enable CloudTrail to enable Macie. After an IAM role is defined and CloudTrail is enabled, we enable Macie:

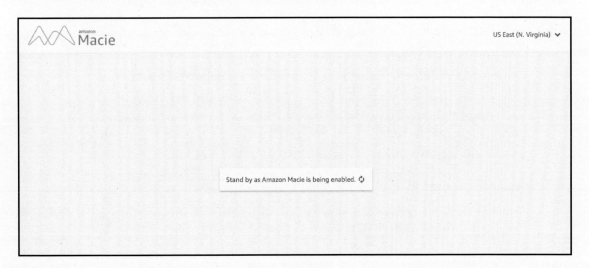

It will take few minutes to enable Macie. Once Macie is enabled, we will go to the Console to see the complete activity in AWS:

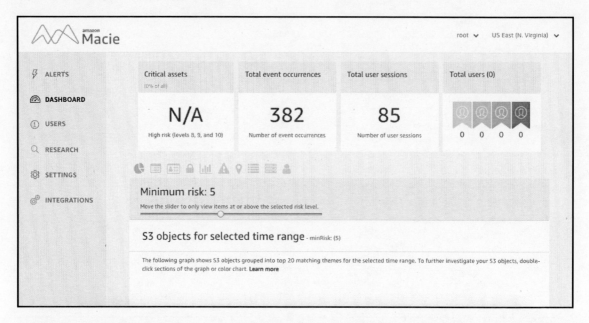

Macie uses machine learning to automatically discover, classify, and protect critical and sensitive data. It also provides you with a dashboard where you can see how data is being accessed and moved. It generates alerts when it finds inappropriate access of data.

AWS Macie provides the following features:

- Continuously monitor new data
- Use artificial intelligence to understand access patterns of data
- Automatically access user activity, applications, and service accounts
- Use **natural language processing** (**NLP**) methods to understand data
- Intelligently classify business-critical data based for your organization
- Create custom security alerts and custom policy definitions

AWS Macie also comes with the following benefits:

- Identifies data types such as **personally identifiable information** (**PII**), **protected health information** (**PHI**), access keys, and secret keys

- Compliance verification using automated logs
- Identity changes in access policies
- Observing users' behavior and receiving actionable alerts
- Receiving alerts and notification when data leaves protected zone
- Detecting when massive business critical data is shared internally and externally

Now, you will be wondering how exactly Macie is doing it all.

Macie basically comes with Macie-curated (or predefined) data types, file extensions, keywords, regular expressions, PII, and PHI. All these Macie-curated details are defined a risk rating of 1-10, where 1 denotes minimum risk and 10 is maximum risk.

For logging, it always uses CloudTrail to monitor all the API calls.

AWS Inspector

As the name suggests, AWS Inspector is a tool that provides an automated security assessment service, which helps improve security and compliance for infrastructure and applications.

As you can see in the following screenshot, it works on IAM roles and then installs agents on AWS EC2 instances to monitor the traffic:

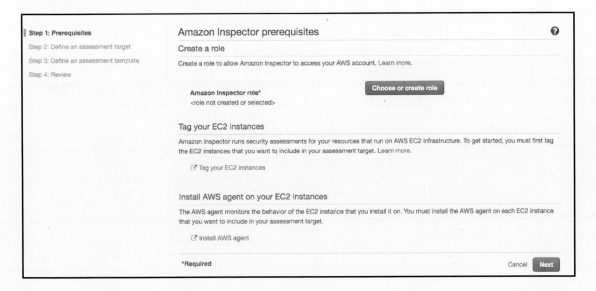

To use AWS Inspector, log in to AWS Console and search for Inspector. On the wizard, select **Choose or create role**, tag your instance, and install the AWS agent.

To install the agent on a Linux machine, we have to run the following commands from the SSH console:

```
wget https://d1wk0tztpsntt1.cloudfront.net/linux/latest/install
sudo bash install
```

After the installation, you will get the following successfully installed message:

```
ETag: "3e1fff6e6ca0f0e949c5aaf66fde70a2"
Accept-Ranges: bytes
Content-Type:
Content-Length: 917
Server: AmazonS3

Installation script completed successfully.

notice:
by installing the Amazon Inspector Agent, you agree that your use is subject to
the terms of your existing
AWS Customer Agreement or other agreement with Amazon Web Services, Inc. or its
affiliates governing your
use of AWS services. You may not install and use the Amazon Inspector Agent unl
ss you have an account in
good standing with AWS.
* * *
Current running agent reports to arsenal endpoint:
Current running agent reports version as: 1.0.1611.0
This install script was created to install agent version:1.0.1611.0
In most cases, these version numbers should be the same.

[root@ip-172-31-42-189 ec2-user]# █
```

Now, after installing the agent, click on **Next** and define an assessment target using the tag we have defined for EC2 instances:

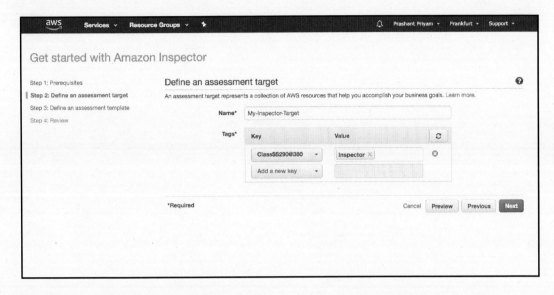

Next, define the template where we specify a name, as mentioned in the following screenshot, and choose from a list of available rule package templates:

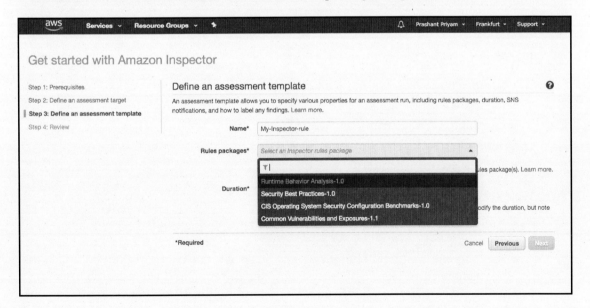

Click on **Next**, and now we can review our configuration and then run the assessment. The assessment only runs if the registered target is in health status:

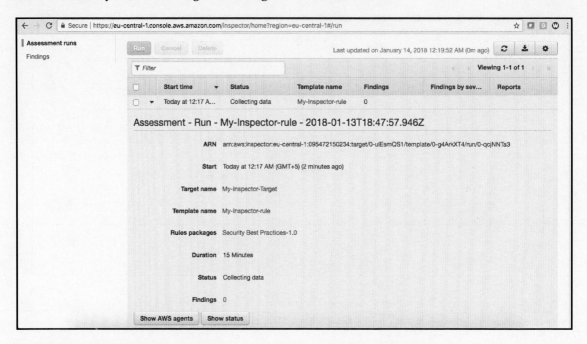

It will run for at least for 15 minutes and then you can see the findings.

AWS Inspector provides the ability to:

- Identify the security in the application
- Integrate with DevOps
- Leverage AWS security
- Streamline security compliance
- Enforce security standards

AWS Inspector has two main parts:

- **Assessment target**: It is a set of all the EC2 instances installed with the Inspector agent.
- **Assessment template**: This allows you to specify the configuration on which the assessment runs. Here, you also specify the duration and rules. It also uses a **Simple Notification Service (SNS)** to send notifications related to assessment process and results.

The Inspector uses CloudTrail to log all the API call and logs, and CloudWatch for real-time monitoring.

For authentication and authorization, it's mandatory to define an IAM role for Inspector.

AWS GuardDuty

In re:Invent 2017, AWS launched one more security service named GuardDuty, which analyzes billions of events in pursuit of trends, patterns, and anomalies that are recognizable signs that something is not right.

It takes input from multiple data streams, including several threat intelligence feeds, staying aware of malicious IP addresses, devious domains, and, more importantly, learning to accurately identify malicious or unauthorized behavior.

GuardDuty takes information from VPC Flow Logs, AWS CloudTrail event logs, and DNS logs. This allows GuardDuty to detect many different types of dangerous and mischievous behavior, including probes for known vulnerabilities, port scans and probes, and access from unusual locations.

Here, you can see the sample report generated by GuardDuty for an environment. It scans your AWS account in depth to identify the loophole:

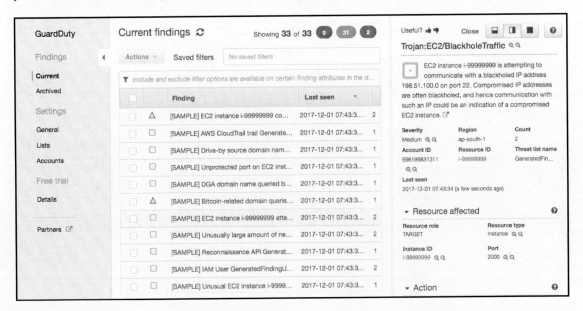

It also allows you to set a trusted IP list, which it won't include during scanning:

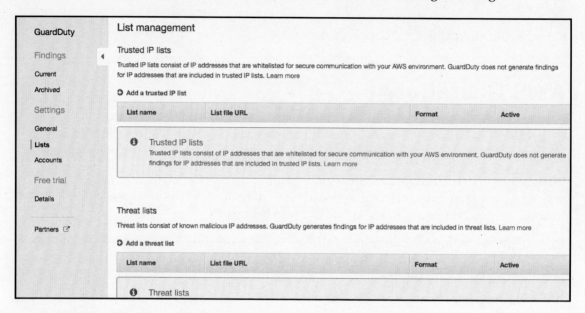

AWS GuardDuty gives in-depth insight of infrastructure in reports:

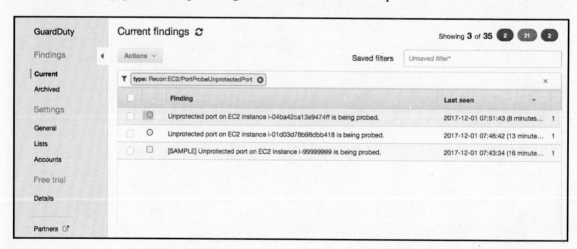

Quick recap

Security is a very important aspect for any organization. IAM plays a vital role in securing your infrastructure and application. In this chapter, you have learned about different aspects of IAM, and also about how to define the access of AWS services and resource-based permissions, cross-account access, and federated access.

Apart from this, you have learned about other AWS security services, such as:

- **AWS WAF and Shield**: AWS WAF and Shield helps you implement security at Layer 7 to secure the application from cross-site scripts, MySQL injections, and DDoS attacks. We define access control policies to access the application.
- **AWS CloudHSM**: It's used to store encryption keys in a highly secure and available environment. It's always deployed in a cluster that lets you download CSR, and then you sign CSR and upload a certificate in a secure environment.
- **AWS Cognito**: Cognito provides a sign in and application authentication process using web identity providers such as Google, Facebook, Amazon for mobile, and web applications. It can get millions of users authenticated with an application at once by using web identity along with a temporary token service, and it also lets users get authenticated using an enterprise identity provider that uses SAML 2.0.
- **AWS Macie**: Macie uses machine learning to automatically discover, classify, and protect critical and sensitive data. It also provides you a dashboard where you can see how data is being accessed and moved. It generates alerts when it finds inappropriate data access.
- **AWS Inspector**: AWS Inspector is a tool that provides an automated security assessment service that helps us improve security and compliance for infrastructure and applications.
- **AWS GuardDuty**: It analyzes billions of events in pursuit of trends, patterns, and anomalies that are recognizable signs that something is not right. It takes feeds from all the logs coming from VPC Flow Logs, AWS CloudTrail event logs, and DNS logs to identify the anomalies.

Summary

In this chapter, you learned about different aspects of IAM and other security mechanisms. In the next chapter, we will study network security in public clouds in depth.

Cloud Network Security

4

Let's first understand what network security is. **Network security** is an activity intended to secure the integrity and usability of one's network and data. It includes a set of policies to prevent and monitor unauthorized access of network resources.

Network security covers a different set of public (internet) and private (local) network, which is used for the transfer of data between business organizations, government agencies, security organizations, and so on.

We could say that it's a set of policies that secure all the data transmission that happens over the network and network resources as well. When we use the network resource, it means all the nodes are connected together through the communication channel to transfer data and information.

Now, the question is, how does it work? Network security defines multiple layers of security in a network perimeter, or in the network. Each layer consists of the list of policies and controls so that only legitimate users can access the network resource, while malicious users are blocked from carrying out exploits and threats.

Here, we define the following types of security:

- **Access control**: This is to define who will access the resource and services
- **Application security**: This is to ensure the security of the application, or Layer 7 security
- **Antivirus and antispam**: This is to ensure safety from viruses and malware attacks
- **Behavioral analytics**: This is to understand the behavior of traffic to stop malicious traffic or DDoS attacks
- **Firewall**: This is to stop unwanted traffic at subnet level

- **Network segmentation**: This is to create isolation, and segment the workload into different tiers for enhanced security
- **Security information and event management**: This is to keep track of all the information about the security patches and events that take place at infrastructure level
- **Web security**: This is to ensure the security of publicly-accessible applications
- **Virtual private network (VPN)**: This is to ensure the security of data in transit

Now that we have a fair idea of what network security is and the types of network security, let's get deeper into it.

The following topics will be covered in this chapter:

- Virtual private cloud
- NACL and security group
- DNS security
- CDN-level security
- Direct Connect
- VPN connection and transit VPN
- Logging and monitoring
- CloudWatch and CloudTrail

Virtual private cloud

Let's understand network security from AWS's perspective. In AWS, we define a network as a **VPC**, which stands for **virtual private cloud**. Before creating an EC2 instance, it's mandatory to define a VPC.

In a VPC, we define subnets, which are called network segments. Here, we break VPC and CIDR into multiple private and public subnets, as per the requirement. In AWS, we can have CIDR of maximum size /16.

In AWS, VPC is an isolated network that is separated from other networks and associated with an AWS account. VPC includes the following:

- Subnets

- Route table
- Internet gateway
- Security group and network ACL

Apart from these, VPC also enables you to have a private connection with an AWS network using the following things:

- VPN
- Private link using VPC endpoint network
- Direct Connect

AWS networking best practices are:

- **Always use security groups**: They provide stateful firewalls for Amazon EC2 instances at the hypervisor level. You can apply multiple security groups to a single instance and a single ENI.
- **Augment security groups with network ACLs (NACLs)**: NACLs are stateless, but they provide fast and efficient controls. NACLs are not instance-specific, so they can provide another layer of control in addition to security groups. NACL works at subnet level, and here return traffic is explicitly allowed. It's different from security group, as security group works at instance level and it is stateful in nature. In security group, return traffic is automatically allowed.
- **Use IPSEC or AWS Direct Connect**: You must use IPSEC (VPN) or AWS Direct Connect as trusted connections for other sites. You must use **virtual private gateway (VGW)** where VPC-based resources require remote network connectivity.
- **Protect data in transit**: This enables encryption on data in transit to ensure the confidentiality and integrity of data.
- **Segregate deployment zones**: For any solution deployment, instead of creating a single layer of network security protection, apply network security at external, DMZ, and internal layers.
- **VPC flow logs**: You must enable VPC flow logs to provide further visibility, as it enables you to capture information about the IP traffic to and from network interfaces in your VPC.

Here, we understood how to secure VPC; now we will go deeper into VPC, and we will see how to enable security at different levels of VPCs.

NACL

NACL is defined at the VPC level. It's stateless in nature. It is an optional security layer in a VPC, which basically works as a firewall to control incoming and outgoing traffic for one or more subnets in a VPC.

When we define a VPC in AWS and create subnets, a default NACL is automatically created. You can see it from the AWS Management Console, under the **VPC** section:

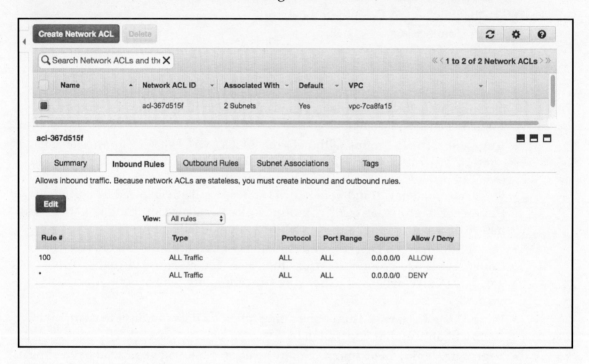

In the preceding screenshot, we can see that NACL rules are defined by the following:

- **Rule #**: All the rules are defined by a number. NACL processes the rules on the basis of sequence, where the rule with the lowest number is applied first. In the preceding screenshot, we have rule number **100** that says to allow **ALL Traffic** from public; then, let's assume that we have rule number **110** saying to allow **ALL Traffic** from a specific CIDR. Here, rule number **100** will be default applicable. It's always advised to leave a gap between the rule numbers so that in the future, you can add a new rule in between if it is required.

- **Type**: Denotes which kind of traffic we want to add into the rule: TCP, UDP, ICMP, or custom rules.

- **Protocol**: Here, we define which protocol we are going to add into the rule. AWS has given a list of almost all the protocols we need for all kinds of workload, apart from the standard TCP and UDP rules.
- **Port range**: What is the port range we want to add in the rule? Just take an example: we want to use port number `1082-1085`, so here, we can define the range.
- **Source**: It denotes the source IP from which the traffic will be generated.
- **Allow/Deny**: This is the action that will be performed on the specified rule.

Similarly, we define a rule for outgoing traffic as well:

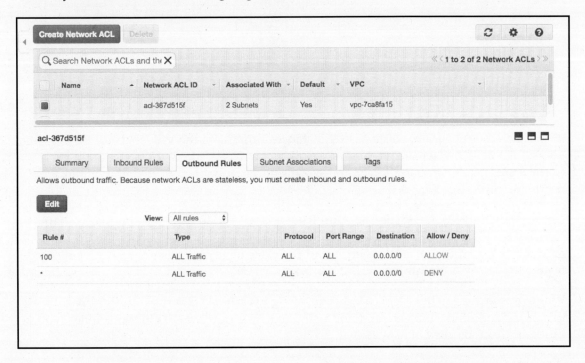

Now, let's understand how it works:

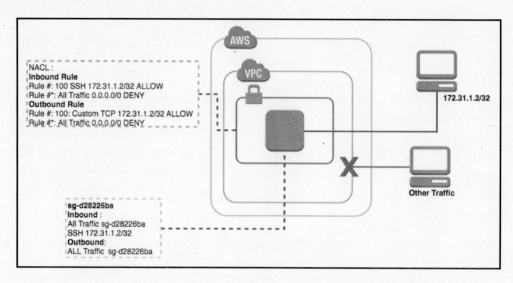

In the preceding diagram, we have EC2 instances running in the VPC with CIDR `10.0.0.0/16`. Now, we want to define a policy on our VPC network so that only SSH traffic from `172.31.1.2` is allowed for EC2 instances, and all other remaining internet traffic should be blocked.

Here, we define **NACL** with an **Inbound Rule** as specified in the diagram, which shares the rule that no **100 SSH** traffic is allowed from `172.31.1.2`, and other remaining traffic is denied from the internet, and in **Outbound Rule**, we have only custom TCP port allowed from `172.31.1.2`. All internet traffic is blocked.

When the machine with IP `172.31.1.2` is trying to access EC2 on SSH port, NACL allows this traffic and sends it to get validated with security group, where other machines with a different IP are blocked at NACL level.

The basic facts of NACL are:

- Once you create a VPC, it automatically creates NACL, which can be modified
- You can associate one or more VPC subnets with one NACL
- You can have multiple NACL
- NACL contains a numbered list of rules, which is evaluated in sequential order
- NACLs are stateless in nature, which means that all the inbound rules depend on the outbound rules, and so on

To ensure security of your infrastructure, you must define inbound and outbound rules of NACL. It helps you control traffic at the perimeter of AWS VPC.

Security group

In AWS, a security group represents a virtual firewall that controls inbound and outbound traffic for instances. It works at the instance level, but not at the subnet level. This is the reason we can associate multiple security groups with one subnet.

When we define VPC and subnets, by default, a security group is created. You can also create your own multiple security groups as per your need.

You can see the details of security groups in the **VPC** section in AWS Management Console:

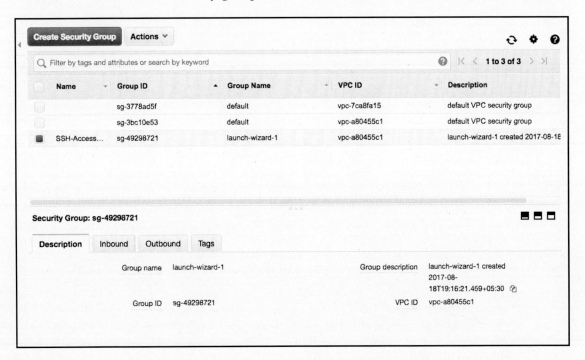

Whenever we create a VPC, it automatically creates a default security group that can be customized. Apart from that, we can also create multiple security groups on the basis of the kind of traffic we want to control. For example, say we just want to allow SSH access on the EC2 instance. To do this, we can create a security group allowing port 22 from public (in this case, we want to access SSH from the internet):

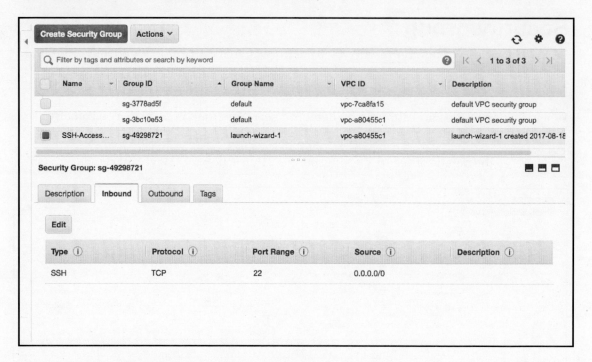

In the security group, we create a rule on the basis of:

- **Type**: What kind of traffic you want to control, such as TCP, UDP, ICMP, and custom TCP.
- **Protocol**: Specify the kind of protocol it is, such as **TCP, UDP**, and **ICMP**.
- **Port range**: Specify the port range.
- **Source**: Here, the security group allows you to define a source as IP or subnet. It helps us control the traffic between subnets; for example, we have app servers deployed in app subnet with CIDR 172.10.1.0/24, and database servers deployed in DB subnet with CIDR 172.10.2.0/24. Now, we want to ensure that the DB subnet only accesses traffic from an app subnet on port 3306. To do this, we need to create a security group that will allow traffic on 3306 from source as app subnet ID.

In the following screenshot, you can see that we have a rule for DB security group, which allows access on port `3306` to `App_SG` ID:

The **Description** field was added recently to keep track of the purpose of the rule; for example, when you have a security group for Cisco CSR, which requires around 15 different kinds of ports to be opened. So here, in **Description,** you can specify the purpose.

Security group best practices are:

- Do not open all the traffic for public
- Must define inbound policy specifying all the granular details, such as port and IPs, along with purpose
- Must define outbound rules
- Must enable VPC flow logs for the logging of all the events at VPC level, including security group
- Delete unused security groups
- Define IAM policy to modify the security group

Let's see an example of how we use the IAM policy to protect various security groups:

```json
{
    "Version": "2012-10-17",
    "Statement": [
      {
          "Sid": "AllowDescribePermissionsonEC2NACLsandSG",
          "Effect": "Allow",
          "Action": [
              "ec2:DescribeInstanceAttribute",
              "ec2:DescribeInstanceStatus",
              "ec2:DescribeInstances",
              "ec2:DescribeNetworkAcls",
              "ec2:DescribeSecurityGroups"
          ],
          "Resource": [
              "*"
          ]
      },
      {
          "Sid": "AllowModificationtoSpecificSecurityGroup",
          "Effect": "Allow",
          "Action": [
              "ec2:AuthorizeSecurityGroupEgress",
              "ec2:AuthorizeSecurityGroupIngress",
              "ec2:RevokeSecurityGroupEgress",
              "ec2:RevokeSecurityGroupIngress"
          ],
          "Resource": [
              "arn:aws:ec2:<region>:<accountid>:security-group/sg-<id>"
          ]
      }
    ]
}
```

In the preceding code block, we have defined a policy that enables users to modify and access security group rules.

VPN connection

Now, to have a secure channel to communicate between your corporate office and AWS VPC, AWS also provides site-to-site VPN connections to connect with your on-premise or other private or public cloud network using VPN connection.

Here, we have the types of VPN connection options available:

- **AWS-managed VPN connection**: In AWS-managed VPN connection, we have the following scenario:
    - **Between AWS network and other networks**: In AWS VPC, we have VGW, which provides two VPN endpoints for automatic failover. And we configure the VPN tunnel between VGW and other networks' firewalls (it can be from any vendor such as Cisco, Juniper, Palo Alto, and Cyberoam). In this case, there will be a single tunnel:

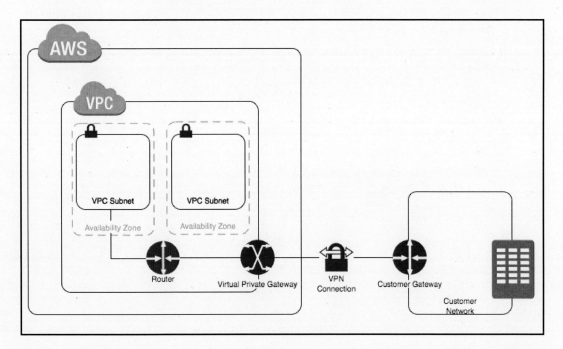

In the preceding diagram, we have a connection between **Virtual Private Gateway** and **Customer Gateway**. These are two major components of a VPC connection. To create a **VPN Connection**, first, we have to create a VGW, which, by default, creates two endpoints. Then, we define the **Customer Gateway** (which is a customer-end device) to establish a connection using a static route, or using BGP protocol. Once it's defined, we modify our route table to send traffic over the IPSEC tunnel; for example, let's assume that we have our VPC CIDR 10.0.0.0/16, and customer CIDR is 172.16.0.0/16. After defining the **VPN Connection**, we have to modify our route table and add entry for 172.16.0.0/16 points to VGW.

- **VPN connection hub**: In this scenario, let's assume that the customer has three different head offices; now, they want to access the AWS resource, or their on-premise workload needs to access AWS-hosted components. Here, we create multiple VPN connections between the VPC virtual gateway and customer office locations.

- **Third-party VPN appliance**: In this case, we establish a VPN connection between other networks and third-party VPN appliances hosted on AWS; for example, we have Sophos, Barracuda, OpenVPN, and software VPN appliance, which we can configure.

- **Transit VPC**: Transit VPC is required when you have multiple AWS accounts running in different regions and you want to connect them to your corporate office network. Using a simple VPN solution, it becomes complex, but transit VPC makes it easier. It basically minimizes the number of connections. Normally, we use VPC peering; it will be very complex, as it does not *support transitive connections*, which means that you need to create full mesh in case of VPC peering; for example, if you have three VPCs named *A*, *B*, and *C*, you must have three connections to communicate between *A*, *B*, and *C*. Connection will be such as *A* to *B*, *A* to *C*, and *B* to *C*. Now, if we had created a transit VPC, we could have done this using only two connections:

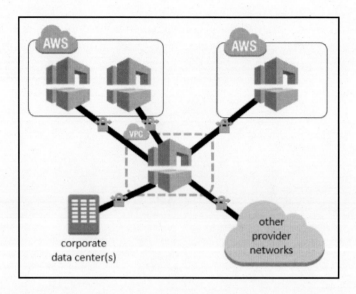

When we create a VPN connection using virtual gateway, it gives us the option to download the configuration for the customer gateway that includes all the details related to the tunnel encryption method.

Apart from the VPN connection, AWS VPC also enables you to define a route between two different AWS VPCs, and we call this **VPC peering**. Earlier, VPC peering was available within the same region, but now it's available for cross-region as well:

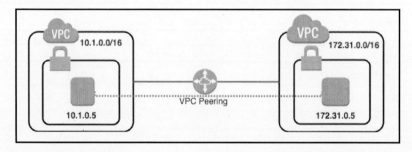

Direct Connect

Direct Connect is dedicated MPLS connectivity between AWS VPC and customer on-premise network. Whenever you want to synchronously transfer critical data (high-volume) from on-premise to AWS, or so on, Direct Connect comes into the picture.

In a Direct Connect connection, a cable is connected to your network, and another is connected to the VPC Direct Connect router. With Direct Connect, we define a virtual interface, which can be public if we want to connect with S3, such as service, or private if we want to connect VPC resources. In every region, there are ISPs that provide a Direct Connect connection:

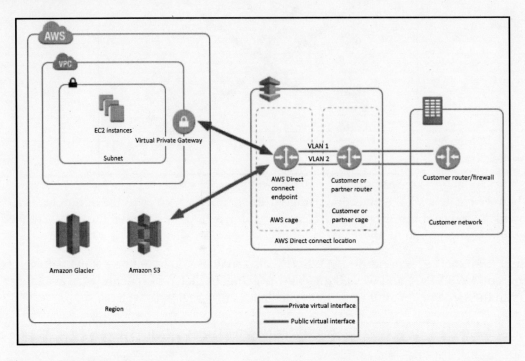

In the preceding diagram, we have a Direct Connect connection which is connected with two **virtual interfaces** (**VIFs**) (one is private, and one is public). On VIF, we define VLAN to transfer the data.

Direct Connect connection can be in active-active mode, or active-passive mode.

Now, to enable security on Direct Connect connection, we can have a VPN tunnel. If it's using public VIF, then we can enable VPN connection using VPC; however, if it's on private VIF, then we must use a third-party router tool such as *Cisco CSR 1000v* to enable the VPN connection.

For a Direct Connect connection:

- We must define an IAM policy to grant access
- We must capture all the logs using CloudTrail
- CloudWatch must be configured for continuous monitoring of the connection

To create Direct Connect connection, first ask your Direct Connect provider to initiate the connection using your AWS account ID. Once a connection is created, you will get a pop-up message in the Direct Connect console. Now log in to the AWS console, and search for direct connection. On the Direct Connect console, you will get a message to accept a newly-created connection—accept it. After acceptance, the connection will be created. You can see it by clicking on **Connections**:

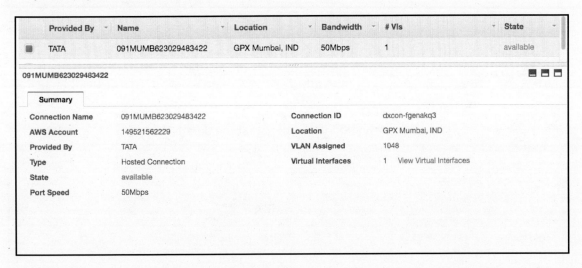

Now, once the connection is created, you need to create a virtual interface. Now click on **Virtual Interfaces** and **Create Virtual Interface**, input the details, and complete the wizard:

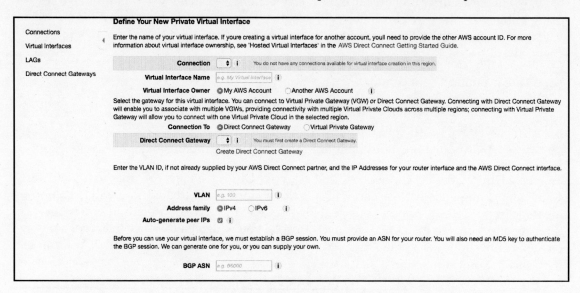

Here, one thing to always keep in mind is whether you need public interface or private interface. **Private interface** is used to access Amazon VPC using private IP addresses, and **public interface** is used to access all AWS public services (including EC2, S3, and DynamoDB) using public IP addresses.

If a connection is defined from the ISP, you will get all the details from the ISP to create the virtual interface:

Summary			
Name	SMBC-GSP-DX-VI-Secondary	Amazon side ASN	7224
ID	dxvif-fgwwbh4a	BGP Status	up
AWS Account	149521562229	BGP ASN	4755
Type	private	BGP Auth Key	T@taN714755
State	available	Your Peer IP	10.6.216.157/30
Connection	dxcon-fg872kar	Amazon Peer IP	10.6.216.158/30
Location	GPX51		
Virtual Gateway	vgw-5b36bb6b		
VLAN Assigned	1048		

If everything is okay, then you will see the interface state is **available**.

Here, once a connection is created, you also then have to make changes in **Route Table** to propagate the route:

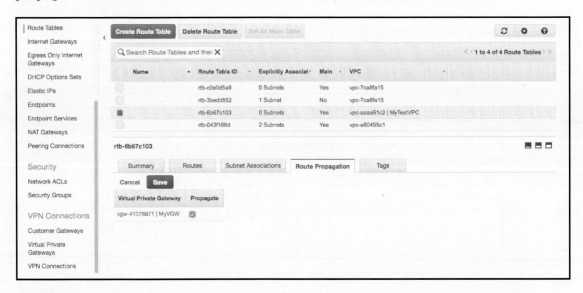

After that, you can then make changes in **Route Table** as per the requirement of your connection.

Now that we've covered the connection, we will now see how to secure the DNS in AWS.

DNS security

In AWS, we have a global DNS solution provided by AWS named **Route 53**. It is a highly available and scalable domain name service that supports both IPv4 and IPv6.

It connects end user requests from the internet to AWS services, and also transfers traffic to external endpoints (outside of AWS) as well.

Route 53 helps you with:

- **DNS management**: It helps you host your new subdomain or existing subdomain while keeping parent domain to other DNSs.

- **Traffic management**: If we have multiple web services running in multiple regions, then it would be a very complex task to define the record sets in Route 53 routing policies. You can define one policy, but combining multiple policies is a very tough task. For this, Route 53 gives you a visual editor where you can create a tree in a fraction of time and save maximum effort. You can define the traffic policy in Route 53 using the AWS Management Console:

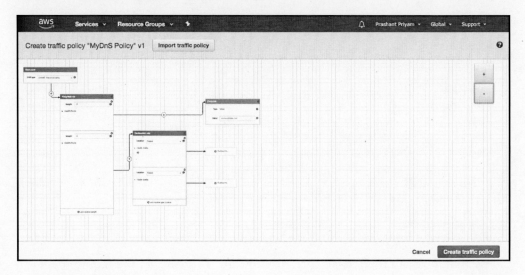

- **Availability monitoring**: Route 53 helps you monitor the health and performance of your web applications. You can define a health check that monitors your web application, CloudWatch alarm status, and status of other health checks as well.
- **Domain registration**: Route 53 also enables you to register a domain from the AWS console.

Route 53 gives you an ample security facility to ensure the security of your DNS:

- **IAM roles**: You can define IAM roles for users who will have the right to modify the DNS-hosted zone entries. In the following policy, the first section allows you to do all the operations related to a hosted zone under the account, and the second section allows you to do all the operations related to health checks:

```
{
    "Version": "2012-10-17",
    "Statement": [
      {
        "Sid" : "AllowPublicHostedZoneAccess",
        "Effect": "Allow",
```

```
        "Action": [
            "route53:CreateHostedZone",
            "route53:UpdateHostedZoneComment",
            "route53:GetHostedZone",
            "route53:ListHostedZones",
            "route53:DeleteHostedZone",
            "route53:ChangeResourceRecordSets",
            "route53:ListResourceRecordSets",
            "route53:GetHostedZoneCount",
            "route53:ListHostedZonesByName"
        ],
        "Resource": "*"
    },
    {
        "Sid" : "AllowHealthCheck",
        "Effect": "Allow",
        "Action": [
            "route53:CreateHealthCheck",
            "route53:UpdateHealthCheck",
            "route53:GetHealthCheck",
            "route53:ListHealthChecks",
            "route53:DeleteHealthCheck",
            "route53:GetCheckerIpRanges",
            "route53:GetHealthCheckCount",
            "route53:GetHealthCheckStatus",
            "route53:GetHealthCheckLastFailureReason"
        ],
        "Resource": "*"
    }
  ]
}
```

- **Enabling DNSSEC on Route 53**: The most common attack we find for the internet application is to hijack traffic by intercepting DNS queries. In this attack, DNS translation returns the IP address of hackers' machines instead of an actual endpoint. As a result, users are redirected to the hacker's IP address in a spoofed response. To tackle such an event, we must enable DNSSEC on Route 53. When we create DNSSEC for Route 53, it creates the chain of trust between intermediate resolvers. This chain of trust starts from TLD registry of the domain, and ends with authoritative name servers at DNS provider.

- **Logging**: It's very important to log all the DNS queries received at Route 53. Queries received at Route 53 include domain or subdomain, date and time of request, DNS records type (A or AAAA), edge location where the query responded, and response code. When we configure query logging, Route 53 sends all the query logs to CloudWatch logs. It contains only the query that has been forwarded to Route 53 for processing.
- **Monitoring health checks using CloudWatch**: You must enable health checks in Route 53 and also enable the alarm using CloudWatch when health status changes.

Let's take an example of how to host a domain in Route 53 and implement security aspects on it.

To host a domain in Route 53, first, log in to the AWS Console and search for Route 53. Select **Hosted zones**, then **Create Hosted Zone**:

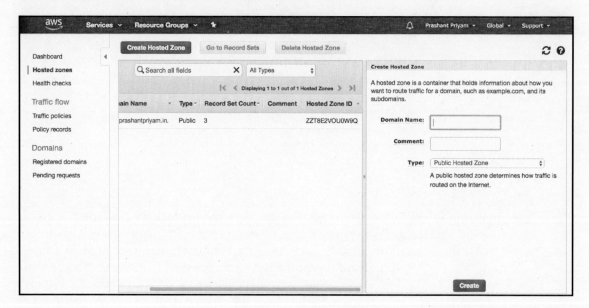

Once a hosted zone is created, you then need to **Create Record Set**:

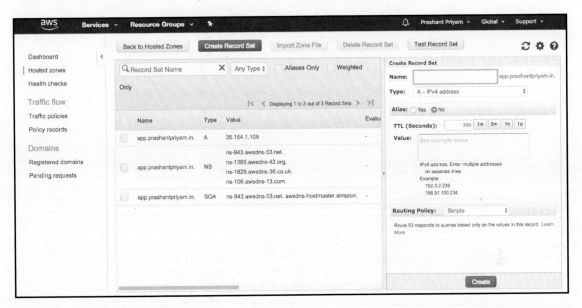

After the hosted zone is created, you then need to make appropriate entries in the domain console. Here, `prashantpriyam.in` is hosted with GoDaddy. So, we need to make the entries of a nameserver in GoDaddy DNS console to use the subdomain named `app.prashantpriyam.in`:

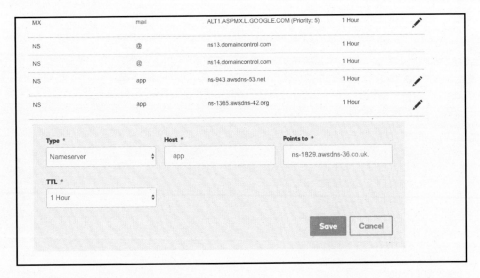

After that, we create a health check for the hosted zone. Now click on the health check and start the configuration of the health check, providing all the required details:

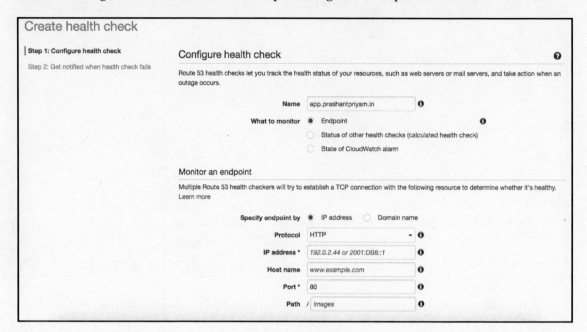

In the **Advanced configuration** section, we define **Request interval**, **Failure threshold**, and other entries required for the health check:

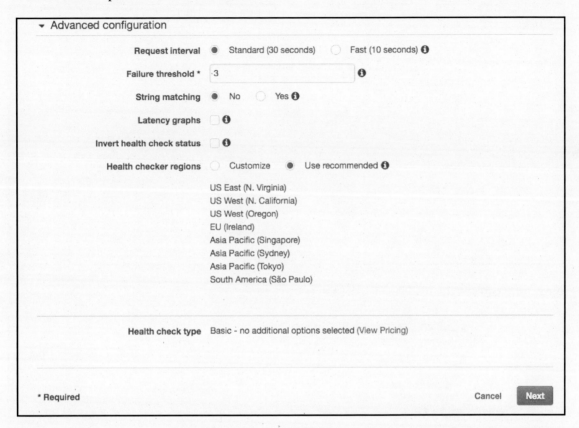

Click on **Next** and define CloudWatch alarm, then click on **Create health check**:

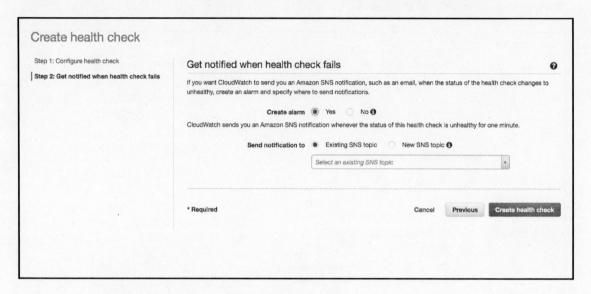

Now, you can see the health status of the hosted zone:

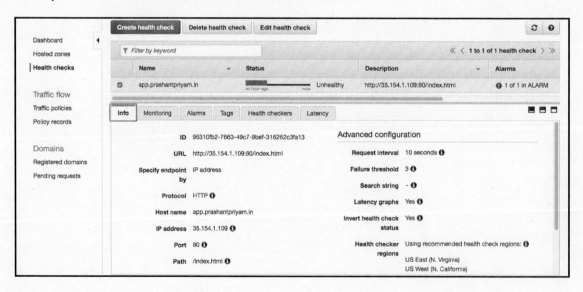

Here, in the **Status** section, the green color denotes the successful access of application, and the red color denotes the error. You can also see the monitoring details, alarm status, and latency:

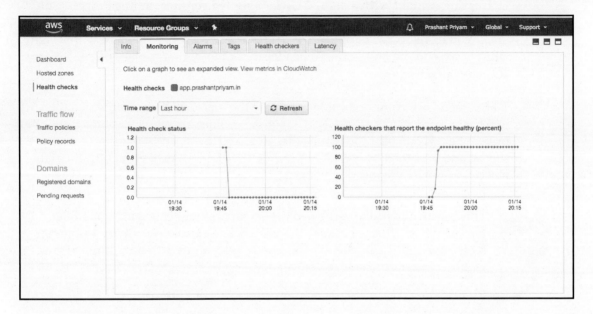

CDN-level security

In AWS, we have CloudFront as **Content Delivery Network** (**CDN**). Let's understand first exactly what the CDN does. CDN delivers your static and dynamic content to the end user with very low latency. Here, you will have a question in mind: how does it deliver content at low latency? CloudFront, or any other CDN, has their edge location across the globe. It actually caches all the static or dynamic content from the origin server. So, when the user hits the application URL, the DNS routes traffic to CDN, and it serves the static or dynamic content for the local/nearest edge location to users.

In AWS, CloudFront caches content from either the S3 bucket or EC2 instances.

Now, let's see how we can secure CloudFront. There are multiple ways available to secure CloudFront:

- **Delivering content with a signed URL or signed cookies**: In this process, you configure CloudFront to deliver content using a signed URL or signed cookies. Then, you develop your application to create and distribute content with a signed URL, or to send the Set-Cookie header to set the signed cookies of authenticated users.

  This signed URL or signed cookies contain the date and time after which the URL will become invalid. Signed URLs or signed cookies are signed using a public and private key. When users send a header to access the object, CloudFront checks the signed and unsigned header; if it matches, then CloudFront grants access to the object, or else invalidates the request.

   This is especially required by an organization that deals with a one-line picture portal. This is because there is always a situation where people can refer your website image to another site, which can increase traffic on your website, or can further use your image.

- **Restricting the access of static content at the origin**: If the origin is S3 bucket for CloudFront, then you can define your policy at S3 bucket so that it can only be accessible using CloudFront. In this case, we create a CloudFront user's named origin identity access and permit the origin identity users to access the bucket object with permission to read and remove other users' access to the bucket.

- **Securing connection to CloudFront**: CloudFront supports both HTTP and HTTPS to serve content. Now it encrypts the connection CloudFront closely associated with the **AWS Certificate Manager** (**ACM**), and it also ensures that data transmission is happening with modern cipher and handshake. Integrating with ACM also enables CloudFront to deploy the certificate on all the edge locations globally, and also helps to renew it automatically.

  You also have an option to use your own custom SSL for CloudFront, which is basically a **Server Name Indicator** (**SNI**) SSL. SNI is an extension of TLS, which ensures to deliver content over HTTPS using your own SSL.

Now it's time to implement security at the CloudFront level. Let's see the procedure, step by step:

1. First, log in to the AWS console and search for `CloudFront`. On the CloudFront console, specify the required details:

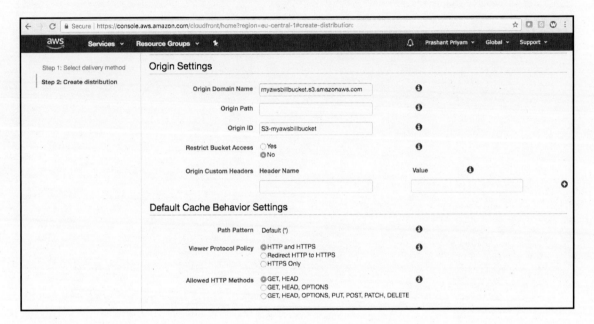

2. Here, we selected to deliver content lying in S3 bucket and allowed viewer policy HTTP and HTTPS both so that the user can access any protocol; but here, we can restrict them to either redirect HTTP requests to HTTPS or only HTTPS:

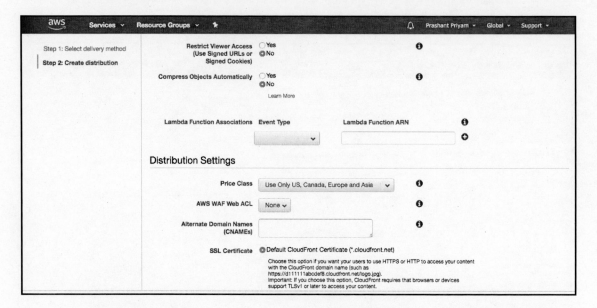

3. Now we can restrict users to access the content using only signed URLs and also associate with WAF ACL if we are using WAF for Layer 7 protection. You have already learned about AWS WAF and Shield in the previous section. An SSL certificate can either be defined for CloudFront, or we can use ACM-stored SSL for this as well, and finally create distribution to access the content.

4. Here, we can also enable login of CloudFront activity, which will get stored in S3 bucket for audit purposes.

5. After provisioning CloudFront, it will take a few minutes to cache the content to edge locations.

6. If you click on the **Distributions** settings on the console, you will get all the details of distribution:

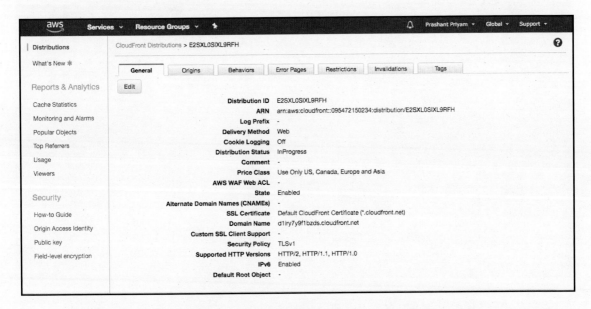

7. Once CloudFront distribution is enabled, then we can see the cache statistics from the console, and also create a CloudWatch alarm for monitoring:

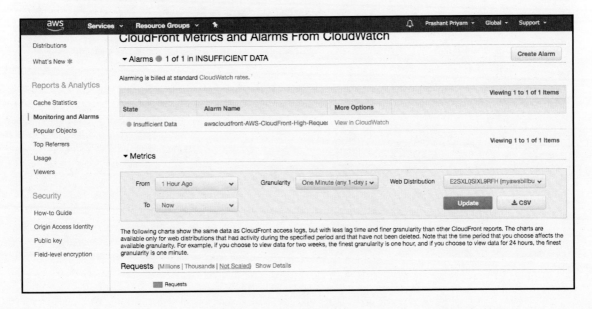

8. Now you can implement security using **Origin Access Identity (OAI)**:

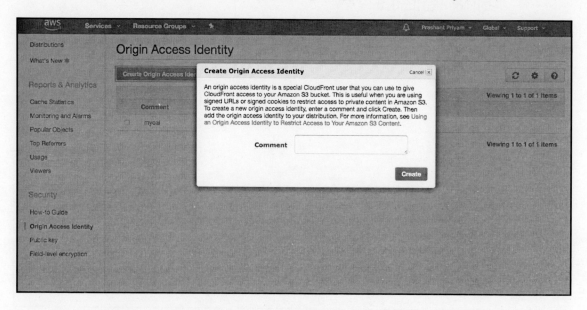

9. After that, you can also add a public key:

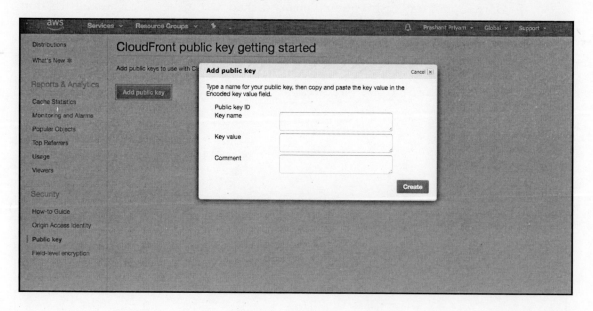

10. And finally, field-level encryption:

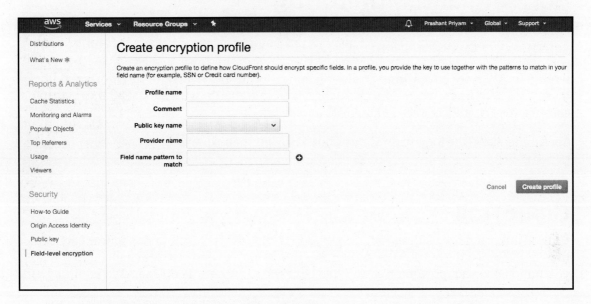

Let's see how CloudFront tackles the vulnerabilities:

- **Cryptographic attacks**: CloudFront frequently reviews the latest security standards, and supports only viewer requests using SSL v3 and TLS v1.0, 1.1, and 1.2. When available, TLS v1.3 will also be supported. CloudFront supports the strongest ciphers (ECDHE, RSA-AES128, GCM-SHA256), and offers them to the client in preferential sequence. Export ciphers are not supported.
- **Patching**: As we know, CloudFront is kind of a PaaS offering. So, all the monitoring and patching works are AWS's responsibility. AWS has a dedicated team who closely monitors the CloudFront infrastructure, and does patching work when required.
- **DDoS attack**: CloudFront has very extensive techniques to mitigate the SSL flood-type request. It disables the SSL renegotiation request. It also improves the performance of SSL with support of session tickets and **Online Certificate Status Protocol (OCSP)** stapling.

If you want to enable further security on CloudFront, then you must enable WAF, where you can define your custom ACL and rules to deliver the content and stop malicious requests or traffic. You learned how to define ACL and rules for WAF in the previous section.

Logging and monitoring

Logging and monitoring is a very important aspect of security management in any infrastructure or cloud. Logging enables you to capture exactly what is happening in your complete system, whereas monitoring lets you observe and raise an alarm if anything goes wrong. In AWS, we have **CloudTrail** for logging and **CloudWatch** for monitoring. Both these tools help us ensure our infrastructure is in compliance with almost all the security compliances, be it PCI, SOC, FEDRAMP, and so on.

Let's understand the logging in CloudTrail first, and then we will dive deep into CloudWatch.

CloudTrail

CloudTrail provides a simple solution to record all AWS API calls and resource changes that help remove the burden of on-premises infrastructure and storage challenges. It helps you build enhanced preventative and detective security controls for the AWS environment.

To see the events in CloudTrail, log in to the AWS Management Console, search for the CloudTrail service, click on **CloudTrail**, and then click on **Dashboard**. You will get the details of events, as seen in the following screenshot:

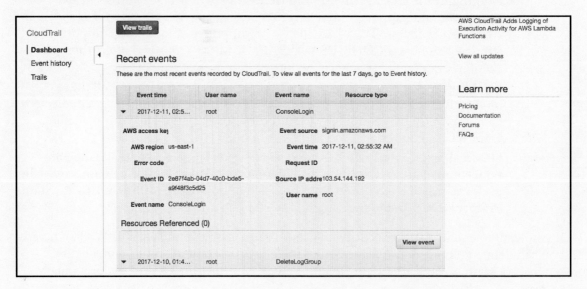

In on-premise infrastructure, logging solutions require installing agents, setting up configuration files and centralized log servers, and building and maintaining expensive, highly durable data stores. CloudTrail continuously captures API calls from multiple servers in a highly available processing pipeline. In AWS, we can ensure the safety of log files using IAM users to define roles to access CloudTrail logs stored in an S3 bucket. CloudTrail provides you with immediate notifications about problems with your logging configuration through the AWS Management Console. It provides visibility into any changes made to your AWS resource, from its creation to deletion, by logging changes made using API calls via the AWS Management Console, the AWS CLI, or the AWS **Software Development Kits (SDKs)**.

By default, all the API logs stored in S3 bucket are encrypted with **server-side encryption (SSE)**. Here, for additional security, you can define IAM users with MFA to control access to and the deletion of records. CloudTrail also ensures the durability of logs by storing them in an S3 bucket, and you can also define a life cycle policy in an S3 bucket to move it to **Glacier** if you want to store it for a longer duration. In CloudTrail, you can generate comprehensive and detailed API call reports by logging the activities performed by all the users who access your logged AWS resources, including root, IAM users, federated users, and any users or services performing activities on behalf of users, using any access method. CloudTrail delivers API calls with a very detailed set of information, such as type, date and time, location, source, and associated user. It helps you identify the user, time of the event, IP address of the user, request parameters provided by the user, response elements returned by the service, and optional error codes and error messages. You can access CloudTrail logs by logging in to the AWS Console and clicking on CloudTrail **Event history**:

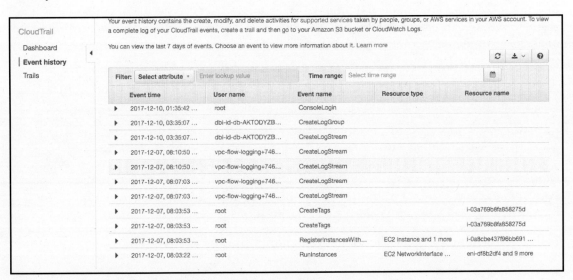

CloudWatch

CloudWatch monitors your AWS resources and the applications you run on AWS in real time. It also enables you to define alerts and alarms for defined metrics or events:

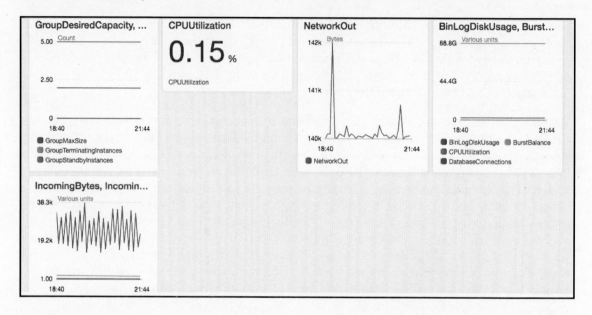

In the preceding screenshot, you can see that we have the dashboard view of CloudWatch showing real-time metrics for EC2 instances and databases. We can secure CloudWatch by defining IAM roles and can also define which actions a user can perform. It also helps you store your application logs in CloudWatch logs, which can be further used for real-time analysis using **Kinesis**.

We can also use AWS CloudWatch logs for further analysis and dashboarding using ELK or **AWS Elasticsearch**. Mostly, we use VPC flow logs to see real-time events and traffic using Elasticsearch.

In CloudWatch, we use SNS or SES to receive notifications of any events. We also use it to manage our AWS billing alerts.

CloudWatch gives you system-wide visibility about resource utilization, application performance, and system health. It's mandatory to enable CloudWatch for your infrastructure, and also define alarms and notifications.

Let's see an example of how CloudWatch monitors your AWS environment.

First, log in to the AWS Console and search for the `CloudWatch` service:

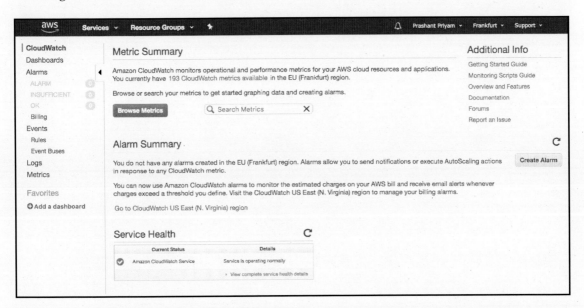

As we can see in the preceding screenshot, we can create a dashboard that is a summarized view of the infrastructure running on AWS:

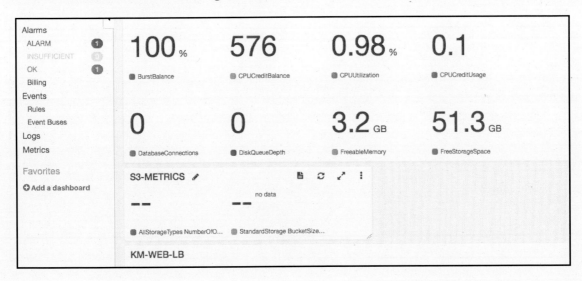

Apart from dashboards, you can create an event rule and add a target using **SNS topic**:

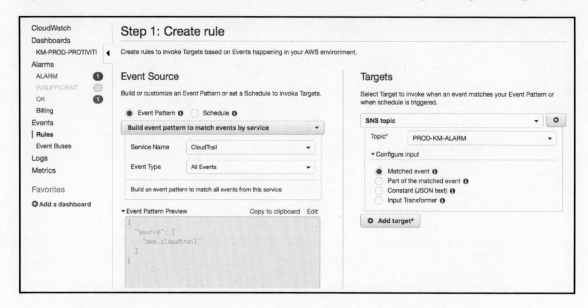

We can also create a log group to store logs from RDS and VPC flow logs (as discussed in the earlier section):

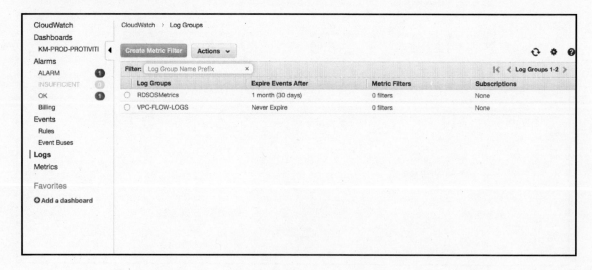

Finally, the metrics by which we monitor the infrastructure. There are many predefined metrics that are defined for AWS services. We create a CloudWatch dashboard using these metrics:

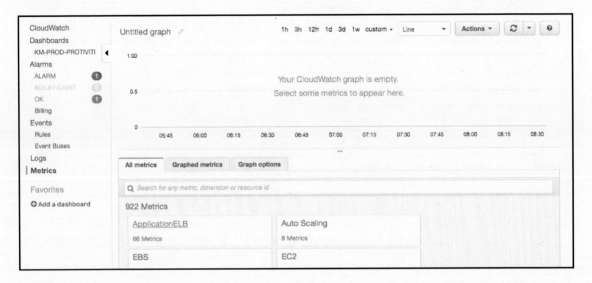

Quick recap

In AWS, we have VPC. It's an isolated boundary under which your infrastructure resides and your application runs. At VPC level, we defined subnets to further isolate traffic by defining DMZ and MZ zones.

NACL and security groups are used to define ingress and egress traffic. The NACL rule works on the basis of sequence number.

To connect the AWS Cloud with on-premise infrastructure, we have the following different methods:

- **VPN connections**: In a VPN connection, we create a site-to-site VPN tunnel between an on-premise infrastructure and AWS using customer gateway and VGW. AWS supports almost all the available firewalls on the market for VPN connections.

- **Direct Connect**: If you want to transfer massive amounts of data to and from the AWS public cloud, there is Direct Connect, which offers a dedicated network connection between the AWS data center and your on-premise infrastructure. If you need to ensure encryption on your direct connection too, you need to create a VPN tunnel between your on-premise infrastructure and AWS VPC using Cisco CSR 1000v, or a software-defined router such as Openswan.

Apart from VPC, we have CloudTrail and CloudWatch to monitor all the network-level activity. We enable VPC flow logs, which are stored in CloudWatch logs, and can be used for further analysis using the Elasticsearch service.

CloudTrail records all the API-level events and stores them in an S3 bucket. Furthermore, you can define monitoring of your instance network interface to detect anomalies, and use SNS to notify the admin to take the appropriate action.

In the same way, using CloudWatch, you can monitor your Direct Connect connection as well.

CloudFront is also used to deliver your application's static and dynamic content globally using CloudFront edge locations.

We can also define security on the CloudFront level using the following:

- Delivering content with signed URLs or signed cookies
- Restricting the access of static content at the origin
- Securing a connection to CloudFront

In addition, we can use WAF to define ACL and rules to monitor the traffic on the Layer 7 level.

AWS also offers a global DNS service named Route 53, which is used to host your domain. It is not only used to host the domain, but also to have the functionality to define traffic flow and monitor the health of the domain.

You can use the CloudWatch alarm to raise an alarm and send an email using SNS notifications to the admin to take action.

Summary

In this chapter, you learned about how to ensure security for cloud networks. Similar to on-premise network infrastructure, in the cloud we have different components, such as NACL, security groups, VPN, and so on, which help us to ensure the security of data in transit. We will learn about different storage options in AWS and their usability in the next chapter.

5
Cloud Storage and Data Security

Until now, we have seen the different security options and methodologies that are available in AWS to ensure the security of your application, infrastructure, and data.

In this chapter, we will dive deep into data security. So, before going into the security aspect, let's look at the kind of storage we have in AWS.

In AWS, we have the following two categories of storage:

- **Ephemeral**: This is volatile in nature. It stores data temporarily but ensures very high performance. Ephemeral storage comes with EC2 instances. We also call it the instance store. The basic reason behind using ephemeral storage is to store the cache in transaction data, which changes very frequently. We cannot store any critical data in ephemeral storage.
- **Persistent**: This is used to store the data you want to access from time to time for operational purposes. For persistent storage, we have the **Elastic Block Store** (**EBS**). Here, you can choose a disk category that is suitable for your workload. You have the following disk types:
  - General Purpose (SSD)
  - Optimized I/O SSD
  - Throughput Optimized HDD (st1)
  - Cold HDD (sc1) volumes

All the storage types are available for EC2 instance-level storage. Apart from this, AWS also offers the following storage options:

- **Simple Storage Service (S3)** storage
- AWS Glacier
- **Elastic File System (EFS)**
- Storage Gateway
- AWS Snowball

Now, let's look at each of the storage options one by one, and also look at how to define security.

EBS

EBS is block-level storage provided by AWS. It can be used as an operating system disk and a data storage disk for EC2 instances. It's network attached storage, which persists independently from your data from the life of the instance. For this, we need to specify it while creating the EC2 instance.

EBS can be used as a separate physical hard drive, where you can specify the filesystem of your own choice after formatting and use the file I/O interface provided by the EC2 instance operating system.

EBS also works as the boot volume for EBS-based AMIs. You can attach multiple EBS volumes to EC2 instances. However, one volume can only be attached to one instance at a time.

EBS also provides you with the ability to create point-in-time snapshots of volumes that are then stored in S3.

Let's see how we can enable data security at the EBS level.

Fault tolerance at EBS

As we know, EBS can be attached to an instance as a physical volume. Here, we can define the **redundant array of independent disk (RAID)** as well, although it will be software-based RAID. RAID basically gives fault tolerance, which means that if anything goes wrong with the volume you will not lose your data.

Here is the trick—while defining RAID, we must see the IOPS and throughput requirements of the application. This is because defining RAID affects your IOPS and throughput.

In AWS, we can define RAID 0 and RAID 1, while RAID 5 and RAID 6 are not recommended.

RAID 0

We use RAID 0 when we need more IOPS, and it's more important than fault tolerance. In RAID 0, data is striped in volumes. So, we can add multiple volumes in RAID 0 to get maximum performance.

For example, suppose that you are running a database instance where a very high number of read and write operations are being performed. In this case, your instance needs more and more IOPS to handle the operation. Currently, your instance has 100 GB GP2 volumes, which gives you around 300 IOPS and 160 MBps throughput, but your machine needs to have around 320 MBps throughput. To achieve this, you can add one more volume and configure RAID 0. After the RAID configuration, you will get 600 IOPS and 320 MBps throughput.

However, there is a disadvantage of RAID 0, wherein once there is a problem with any of the volume in the array, you will lose the complete data.

RAID 1

We consider RAID 1 when fault tolerance is more of a priority than performance. In RAID 1, data is mirrored into volumes. It's required for critical applications. Just assume that we have a critical application where we are not in a position to lose any data. For this, we must use RAID 1. In RAID 1, if we have added two volumes with 100 GB GP2 that have 160 MBps of throughput, unlike RAID 0 it will give you only 100 GB storage with 160 MBps of throughput.

Now, let's see how to define RAID on AWS. First, log in to the AWS Console and search for an EC2 instance where you want to define RAID. Here, we will go with RAID 0. To do this, we will add two identical volumes to the EC2 instance:

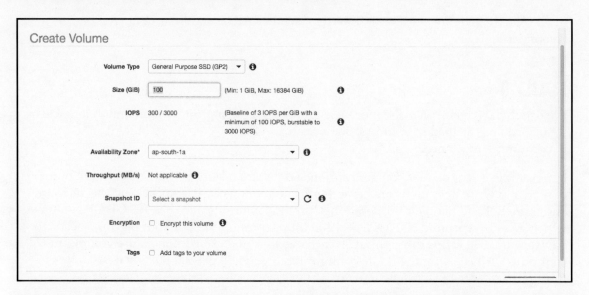

Once the volume is created, we need to attach this volume to the EC2 instance:

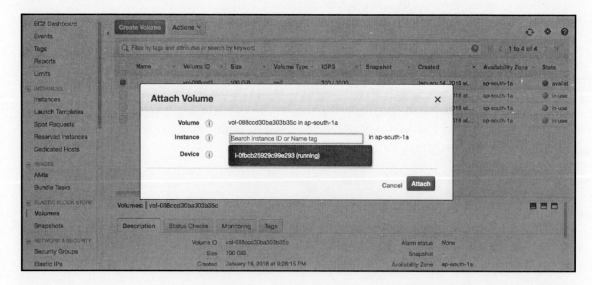

Now, the volume is attached with the instance. Let's access the SSH or RDP of your EC2 instances as per your operating system.

For Linux, we need to run the following command to configure RAID:

```
sudo mdadm --create --verbose /dev/md0 --level=1 --name=MY_RAID --raid-
devices=number_of_volumes device_name1 device_name2
```

To learn about volume details, you need to run the following command in the Terminal:

```
sudo lsblk
```

After we run both the commands, you will find that RAID has been configured:

```
[root@ip-172-31-19-126 ec2-user]# lsblk
NAME      MAJ:MIN RM SIZE RO TYPE MOUNTPOINT
xvda      202:0    0   8G  0 disk
`-xvda1 202:1    0   8G  0 part /
xvdf      202:80   0   8G  0 disk
xvdg      202:96   0   8G  0 disk
[root@ip-172-31-19-126 ec2-user]# mdadm --create --verbose /dev/md0 --level=0 --
name=MY_RAID --raid-devices=2 /dev/xvdg /dev/xvdf
mdadm: chunk size defaults to 512K
mdadm: Defaulting to version 1.2 metadata
mdadm: array /dev/md0 started.
[root@ip-172-31-19-126 ec2-user]# 
```

Now, after the creation of the RAID volume, you can mount it and make an /etc/fstab entry for the use.

Encryption in EBS

In AWS, we enable encryption at the EBS volume to ensure data security. It's a simple encryption solution that works without the need to build, create, and maintain your key management infrastructure.

Once we enable encryption on the EBS volume, it encrypts the following:

- Data at rest from volume
- All data moving between the volume and the instance
- All snapshots created from the volume
- All volumes created from these snapshots

The encryption operation occurs at host level, which hosts the EC2 instances and ensures encryption of data in transit and data at rest between EC2 instances and the attached volume.

All the EBS volumes support data encryption. There may be performance jitters (which are very, very significant) in the volumes after encryption.

Now, you will be asking how the application will access the data when the volume is encrypted.

Here, your application does not have to play any role in the encryption and decryption of data. It's being handled at the host level. Your application can seamlessly access the data stored in the encrypted volume.

In AWS, public snapshots of encrypted volumes are not supported, but you can share an encrypted snapshot with specific accounts.

Customer master keys (**CMKs**) are used to create encrypted EBS volumes and snapshots of volumes, which are also encrypted, and this CMK is managed by the AWS **Key Management Service** (**KMS**). A unique AWS-managed CMK is automatically created in each region. This AWS-managed CMK is used for Amazon EBS encryption. However, here you can also specify a customer-managed CMK that is created separately using AWS KMS for EBS encryption.

To use create encryption keys in KMS, log in to the AWS Console, search for the IAM section, and click on **Encryption keys**:

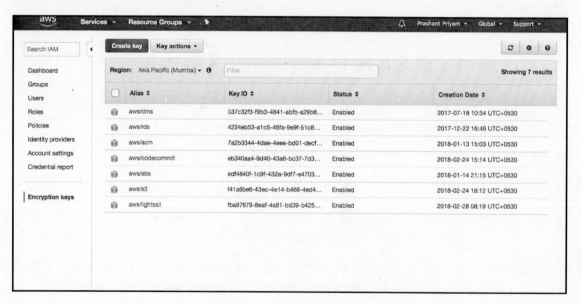

Here you will get list of all the keys. Now, to create new keys click on **Create key**. On the Console, specify the name and description of the key and click on **Advanced Options**. Here, you have to choose options for the **Key Material Origin**, and you can either select **KMS** or **External**. If you check **External** it will ask you to upload the key:

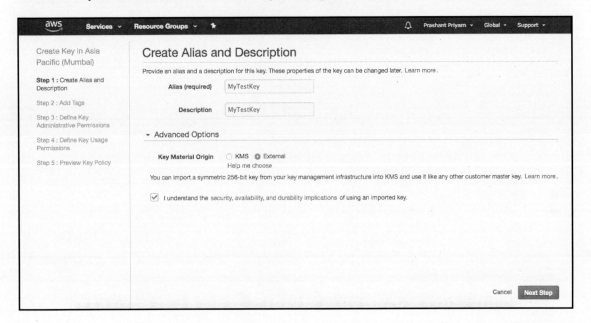

Now, click on **Next Step**, specify **Tag** and **Value** on the Console, and click on **Next Step**. Here, you need to choose administrative permissions from the list of users and roles:

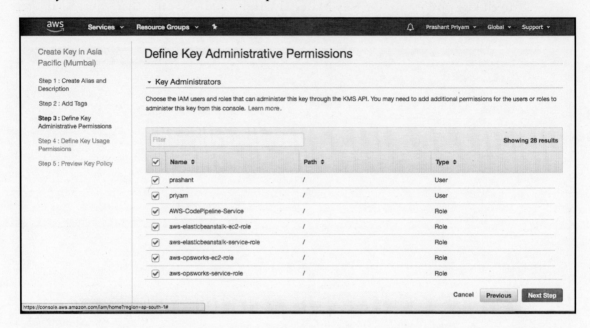

Now, click on **Next Step** and select key usage permissions:

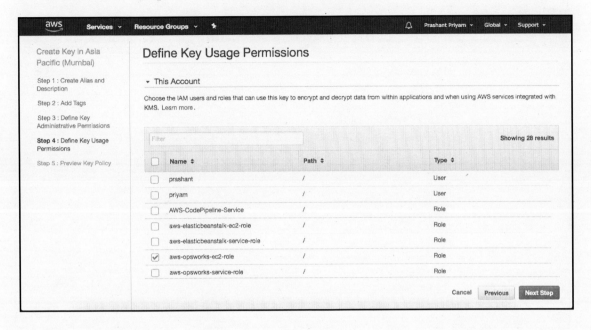

After selecting the role, click on **Next Step** and it will automatically generate the IAM policy for the key:

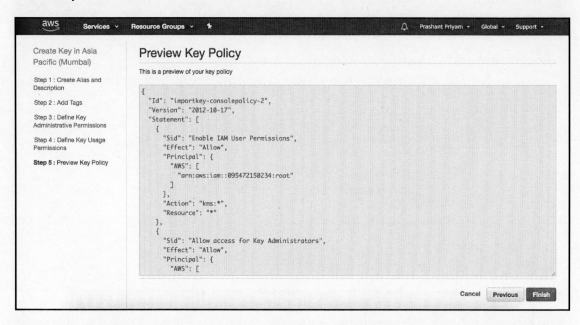

Now click on **Finish**, which will create a key and a new window to import the key material:

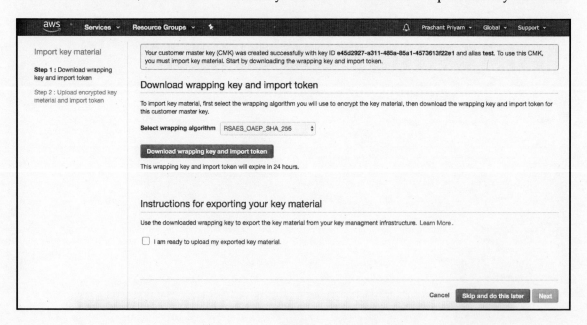

Now you can download a wrapping key, import a token, and check **I am ready to upload my exported key material**. However, if you want to do it later you can click on **Skip and do this later**; otherwise, click on **Next**.

Now it will ask you to import the key and token. Here, you can specify a key expiry period as well:

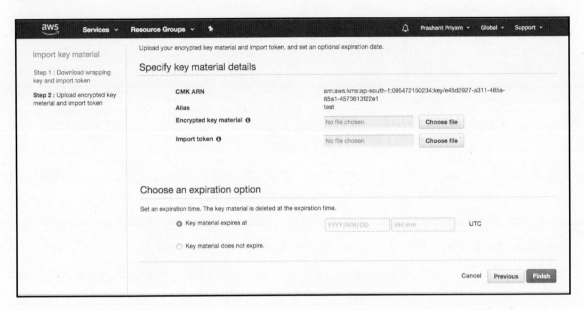

After a successful upload, you can get this key listed inside the encryption keys list.

You cannot change the CMK for exiting an encrypted snapshot and volume. Here, again you will be asking how to modify the CMK. To do this, you can associate a different CMK during a snapshot copy operation so that the newly copied snapshot can use the new CMK.

One more very important question is, how do you remove encryption from the encrypted volume? Here, you cannot remove/disable encryption from the encrypted volume, but you can copy data from the encrypted volume to an unencrypted volume. Now, let's see how to enable encryption on the EBS volume while creating an instance.

First, log in to the AWS Management Console and search for the EC2 service. Now, click on **Launch Instance** and select an **Amazon Machine Image (AMI)**. AMI is a VM template, which is used to create a virtual machine:

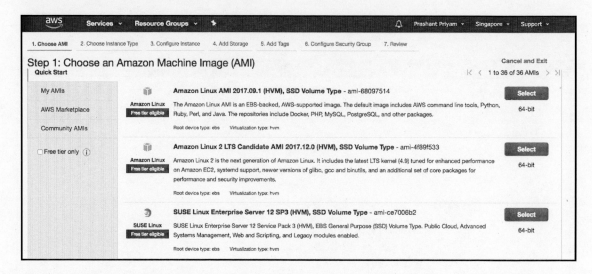

After the selection of the AMI, we need to choose the compute type:

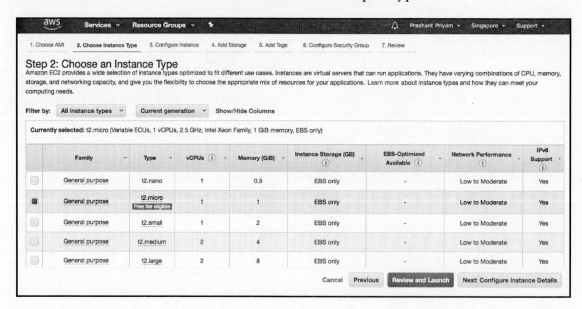

After the selection of the compute type, click on **Next: Configure Instance Details**, specify information about the VPC and subnet, and assign a public IP, IAM roles, and tenancy (this says how you want to run your instance, such as whether it will be run on shared hardware or dedicated hardware):

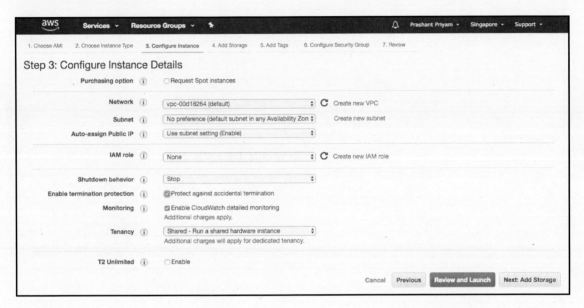

Now click on **Add Storage**:

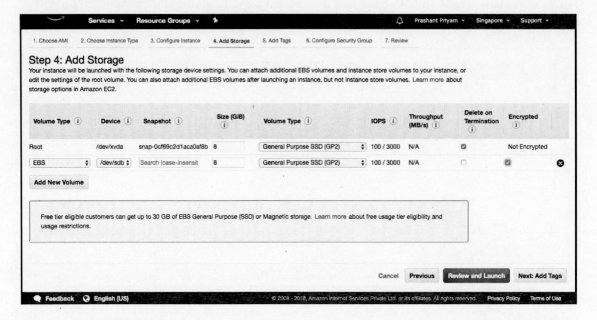

Here, we allocate storage for the root volume (we cannot encrypt the root volume of EC2). Now, as we need to encrypt the volume, we will add one additional volume by clicking on the **Add New Volume** button.

Finally, click on **Review and Launch** to review and launch the instance. Now, once the instance is created, it will be up with an additional encrypted volume.

S3

AWS provides you with S3 as the object storage, where you can store your object files from 1 KB to 5 TB in size at a low cost. It's highly secure, durable, and scalable, and has unlimited capacity. It allows concurrent read/write access to objects by separate clients and applications. You can store any type of file in AWS S3 storage.

 AWS keeps multiple copies of all the data stored in the standard S3 storage, which are replicated across devices in the region to ensure durability of 99.999999999%. S3 cannot be used as block storage.

AWS S3 storage is further categorized into three different sections:

- **S3 Standard**: This is suitable when we need durable storage for files with frequent access.
- **Reduced Redundancy Storage**: This is suitable when we have less critical data that is persistent in nature.
- **Infrequent Access (IA)**: This is suitable when you have durable data with nonfrequent access. You can opt for Glacier. However, in Glacier you have a very long retrieval time. So, S3 IA becomes a suitable option. It provides the same performance as the S3 Standard storage.

AWS S3 has in-built error correction and fault tolerance capabilities. Apart from this, in S3 you have an option to enable versioning and cross-region replication (**cross-origin resource sharing (CORS)**).

 If you want to enable versioning on any existing bucket, versioning will be enabled only for new objects in that bucket, not for existing objects. This also happens in the case of CORS, where you can enable cross-region replication, but it will be applicable only for new objects.

Security in S3

S3 is highly secure storage. Here, we can enable fine-grained access policies for resource access and encryption.

To enable access-level security, you can use the following:

- S3 bucket policy
- IAM access policy
- MFA for object deletion

The S3 bucket policy is a JSON code that defines what will be accessed by whom and at what level:

```
{
  "Version": "2008-10-17",
  "Statement": [
    {
      "Sid": "AllowPublicRead",
      "Effect": "Allow",
      "Principal": {
        "AWS": "*"
```

```
      },
      "Action": [
        "s3:GetObject"
      ],
      "Resource": [
        "arn:aws:s3:::prashantpriyam/*"
      ]
    }
  ]
}
```

In the preceding JSON code, we have just allowed read-only access for all the objects (as defined in the `Action` section) for an S3 bucket named `prashantpriyam` (defined in the `Resource` section).

Similar to the S3 bucket policy, we can also define an IAM policy for S3 bucket access:

```
{
  "Version": "2012-10-17",
  "Statement": [
    {
      "Effect": "Allow",
      "Action": [
        "s3:GetBucketLocation",
        "s3:ListAllMyBuckets"
      ],
      "Resource": "arn:aws:s3:::*"
    },
    {
      "Effect": "Allow",
      "Action": ["s3:ListBucket"],
      "Resource": ["arn:aws:s3:::prashantpriyam"]
    },
    {
      "Effect": "Allow",
      "Action": [
        "s3:PutObject",
        "s3:GetObject",
        "s3:DeleteObject"
      ],
      "Resource": ["arn:aws:s3:::prashantpriyam/*"]
    }
  ]
}
```

In the preceding policy, we want to give the user full permissions on the S3 bucket from the AWS console as well.

In the following section of policy (JSON code), we have granted permission to the user to get the bucket location and list all the buckets for traversal, but here we cannot perform other operations, such as getting object details from the bucket:

```
{
    "Version": "2012-10-17",
    "Statement": [
      {
        "Effect": "Allow",
        "Action": [
          "s3:GetBucketLocation",
          "s3:ListAllMyBuckets"
        ],
        "Resource": "arn:aws:s3:::*"
      },
      {
        "Effect": "Allow",
        "Action": ["s3:ListBucket"],
        "Resource": ["arn:aws:s3:::prashantpriyam"]
      },
```

While in the second section of the policy (specified as follows), we have given permission to users to traverse into the `prashantpriyam` bucket and perform PUT, GET, and DELETE operations on the object:

```
{
        "Effect": "Allow",
        "Action": [
          "s3:PutObject",
          "s3:GetObject",
          "s3:DeleteObject"
        ],
        "Resource": ["arn:aws:s3:::prashantpriyam/*"]
    }
```

MFA enables additional security on your account where, after password-based authentication, it asks you to provide the temporary code generated from AWS MFA. We can also use a virtual MFA such as Google Authenticator.

AWS S3 supports MFA-based API, which helps to enforce MFA-based access policy on S3 bucket.

Let's look at an example where we are giving users read-only access to a bucket while all other operations require an MFA token, which will expire after 600 seconds:

```
{
    "Version": "2012-10-17",
    "Statement": [
      {
        "Sid": "",
        "Effect": "Deny",
        "Principal": "*",
        "Action": "s3:*",
        "Resource": "arn:aws:s3:::prashantpriyam/priyam/*",
        "Condition": {"Null": {"aws:MultiFactorAuthAge": true }}
      },
      {
        "Sid": "",
        "Effect": "Deny",
        "Principal": "*",
        "Action": "s3:*",
        "Resource": "arn:aws:s3:::prashantpriyam/priyam/*",
        "Condition": {"NumericGreaterThan":
          {"aws:MultiFactorAuthAge": 600 }}
      },
      {
        "Sid": "",
        "Effect": "Allow",
        "Principal": "*",
        "Action": ["s3:GetObject"],
        "Resource": "arn:aws:s3:::prashantpriyam/*"
      }
    ]
}
```

In the preceding code, you can see that we have allowed all the operations on the S3 bucket if they have an MFA token whose life is less than 600 seconds.

Apart from MFA, we can enable versioning so that S3 can automatically create multiple versions of the object to eliminate the risk of unwanted modification of data. This can be enabled with the AWS Console only.

You can also enable cross-region replication so that the S3 bucket content can be replicated to the other selected regions. This option is mostly used when you want to deliver static content into two different regions, but it also gives you redundancy.

For infrequently accessed data you can enable a life cycle policy, which helps you to transfer the objects to a low cost archival storage called Glacier.

Let's see how to secure the S3 bucket using the AWS Console. To do this, we need to log in to the S3 bucket and search for S3. Now, click on the bucket you want to secure:

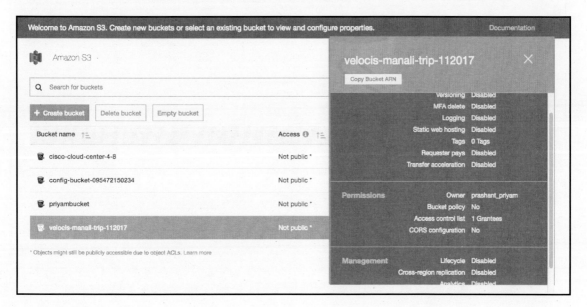

In the screenshot, we have selected the bucket called `velocis-manali-trip-112017` and, in the bucket properties, we can see that we have not enabled the security options that we have learned so far. Let's implement the security.

Now, we need to click on the bucket and then on the **Properties** tab. From here, we can enable **Versioning**, **Default encryption**, **Server access logging**, and **Object-level logging**:

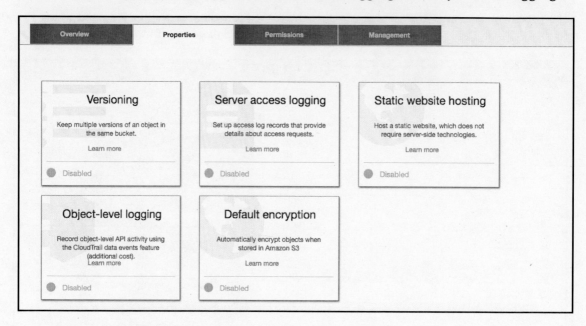

To enable **Server access logging**, you need to specify the name of the bucket and a prefix for the logs:

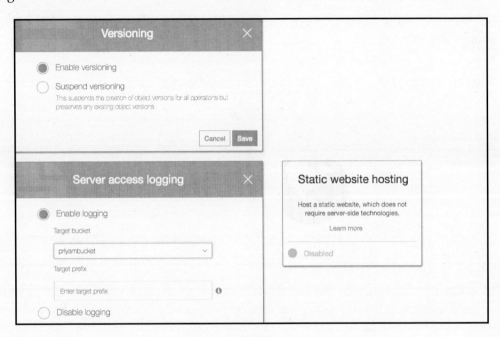

To enable encryption, you need to specify whether you want to use AES 256 or AWS KMS based encryption.

Now, click on the **Permission** tab. From here, you will be able to define the **Access Control List**, **Bucket Policy**, and **CORS configuration**:

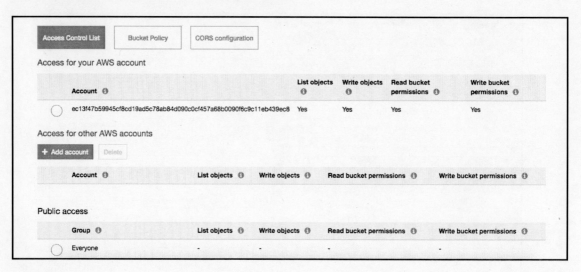

In **Access Control List**, you can define who will access what and to what extent, in **Bucket Policy** you define resource-based permissions on the bucket (like we have seen in the example for bucket policy), and in **CORS configuration** we define the rule for CORS.

Let's look at a sample CORS file:

```
<!-- Sample policy -->
<CORSConfiguration>
  <CORSRule>
    <AllowedOrigin>*</AllowedOrigin>
    <AllowedMethod>GET</AllowedMethod>
    <MaxAgeSeconds>3000</MaxAgeSeconds>
    <AllowedHeader>Authorization</AllowedHeader>
  </CORSRule>
</CORSConfiguration>
```

It's an XML script that allows read-only permission to all the origins. In the preceding code, instead of a URL, the origin is the wildcard *, which means anyone.

Now, click on the **Management** section. From here, we define the life cycle rule, replication, and so on:

In life cycle rules, an S3 bucket object is transferred to the Standard-IA tier after 30 days and transferred to Glacier after 60 days.

This is how we define security on the S3 bucket.

AWS Glacier

AWS Glacier is an archival solution, where we store data that is not accessed frequently. You can use it to transfer data directly from S3 using a life cycle policy.

In AWS Glacier, you can store a file with a maximum size of 40 TB. It also has unlimited storage, like S3, where you can store unlimited files and an unlimited volume of data.

Security in AWS Glacier

In AWS, Glacier stores data into a vault. It's only accessible to the users who created the vault. All the data stored Glaciers are encrypted, and they also support data in transit encryption using SSL.

Any data stored in the Glacier vault is immutable. This means that data stored in a Glacier cannot be updated. For access control and management you can use IAM policies.

To add more security, you can use request signing, whereas to authenticate requests, you need to sign your request using hash keys. A cryptographic hash is a function that returns a unique hash value based on the input. In input, we pass secret access keys along with the request text. The hash function returns a hash value that you include in the request as your signature. It looks like hexadecimal keys:

```
3ce5b2f2fffac9262b4da9256f8d086b4aaf42eba5f111c21681a65a127b7c2a
```

EFS

AWS also offers scalable file storage to use with EC2 using the NFS protocol. In EFS, the storage capacity is elastic, therefore it grows and shrinks when you add or remove files, respectively.

You can use EFS with multiple EC2 instances as a common data source for the same point of time. All of them can concurrently access the EFS stored files.

We can use it with an on-premise server as well when we have a direct connection between the on-premise server and VPC.

To use EFS, you need to log in to the AWS Console and search for EFS. Now, from the EFS Console we define the filesystem access policy. In the EFS Console, it is not mandatory to have optional configuration but, if you want, you can define the optional settings:

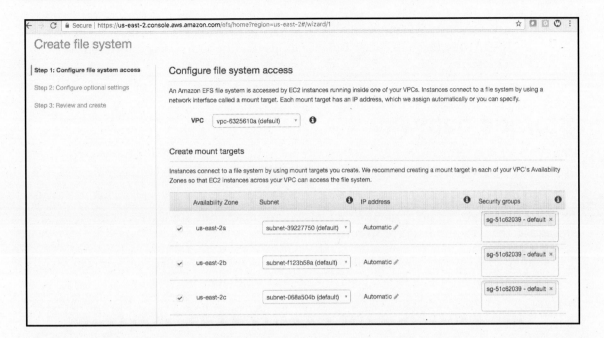

In the preceding screenshot, which shows what you can see while creating the EFS, we need to specify the availability zone and security.

We can use EFS for database backup, to store web app files, and for cloud burst and enterprise applications that need to have shared storage.

Now, let's see the security options in EFS.

Security in EFS

EFS also comes inside the VPC; so, the following are the options for security:

- **Security group**: We must open only the NFS port in the security group to access EFS on a specific IP in order to get it mounted.
- **Read write and execute permission**: EFS works as Unix-style read, write, and execute permissions based on the user and group ID asserted by the mounting NFSv4.1 client. So, you can define file- and folder-level permissions to users.
- **Encryption**: In EFS, you can define encryption for metadata and data at rest. For this, you need to enable encryption while creating the filesystem. It can be enabled using Console, CLI, and SDK.

- **API calls**: You can define the IAM policy for EFS access to users and API calls. The IAM policy will check the operations that the users can perform on the filesystem.

Storage gateway

The AWS storage gateway helps you to create hybrid cloud storage that your own premise application can utilize. You can use it for backup, disaster recovery, cloud bursting, and storage migration.

For this, AWS provides an appliance that lets you connect your application with cloud storage on the NFS and iSCSI protocols.

The storage gateway includes a highly-optimized data transfer mechanism with bandwidth management, automated network resilience, and efficient data transfer.

It also provides an optional local cache for low-latency, on-premises access to your most active data:

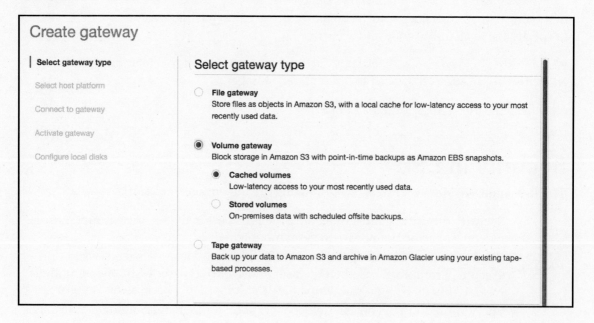

In the preceding screenshot, you can see that we can use the storage gateway in the following ways:

- **File gateway**: This works on NFS, where you can directly store your files on AWS S3 using the file gateway.
- **Volume gateway**: This works on iSCSI, and data in these volumes can be transferred into Amazon S3 Cloud storage and accessed through the volume gateway.
- **Tape gateway**: This is used for archiving the tape-based backup to AWS Glacier for archival. Tape gateway is a virtual tape infrastructure that scales seamlessly with your business needs and eliminates the operational burden of provisioning, scaling, and maintaining a physical tape infrastructure.

Security in the storage gateway

In storage gateway, your iSCSI initiators connect your volume to the iSCSI targets. For security, storage gateway uses CHAP-based authentication to authenticate iSCSI and its initiator connection.

CHAP provides protection against playback attacks by requiring authentication to access storage volume targets.

You can define one or more of the CHAP credentials:

Apart from this, we can use IAM for security. Here, you also have an IAM policy to define the permission needed to access the storage gateway.

Let's look at an example:

```
{
    "Version": "2012-10-17",
    "Statement": [
        {
            "Sid": "AllowsSpecifiedActionsOnAllGateways",
            "Effect": "Allow",
            "Action": [
                "storagegateway:ActivateGateway",
                "storagegateway:ListGateways"
            ],
            "Resource":
              "arn:aws:storagegateway:us-west-2:095472150234:gateway/*"
        },
        {
            "Sid": "AllowsEC2ActionsGateways",
            "Effect": "Allow",
            "Action": [
                "ec2:DescribeSnapshots",
                "ec2:DeleteSnapshot"
            ],
            "Resource": "*"
        }
    ]
}
```

In the preceding policy, we have two sections. In the first section, we have allowed users to activate a storage gateway connection and list the activated gateway under the specified account ID.

In the second section, we have given EC2 permission to describe the snapshots and then delete them. The storage gateway volumes create snapshots and store them into EBS. Now, to access these snapshots, we need to give this EC2 permission.

AWS Snowball

AWS Snowball is a service used to migrate your data from the on-premise datacenter to AWS. It has a petabyte-scale data transport solution that uses secure appliances to transfer data in and out of AWS.

Snowball comes into the picture when you have massive scale of data that cannot be transferred using network connections due to time limits, cost limits, and major security concerns.

It's a very simple device that you request from AWS to get it shipped to your location. After that, you start the appliance and copy all your data, and send it back to AWS to be uploaded to AWS S3.

You can see the details of each activity using the AWS Management Console.

It comes in the following three sizes:

- **Snowball**: The Snowball device has a capacity of 50 TB (only US) and 80 TB. On the physical interface, there is a link display, which helps to configure the IP and is also used to track shipping information.
- **Snowball Edge**: Snowball Edge has a higher data storage capacity than Snowball. It comes in a size of 100 TB.
- **Snowmobile**: This is a large truck carrying your petabytes of data.

To transfer the data to Snowball, you need to insert the power plug and boot the device. Once the device starts, it will show you the following screen:

Now you can attach your network cable and define the network settings, such as IP address, subnet mask, and gateway.

Now, to transfer your data you have the following two options:

- **Using Snowball client**: This is a terminal application that allows you to transfer data. It's very simple to use, so you do not need to be a programmer or an expert to use it.
- **Using S3 adaptor**: This lets you push the data programmatically using the CLI and SDK.

There are few best practices for the use of Snowball, which are listed as follows:

- It says that if you find anything suspicious, do not use it and instead make a request to AWS to replace it.
- Do not save a copy of the unlock code in the same location in the workstation as the manifest for that job. This helps you to prevent an unauthorized party from accessing Snowball.
- Always delete the logs from your workstation once the copy process completes.
- It's always advised to attach Snowball with localhost to transfer the data.
- Make sure that your workstation system is powerful in terms of RAM and CPU (such as a 16-core CPU and 16 GB RAM).
- Do not disconnect Snowball during data transfer.
- The file must be in static state for the transfer to Snowball.

Security in Snowball

Snowball provides the safest way to transfer your data to the AWS Cloud. We can define security parameters for Snowball using IAM. IAM lets you authorize the users to create a Snowball job, and also access controls.

Before using Snowball, users must get authenticated with IAM. Once the user is authenticated, they should have sufficient privileges to access the AWS Snowball Management Console.

To use the Snowball Management Console, users must have the following access permissions defined in IAM:

- List all S3 buckets or create a new bucket, if required
- Create SNS topics to send notification
- Select AWS KMS keys
- Create an IAM role

Let's see an example of an IAM policy defined for Snowball:

```
{
    "Version": "2012-10-17",
    "Statement": [
        {
            "Effect": "Allow",
            "Action": [
                    "s3:ListBucket",
                    "s3:GetBucketPolicy",
                    "s3:GetBucketLocation",
                    "s3:ListBucketMultipartUploads",
                    "s3:ListAllMyBuckets",
                    "s3:CreateBucket"
            ],
            "Resource": [
                "*"
            ]
        },
        {
            "Effect": "Allow",
            "Action": [
                    "kms:DescribeKey",
                    "kms:ListAliases",
                    "kms:ListKeys",
                    "kms:CreateGrant"
            ],
            "Resource": [
                "*"
            ]
        },
        {
            "Effect": "Allow",
            "Action": [
                "iam:AttachRolePolicy",
                "iam:CreatePolicy",
                "iam:CreateRole",
                "iam:ListRoles",
                "iam:ListRolePolicies",
                "iam:PutRolePolicy"
            ],
            "Resource": [
                "*"
            ]
        },
        {
            "Effect": "Allow",
            "Action": [
```

```
                    "sns:CreateTopic",
                    "sns:GetTopicAttributes",
                    "sns:ListSubscriptionsByTopic",
                    "sns:ListTopics",
                    "sns:Subscribe",
                    "sns:SetTopicAttributes"
                ],
                "Resource": [
                    "*"
                ]
            },
            {
                "Effect": "Allow",
                "Action": [
                    "snowball:*",
                    "importexport:*"
                ],
                "Resource": "*"
            }
        ]
    }
```

In the preceding code, we have defined following:

- In the first section, we have given permissions for the S3 bucket as `ListBucket`, `GetBucketPolicy`, `GetBucketLocation`, `ListBucketMultipartUploads`, `ListAllMyBuckets`, and `CreateBucket`
- In the second section, we have granted permissions on AWS KMS level so that they can `DescribeKey`, `ListAliases`, `ListKeys`, and `CreateGrant` for KMS keys
- In the third section, we have allowed them to define IAM roles and attach the policy
- In the fourth section, the SNS-level access policy is defined so that users can create SNS topics for notification
- Finally, we have defined access to Snowball and created import-export tasks

When we choose to import data from Snowball to S3, it has two layers of encryption:

- The first layer of encryption is applied in the memory of your local workstation. It is applied irrespective of whether we are using the Snowball client or the S3 adapter for Snowball.
- SSL encryption is a second layer of encryption for all data going into or out of a standard Snowball.

AWS Snowball supports server-side encryption with S3-managed server-side encryption keys. Server-side encryption is about protecting data at rest and SSE-S3 has strong, multi-factor encryption to protect your data at rest in Amazon S3.

AWS Snowball also uses signing to ensure security of data being transferred from your workstation to the Snowball appliance. It's applicable only when we use the S3 adaptor for data transfer. Here, signing is only for data transfer between the workstation and Snowball. So it does not factor into the encryption keys used to encrypt your data on Snowball.

Snowball does not store any AWS-access credentials.

A quick recap

In this chapter, we have learned about different storage options in AWS and their usability.

In short, we have following storage options in AWS—for EC2 instances:

- Ephemeral storage or instance store
- EBS

For security at the EC2 level, we can ensure data security and safety using encryption, snapshots, and by defining RAID.

Defining encryption at the volume level does impact your application's code, but if we take a snapshot of an encrypted volume, that also becomes encrypted. It encrypts data at rest and data transition between volumes and instances.

Defining RAID gives you fault tolerance at the volume level.

Ephemeral storage, or instance store, is high-performance volatile storage that is used to store temporary data. So, it is always advisable to store persistent data into a persistent volume.

For static content, we have S3 storage, which is object storage with unlimited capacity. To ensure the security of S3 storage, we have multiple options, such as defining an IAM policy, S3 bucket policy, cross-region replication, versioning, and encryption.

For archival data, we have AWS Glacier, which stores data in a vault. All the data stored in the vault is encrypted by default. We can use the IAM policy to define the accessibility of the Glacier vault object.

For shared filesystems, AWS has the EFS service, which works on the NFS protocol and allows you to seamlessly mount it with multiple instances to access the data. You can also mount it with on-premise servers using direct connect. For security at the EFS level, we can use security groups, an IAM policy, and encryption.

For hybrid storage, we have a storage gateway, which lets us connect the on-premise storage to AWS Cloud using a virtual appliance. We use its storage gateway for data migration, cloud bursting, backup, and disaster recovery scenario.

At the storage gateway, we again define security groups, CHAP-based authentication for the iSCSI initiator validation, and IAM policies.

Finally, in storage we have AWS Snowball, which is a petabyte-scale data migration service. Here, we get a Snowball device shipped from AWS to our on-premise location to copy data from on-premise server/storage and then ship it to get uploaded on the S3 bucket.

For security at Snowball, we have SSE, IAM policies, and signing to ensure the security of data at rest and in transit. We have also learned about the best practices of using Snowball.

Summary

In this chapter, we talked about cloud storage and data security. In the next section, we will learn about cloud platform security. We will see how to ensure security for PaaS services, such as database and analytics services.

6
Cloud Platform Security

In the cloud, we have three major offerings—**Infrastructure as a Service (IaaS)**, **Platform as a Service (PaaS)**, and **Software as a Service (SaaS)**. Till now, you have learned about security from an IaaS perspective.

Now, we will see how to ensure security at the PaaS level. In AWS, we have many PaaS services. One of the most popular PaaS services is **Relational Database Service (RDS)**. Apart from that, we have DynamoDB, Redshift, ElastiCache, **Elastic Container Service (ECS)**, and **Simple Queue Service (SQS)**. In this chapter, you will learn to secure all these services.

In PaaS, we do not need to worry about OS and underlying platform management, as it is part of AWS responsibility; you can say that the complete platform is being managed by AWS. We just need to manage our own services that are running on this platform. For the security too, we need to work on securing our services that are running on top of the PaaS services.

We will cover the following topics in this chapter:

- RDS
- AWS Redshift
- AWS DynamoDB
- ElastiCache
- AWS ECS
- SQS

Let's start with RDS.

RDS

AWS RDS is a highly available, scalable, and managed database service. It's a cost-efficient, resizable capacity database wherein AWS manages common database administration tasks.

As we know, the database is the most critical component for any application. That's why we always define a private subnet to host a database and only allow connections from the specific subnet or IP on a specific database port.

In the case of RDS, we apply the same, although we have more security components to ensure the security and safety of the database instance.

For RDS, we have two models to provision:

- **Single Availability Zone**: In this model, you have only one database (master database) running in a single **Availability Zone** (**AZ**). However, it's not fault-tolerant, which means that if there is any problem or maintenance activity being performed on the database, your application can face downtime.
- **Multi AZ**: In this model, you have two database instances running in two different AZs in master and standby fashion, where the standby instance is being synchronously replicated to the master instance. If anything goes wrong with the master database, your standby automatically takes over to ensure zero downtime.

Apart from these, RDS has one more model named **read replica**. Read replica is used to give you scaling features where you can add multiple read replica with your master database to perform read-only queries. It's a horizontal mode of scaling for a database.

In AWS, RDS supports the following databases:

- MySQL
- MariaDB
- MS SQL Server
- Oracle
- Postgres
- Amazon Aurora DB

For NoSQL database, we have DynamoDB in AWS as PaaS. Now, let's look at the security in RDS.

Security in RDS

Security in RDS can be defined at different levels such as:

- Using a security group, we can define security at the network level
- IAM role and policies can be used to define security at the database management and user access levels
- Encryption can be used to ensure the encryption of data-at-rest, and **Secure Socket Layer** (**SSL**)-based encryption can be used to ensure data-in-transit

Using security groups

RDS has its scope bounded to VPC. We use a security group for database security to control the traffic.

RDS can be associated with the **database** (**DB**) security group to control open public traffic, and associated with the VPC security group when RDS is used inside the VPC and EC2 security group.

In the DB security group, you need to specify the ports, while in VPC security you need to specify the port and IPs from which traffic will come to RDS instances.

You can define the security group from your AWS VPC console and associate it while creating a DB instance:

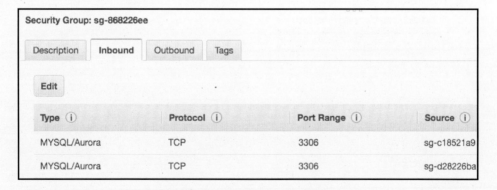

Using IAM

We use IAM to ensure the security of RDS. We use IAM policies to control the RDS actions to specially create, modify, and delete the RDS database, RDS security groups, option groups, and parameter groups. Apart from this, we also control the backup and restore operations for the database.

There are many predefined policies available in the IAM management console, which you can access in the **Policy** section:

Let's see inside a predefined IAM policy for RDS named **AmazonRDSReadOnlyAccess**:

```
{
  "Version": "2012-10-17",
  "Statement": [
    {
      "Action": [
        "rds:Describe*",
        "rds:ListTagsForResource",
        "ec2:DescribeAccountAttributes",
        "ec2:DescribeAvailabilityZones",
        "ec2:DescribeInternetGateways",
        "ec2:DescribeSecurityGroups",
        "ec2:DescribeSubnets",
        "ec2:DescribeVpcAttribute",
        "ec2:DescribeVpcs"
      ],
      "Effect": "Allow",
      "Resource": "*"
    },
    {
      "Action": [
        "cloudwatch:GetMetricStatistics",
        "logs:DescribeLogStreams",
        "logs:GetLogEvents"
      ],
```

```
      "Effect": "Allow",
      "Resource": "*"
    }
  ]
}
```

In the previous IAM code, you can see that we have to allow read-only access to RDS resources and read-only access to EC2-level resources.

In the next section, we have allowed users to get read-only access to logs and monitoring of RDS resources using CloudWatch actions.

For best practices, one must create an IAM account to access RDS with minimal access rights, to access the database and regularly rotate IAM credentials.

Apart from this, we can use IAM authentication for databases such as MySQL and Amazon Aurora with MySQL compatibility. For this authentication, we do not need a database password. Here, an IAM authentication token is used for database authentication.

An **authentication token** is a unique string of characters that Amazon RDS generates on request with 15 minutes of lifetime. After 15 minutes, it automatically expires. Here, we need not store the database credential for authentication. Apart from this, we can use standard database authentication.

There are the following benefits to using IAM authentication:

- Network traffic to and from the database is encrypted using SSL
- One can use IAM to manage database resources centrally instead of managing access to each database instance and cluster
- Applications running on EC2 can access the database using an IAM role instead of hardcoding the password

However, this has some limitations as well; for example, if you have the maximum number of connections on the database, then it can create network throttling.

Using SSL to encrypt database connections

AWS RDS also enables you to encrypt database connections using SSL. Here, all the database flavors, such as MySQL, MariaDB, SQL Server, Oracle, and Postgres, have their own way of implementing the SSL.

AWS RDS creates an SSL certificate and installs the certificate on the database instance while provisioning the instance. These certificates are signed by a **certificate authority (CA)**. The SSL certificate includes the DB instance endpoint URL as the **common name (CN)** for the SSL certificate.

 The public key is stored at `https://s3.amazonaws.com/rds-downloads/rds-combined-ca-bundle.pem`.

Now, to implement these keys, we use the following script:

```
mysql -h <specify you mysqlRDS endpoint url> --ssl-
ca=https://s3.amazonaws.com/rds-downloads/rds-combined-ca-bundle.pem --ssl-
mode= VERIFY_IDENTITY


GRANT USAGE ON *.* TO 'encrypted_user'@'%' REQUIRE SSL
```

In the first block, we implement the SSL certification, and in the next section, we grant permission to use SSL for all the connections.

This is applicable for MySQL and MySQL-compatible Aurora DB.

MS SQL Server has a different mechanism for implementing SSL, and also, we can specify whether all the connections use SSL or just a specific connection uses SSL.

When you force SSL for all the connections, it happens transparently to the client.

To force SSL for all clients, we must use the `rds.force_ssl` parameter and modify its value in the parameter group. By default, the `rds.force_ssl` parameter value is `false`. Here, we have to set the `rds.force_ssl` parameter to `true` to force connections to use SSL. The `rds.force_ssl` parameter is static; after modifying the parameter value, we must reboot the DB instance for the change to take effect.

To use SSL on specific connections, we need to get a certificate for the client computer, import certificates to the client computer, and then encrypt the connections from the client computer.

We can get a root certificate that works for all regions from `https://s3.amazonaws.com/rds-downloads/rds-ca-2015-root.pem`. We can also download a certificate bundle that contains both the old and new root certificates from `https://s3.amazonaws.com/rds-downloads/rds-combined-ca-bundle.pem`.

For an Oracle database, we have many options to enable encryption. Let's see what they are.

To protect database files, RDS allows the use of **Transparent Data Encryption** (**TDE**). But now the question is: *what is TDE?* TDE is an encryption method that encrypts all sensitive data stored in data files. To stop the data security during decryption, TDE stores the encryption keys in a security module external to the database.

TDE helps you encrypt all critical data such as financial details, payment information, and credit or debit card information stored in tables and tablespaces. Data encrypted using TDE is transparently decrypted for a database user or application that has permission to access the data. TDE also lets you protect your critical data stored on secondary storage devices as well as protecting it from data theft.

One cannot disable TDE from a DB instance once that instance is associated with an option group with the Oracle TDE option.

We can enable the TDE option for AWS RDS by modifying or creating the option group and associating it with running DB instances.

To enable and use Oracle TDE, RDS also supports the use of AWS CloudHSM with an Oracle Enterprise Edition DB instance to store TDE keys.

One can enable an RDS DB instance to use AWS CloudHSM only after:

- Setting up an HSM appliance
- Setting the proper permissions for cross-service access
- Setting up Amazon RDS and the DB instance, which will use AWS CloudHSM

To use AWS CloudHSM Classic with an Oracle DB instance using Oracle TDE, one must do the following:

1. Have a security group attached to the Oracle DB instance that allows HSM port 1792.
2. Create a DB subnet group that uses the same subnets defined in VPC used by your HSMs and then assign that DB subnet group to Oracle DB instance.
3. Set up the Amazon RDS CLI.
4. Add IAM permissions for RDS to use to access AWS CloudHSM Classic.
5. Add the TDE_HSM option to the option group associated with your Oracle DB instance. This can be added using AWS CLI.

6. Add two new parameters to the Oracle DB instance that will use AWS CloudHSM Classic. The `tde-credential-arn` parameter is the **Amazon Resource Name (ARN)** of the **high availability (HA)** partition group returned after running the `create-hapg` command. The `tde-credential-password` is the partition password you used while initializing the HA partition group.

The best practice for using AWS CloudHSM Classic with Amazon RDS is to use three AWS CloudHSM Classic appliances configured into a HA partition group. A minimum of three HSMs are suggested for HA purposes. Even if two of your HSMs are unavailable, your keys will still be available to Amazon RDS.

Postgres also supports SSL-based encryption to encrypt connections between application and Postgres RDS. Here, we can force all connections to use SSL-based encryption.

We can enable SSL encryption for Postgres database too, by creating a new option group or modifying an existing option group. Here, we modify the `rds.force_ssl` parameter, which is by default 0, to 1 and modify the database instance's `pg_hba.conf` file to support the new SSL configuration.

Security best practices for AWS RDS

There are a few best practices that have been specified by AWS for RDS services. They are:

- Run your RDS under VPC for greater network access control
- Use an IAM policy to grant a specific permission to users to perform actions on databases
- Use a security group to control and manage the traffic to and from the database
- Use SSL for connection encryption
- Use RDS encryption to secure your database instances and snapshots at rest
- For Oracle database, use Oracle Native Network Encryption and transport data protection
- Use the security features of your DB engine to control who can log in to the databases on a DB instance

Back up and restore database

AWS RDS also supports automated backup of your database. It basically takes volume snapshot-based backup of your database instance on defined backup windows. You can restore it from whenever it is required. You also specify the backup retention period.

Monitoring of RDS

AWS RDS gives you complete insight of your database instance using CloudWatch. You can access the monitoring of RDS database from AWS Console and can also define custom alarms on your custom metrics such as CPU utilization, read/write IOPS, and network throughput.

You can get basic monitoring for RDS console as follows:

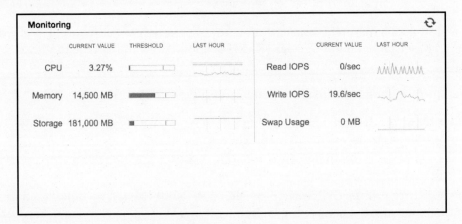

In this section, you have learned about RDS. In the next section, you will learn about Redshift.

AWS Redshift

Amazon Redshift is a petabyte data warehousing solution, available as PaaS, where the complete underlying infrastructure is managed by AWS.

In AWS Redshift, we create a cluster that combines a set of nodes. Once you have a Redshift cluster, you can start running queries to get insight from your database. Redshift offers you very fast query performance for data analysis.

As with other services, AWS Redshift can be managed using console, SDK, and APIs.

Now, let's see how we can secure the Redshift cluster. As we know, in Redshift too, we have databases. First, let's see how to secure a database in Redshift and then how to configure security for a Redshift database.

Security in Redshift

In Redshift, you can enable encryption for a database to ensure the security of data-at-rest. When you enable encryption for Redshift cluster, it automatically encrypts data block, metadata of systems, and its snapshots as well.

Encryption is an optional setting for Redshift but you must be careful while enabling it, as it is immutable in nature. This means that you cannot change it after enabling it. It's recommended to enable encryption for sensitive data.

AWS Redshift uses a hierarchy of encryption keys to encrypt the database. Here, we can use either AWS **Key Management Service (KMS)** or CloudHSM to manage top-level encryption.

There are the following ways to secure and protect your RDS infrastructure:

- **Sign in credential**: Users logging into AWS Redshift console must have sufficient privileges to access the Redshift cluster.
- **IAM roles and policies**: IAM roles and policies must be defined to control access to Redshift resources.
- **Security groups**: When we provision a Redshift cluster, by default, all the traffic is blocked. So when we are launching it in VPC, we need to create a security group and assign it to a cluster. We can manage the security group for RDS programmatically as well.
- **VPC**: If we are creating a Redshift cluster inside VPC, then we can control network-level access of VPC cluster using private subnets.
- **Encryption**: To encrypt user data in tables, we must enable encryption while creating the cluster, but once enabled, you cannot disable encryption.
- **SSL-based encryption**: To define security for data-in-transit, we use SSL-based encryption to secure the connection between the SQL client and the Redshift cluster.

- **Load data encryption**: To upload data from the S3 bucket to the Redshift cluster, we can use **server-side encryption** (**SSE**) or client-side encryption. For SSE, S3 handles the decryption process, while for client-side encryption, Redshift decrypts data using the copy command while loading data into tables.
- **Data-in-transit**: To protect data-in-transit within AWS Cloud, RDS uses hardware-accelerated SSL to communicate with Amazon S3 or DynamoDB for copy, upload, backup, and restore operations.

Now, let's see how we can control the access to Redshift resources. Redshift resource access can be controlled at the following levels:

- **Cluster management**: AWS user or accounts associated with security credential have the rights to create, configure, and delete clusters. AWS users with the required permissions can use the AWS Management Console, AWS CLI, or Amazon Redshift API to manage the clusters. This access is managed using IAM policies. For example, we have an IAM policy that allows users to perform all the operations on a Redshift cluster but not to delete a cluster whose name starts with `protected`:

```
{
  "Version": "2012-10-17",
  "Statement": [
    {
      "Sid":"AllowClusterManagement",
      "Action": [
        "redshift:CreateCluster",
        "redshift:DeleteCluster",
        "redshift:ModifyCluster",
        "redshift:RebootCluster"
      ],
      "Resource": [
        "*"
      ],
      "Effect": "Allow"
    },
    {
      "Sid":"DenyDelete",
      "Action": [
        "redshift:DeleteCluster"
      ],
      "Resource": [
        "arn:aws:redshift:us-east-1:
         XXXXXXXXX:cluster:production*"
      ],
      "Effect": "Deny"
```

```
            }
        ]
    }
```

- **Cluster connectivity**: Here, the Redshift security group defines how the EC2 instance will connect with the Redshift cluster.
- **Database access**: AWS Redshift also controls the accessibility of database objects such as tables and views to users. Users can only access resources in the database that their user accounts have been granted permission to access.

For monitoring and logging, we can use CloudWatch and CloudTrail. Using CloudWatch, we can define metrics to get details about the performance of the Redshift cluster. We define metrics such as CPU utilization, read IOPS, and write IOPS.

For logs, we can enable audit logs and store them to S3 buckets to get details about the accessibility.

AWS DynamoDB

Amazon DynamoDB is NoSQL DB, which is very fast and scalable. It provides your application very low latency at any scale. DynamoDB is PaaS (available on AWS), which works on document and key value stores. For huge amounts of requests, AWS offers the **DynamoDB Accelerator** (**DAX**) service to give you microsecond latency.

To secure DynamoDB, we use IAM extensively. Let's look at methods of securing DynamoDB.

Security in DynamoDB

We use IAM for authentication and access management for DynamoDB.

For signing from the console, we define users that have sufficient privileges to access DynamoDB resources.

We use IAM roles and policies to access the DynamoDB tables to perform read/write operations. When we use IAM roles, it creates temporary tokens to authenticate and provide access to DynamoDB resources.

If we have applications running on EC2 instances, we can map the IAM roles to grant permission to access the DynamoDB resources.

When we define an IAM policy to grant permission on DynamoDB, we can define conditions on which permissions take effect.

Let's understand a few permission use cases:

- **Grant permissions on a table, but restrict access to specific items in that table based on certain primary key values**: This case is useful when we have a social media gaming application using DynamoDB where all users' saved game data is stored in a single table, but no user can access data items that they do not own.
- **Abstraction of attribute data so that only subsets of attributes are visible to users**: This case is useful when we have an application for flight information. It displays flight data, such as airline names, arrival and departure times, and flight numbers for nearby airports, based on the user's location. However, other attributes, such as pilot names or the number of passengers, are hidden.

Suppose that we have a mobile gaming application that uses DynamoDB as a database where players have the option to select and play from a variety of available games. The application uses a DynamoDB table named GameRecord to store the scores and other user information. Here, user ID and game name are used to identify the items in the table; we can say that this table has a primary key consisting of user ID and game name. Players only have access to their own data. Now, let's define an IAM role so that players can access their own data from the DynamoDB:

```
{
    "Version": "2012-10-17",
    "Statement": [
        {
            "Effect": "Allow",
            "Action": [
                "dynamodb:GetItem",
                "dynamodb:BatchGetItem",
                "dynamodb:Query",
                "dynamodb:PutItem",
                "dynamodb:UpdateItem",
                "dynamodb:DeleteItem",
                "dynamodb:BatchWriteItem"
            ],
            "Resource": [
                "arn:aws:dynamodb:us-west-2:
                123456789012:table/GameRecord"
            ],
            "Condition": {
                "ForAllValues:StringEquals": {
                    "dynamodb:LeadingKeys": [
                        "${www.facebook.com:user_id}"
```

```
                    ],
                    "dynamodb:Attributes": [
                        "UserId",
                        "GameTitle",
                        "Wins",
                        "Losses",
                        "TopScore",
                        "TopScoreDateTime"
                    ]
                },
                "StringEqualsIfExists": {
                    "dynamodb:Select": "SPECIFIC_ATTRIBUTES"
                }
            }
        }
    ]
}
```

In this IAM policy, we have defined two conditions:

- dynamodb:LeadingKeys: This condition key allows users to access only the items where the partition key value matches their user ID where ${www.facebook.com:user_id} is substation variable. Basically, here users are getting authenticated via Facebook from their mobile devices, which in return generate a **Security Token Service** (**STS**) for application access to play the game.
- dynamodb:Attributes: This condition key limits access to the defined attributes so that only the actions listed in the permissions policy can return values for these attributes.

Also, we can use client-side encryption to ensure the security of data-at-rest using the application code.

Amazon DynamoDB is accessible via SSL-encrypted endpoints. The encrypted endpoints are accessible from both the internet and from within Amazon EC2.

For monitoring and management, we can use CloudWatch to keep eyes on DynamoDB resources, and we can also use SNS notification. Notification will be triggered on defined events at CloudWatch for DynamoDB services.

Now we will see how to secure all these services.

ElastiCache

AWS offers services to handle the cache management process. Earlier, we were using Memcached or Redis installed on VM, which was a very complex and tough task to manage in terms of ensuring availability, patching, scalability, and security.

On AWS, we have this service available as ElastiCache. This gives you the option to use any engine (Redis or Memcached) to manage your cache. It's a scalable platform that will be managed by AWS in the backend.

ElastiCache provides a scalable and high-performance caching solution. It removes the complexity associated with creating and managing distributed cache clusters using Memcached or Redis.

Now, let's look at how to secure ElastiCache.

Securing ElastiCache

For enhanced security, we deploy ElastiCache clusters inside VPC. When they are deployed inside VPC, we can use a security group and NACL to add a level of security on the communication ports at network level.

Apart from this, there are multiple ways to enable security for ElastiCache.

VPC-level security

Using a security group at VPC—when we deploy AWS ElastiCache in VPC, it gets associated with a subnet, a security group, and the routing policy of that VPC. Here, we define a rule to communicate with the ElastiCache cluster on a specific port.

ElastiCache clusters can also be accessed from on-premise applications using VPN and Direct Connect.

Authentication and access control

We use IAM in order to implement the authentication and access control on ElastiCache. For authentication, you can have the following identity type:

- **Root user**: It's a superuser that is created while setting up an AWS account. It has super administrator privileges for all the AWS services. However, it's not recommended to use the root user to access any of the services.
- **IAM user**: It's a user identity in your AWS account that will have a specific set of permissions for accessing the ElastiCache service.
- **IAM role**: We also can define an IAM role with a specific set of permissions and associate it with the services that want to access ElastiCache. It basically generates temporary access keys to use ElastiCache.

Apart from this, we can also specify federated access to services where we have an IAM role with temporary credentials for accessing the service.

To access ElastiCache, service users or services must have a specific set of permissions such as create, modify, and reboot the cluster.

For this, we define an IAM policy and associate it with users or roles.

Let's see an example of an IAM policy where users will have permission to perform system administration activity for ElastiCache cluster:

```
{
    "Version": "2012-10-17",
    "Statement":[{
        "Sid": "ECAllowSpecific",
        "Effect":"Allow",
        "Action":[
            "elasticache:ModifyCacheCluster",
            "elasticache:RebootCacheCluster",
            "elasticache:DescribeCacheClusters",
            "elasticache:DescribeEvents",
            "elasticache:ModifyCacheParameterGroup",
            "elasticache:DescribeCacheParameterGroups",
            "elasticache:DescribeCacheParameters",
            "elasticache:ResetCacheParameterGroup",
            "elasticache:DescribeEngineDefaultParameters"],
        "Resource":"*"
        }
    ]
}
```

Authenticating with Redis authentication

AWS ElastiCache also adds an additional layer of security with the Redis authentication command, which asks users to enter a password before they are granted permission to execute Redis commands on a password-protected Redis server.

When we use Redis authentication, there are the following few constraints for the authentication token while using ElastiCache:

- Passwords must have at least 16 and a maximum of 128 characters
- Characters such as @, ", and / cannot be used in passwords
- Authentication can only be enabled when you are creating clusters with the in-transit encryption option enabled
- The password defined during cluster creation cannot be changed

To make the policy harder or more complex, there are the following rules related to defining the strength of a password:

- A password must include at least three characters of the following character types:
    - Uppercase characters
    - Lowercase characters
    - Digits
    - Non-alphanumeric characters (!, &, #, $, ^, <, >, -)
- A password must not contain any word that is commonly used
- A password must be unique; it should not be similar to previous passwords

Data encryption

AWS ElastiCache and EC2 instances have mechanisms to protect against unauthorized access of your data on the server.

ElastiCache for Redis also has methods of encryption for data run-in on Redis clusters. Here, too, you have data-in-transit and data-at-rest encryption methods.

Data-in-transit encryption

ElastiCache ensures the encryption of data when in transit from one location to another. ElastiCache in-transit encryption implements the following features:

- **Encrypted connections**: In this mode, SSL-based encryption is enabled for server and client communication
- **Encrypted replication**: Any data moving between the primary node and the replication node are encrypted
- **Server authentication**: Using data-in-transit encryption, the client checks the authenticity of a connection—whether it is connected to the right server
- **Client authentication**: After using data-in-transit encryption, the server can check the authenticity of the client using the Redis authentication feature

Data-at-rest encryption

ElastiCache for Redis at-rest encryption is an optional feature that increases data security by encrypting data stored on disk during sync and backup or snapshot operations.

However, there are the following few constraints for data-at-rest encryption:

- It is supported only on replication groups running Redis version 3.2.6. It is not supported on clusters running Memcached.
- It is supported only for replication groups running inside VPC.
- Data-at-rest encryption is supported for replication groups running on any node type.
- During the creation of the replication group, you can define data-at-rest encryption.
- Data-at-rest encryption, once enabled, cannot be disabled.

AWS ECS

Now, organizations have started utilizing the power of containers for their application. So, here, you must have a question; what is a container? A container is a standardized unit of software development, containing everything that your software application needs to run: code, runtime, system tools, system libraries, and so on. Containers are created from a read-only template named an **image**.

Images are created from Dockerfile, which is a text file that includes all the components and configuration required for a container.

Let's see the example of a Dockerfile for JBoss WildFly, running a Java application.

For this, we have created a Dockerfile for the hello world application:

```
FROM jboss/wildfly:latest

ARG APP_FILE=helloworld.war

ADD ${APP_FILE} /opt/jboss/wildfly/standalone/deployments/${APP_FILE}

RUN /opt/jboss/wildfly/bin/add-user.sh admin admin123 --silent
```

In the preceding code block, you can see that on top there is the app server (JBoss/WildFly). Here, `jboss/wildfly` is a Docker image (which will be pulled from Docker Hub) and after that it will deploy the `helloworld.war` file and create an admin user in JBoss server with the password `admin123`. Let's see how it works.

Now, we need to create a Docker image first, using the following command:

```
docker build -t helloworld
```

The preceding command will create a Docker image named `helloworld` using the previously-mentioned Dockerfile:

```
sh-3.2# cat Dockerfile
FROM jboss/wildfly:latest

ARG APP_FILE=helloworld.war

ADD ${APP_FILE} /opt/jboss/wildfly/standalone/deployments/${APP_FILE}

RUN /opt/jboss/wildfly/bin/add-user.sh admin admin123 --silent
sh-3.2# ls
Dockerfile      helloworld.war
sh-3.2# docker build -t helloworld .
Sending build context to Docker daemon  8.704kB
Step 1/4 : FROM jboss/wildfly:latest
 ---> d4b4d01b53bd
Step 2/4 : ARG APP_FILE=helloworld.war
 ---> Using cache
 ---> 71e1fa5950bb
Step 3/4 : ADD ${APP_FILE} /opt/jboss/wildfly/standalone/deployments/${APP_FILE}
 ---> efea512842fb
Step 4/4 : RUN /opt/jboss/wildfly/bin/add-user.sh admin admin123 --silent
 ---> Running in dd55c4cba704
Removing intermediate container dd55c4cba704
 ---> 0afbfd72a4c9
Successfully built 0afbfd72a4c9
Successfully tagged helloworld:latest
sh-3.2# docker run -it -p 8080:8080 helloworld
```

Now, once we have created the image, let's run it using the following command:

```
docker run -it -p 8080:8080 helloworld
```

In the preceding command, we have defined the port to run this application on, `8080`:

```
sh-3.2# docker run -it -p 8080:8080 helloworld
=========================================================================

  JBoss Bootstrap Environment

  JBOSS_HOME: /opt/jboss/wildfly

  JAVA: /usr/lib/jvm/java/bin/java

  JAVA_OPTS:  -server -Xms64m -Xmx512m -XX:MetaspaceSize=96M -XX:MaxMetaspaceSize=256m -Djava.net.preferIPv4Stack=true -Djboss.modules.system
.pkgs=org.jboss.byteman -Djava.awt.headless=true

=========================================================================

20:38:07,519 INFO  [org.jboss.modules] (main) JBoss Modules version 1.5.2.Final
20:38:08,217 INFO  [org.jboss.msc] (main) JBoss MSC version 1.2.6.Final
20:38:08,395 INFO  [org.jboss.as] (MSC service thread 1-1) WFLYSRV0049: WildFly Full 10.1.0.Final (WildFly Core 2.2.0.Final) starting
20:38:12,439 INFO  [org.jboss.as.repository] (ServerService Thread Pool -- 2) WFLYDR0001: Content added at location /opt/jboss/wildfly/standa
lone/data/content/08/38a8293c85177951a346326fb2367a0b856e10/content
20:38:12,575 INFO  [org.jboss.as.server] (Controller Boot Thread) WFLYSRV0039: Creating http management service using socket-binding (managem
ent-http)
20:38:12,660 INFO  [org.xnio] (MSC service thread 1-2) XNIO version 3.4.0.Final
20:38:12,714 INFO  [org.xnio.nio] (MSC service thread 1-2) XNIO NIO Implementation Version 3.4.0.Final
20:38:12,900 INFO  [org.jboss.as.clustering.infinispan] (ServerService Thread Pool -- 38) WFLYCLINF0001: Activating Infinispan subsystem.
20:38:12,956 INFO  [org.jboss.as.naming] (ServerService Thread Pool -- 46) WFLYNAM0001: Activating Naming Subsystem
20:38:12,943 INFO  [org.jboss.as.jsf] (ServerService Thread Pool -- 44) WFLYJSF0007: Activated the following JSF Implementations: [main]
20:38:13,029 WARN  [org.jboss.as.txn] (ServerService Thread Pool -- 54) WFLYTX0013: Node identifier property is set to the default value. Ple
ase make sure it is unique.
20:38:13,012 INFO  [org.jboss.as.security] (ServerService Thread Pool -- 53) WFLYSEC0002: Activating Security Subsystem
20:38:13,099 INFO  [org.jboss.as.webservices] (ServerService Thread Pool -- 56) WFLYWS0002: Activating WebServices Extension
20:38:13,205 INFO  [org.wildfly.extension.io] (ServerService Thread Pool -- 37) WFLYIO001: Worker 'default' has auto-configured to 2 core thr
eads with 16 task threads based on your 1 available processors
20:38:13,242 INFO  [org.jboss.as.remoting] (MSC service thread 1-2) JBoss Remoting version 4.0.21.Final
20:38:13,390 INFO  [org.jboss.as.connector.subsystems.datasources] (ServerService Thread Pool -- 33) WFLYJCA0004: Deploying JDBC-compliant dr
iver class org.h2.Driver (version 1.3)
20:38:13,448 INFO  [org.jboss.as.security] (MSC service thread 1-1) WFLYSEC0001: Current PicketBox version=4.9.6.Final
```

Now, the container is deployed and running. Let's check the same in the browser:

Here, we can see that WildFly is running on port 8080. Now, let's access the application:

With very few lines of code, we can deploy the hello world application in Docker.

Now you have an idea about why using containers is becoming so popular.

To run your containers, AWS has a service named ECS, which is a highly scalable, fast container management service that makes it easy to run, stop, and manage Docker containers on a cluster. It enables you to launch and stop container-based applications with simple API calls. ECS clusters are logical groups of tasks or services.

At the backend, all the infrastructure and environments are managed and maintained by AWS.

Securing ECS

AWS ECS always gets created in VPC, where you define subnets and security groups to ensure network-level security to ECS instances. Similar to EC2 instances, here also we specify a key pair to access the SSH of ECS instances.

In the security group, we define CIDR for incoming traffic on a specific port, or a range of contiguous ports, to open on the container instance.

Apart from the security group, we use IAM roles and policies heavily to ensure the security of ECS clusters.

Let's take some example IAM policies that allow a user to perform all the management activity on the ECS cluster:

```
{
  "Version": "2012-10-17",
  "Statement": [
    {
      "Action": [
        "ecs:Describe*",
        "ecs:List*"
      ],
      "Effect": "Allow",
      "Resource": "*"
    },
    {
      "Action": [
        "ecs:DeleteCluster",
        "ecs:DeregisterContainerInstance",
        "ecs:ListContainerInstances",
        "ecs:RegisterContainerInstance",
```

```
      "ecs:SubmitContainerStateChange",
      "ecs:SubmitTaskStateChange"
    ],
    "Effect": "Allow",
    "Resource": "arn:aws:ecs:us-east-1:XXXXXXX:cluster/default"
  },
  {
    "Action": [
      "ecs:DescribeContainerInstances",
      "ecs:DescribeTasks",
      "ecs:ListTasks",
      "ecs:UpdateContainerAgent",
      "ecs:StartTask",
      "ecs:StopTask",
      "ecs:RunTask"
    ],
    "Effect": "Allow",
    "Resource": "*",
    "Condition": {
      "ArnEquals": {
        "ecs:cluster": "arn:aws:ecs:us-east-1:
        XXXXXXX:cluster/default"
      }
    }
  }
  ]
}
```

Apart from this, we use IAM roles to define the accessibility of other AWS services to ECS, such as ECS services that make calls to EC2, and the ELB API to register and de-register container instances.

Let's see an example of an IAM policy attached to an ECS role which allows access to EC2 and ELB:

```
{
  "Version": "2012-10-17",
  "Statement": [
    {
      "Effect": "Allow",
      "Action": [
        "ec2:AuthorizeSecurityGroupIngress",
        "ec2:Describe*",
        "elasticloadbalancing:DeregisterInstancesFromLoadBalancer",
        "elasticloadbalancing:DeregisterTargets",
        "elasticloadbalancing:Describe*",
        "elasticloadbalancing:RegisterInstancesWithLoadBalancer",
```

```
            "elasticloadbalancing:RegisterTargets"
        ],
        "Resource": "*"
    }
  ]
}
```

SQS

We are all aware of the basic solution architecture principle that states you should always make your solutions loosely coupled or decoupled to ensure maximum availability and reliability.

Message queue is one of the services that help us deploy the solutions in a decoupled environment, where all the components communicate with each other using message queue.

For this, we have many queuing services, such as RabbitMQ and Qpid.

On AWS, we have SQS. This is also the oldest service of AWS. It's a managed, reliable, and highly scalable service. It moves data between distributed application components and helps you decouple these components.

Now let's understand how to secure SQS services. The complete SQS platform is managed by AWS in the backend according to the shared responsibility model.

Securing SQS

In SQS, we define security using IAM for authentication and access control and SSE. Let's see both methods in detail:

- Authentication and access control—access to SQS requires users to get authenticated with AWS Console and have sufficient privileges to access the services. For authentication, we can have the following identities:
  - **IAM root user**: It's strongly recommended not to use root user.
  - **IAM user**: These are the IAM users who have permission to access SQS services and messages.
  - **IAM roles**: IAM role is same as IAM user, but it's not associated with the account. It is associated with the service that you want to access via temporary access keys.

- For access control, we have the SQL resource-based access policy, which is defined similar to IAM policies to give access to SQS resources:

```
{
    "Version": "2012-10-17",
    "Statement": [{
        "Sid":"MyQueue_AllActions",
        "Effect": "Allow",
        "Principal": {
            "AWS": [
                "arn:aws:iam::xxxxxxxxx:role/sqsrole",
                "arn:aws:iam::xxxxxxxxx:user/sqsuser"
            ]
        },
        "Action": "sqs:*",
        "Resource": "arn:aws:sqs:us-east-3:XXXXXXXXX:myqueue1"
    }]
}
```

In this policy, we have allowed one user named `sqsuser` and one role named `sqsrole` to access the SQS queue named `queue1` running in the `us-east` region.

- Queue encryption—apart from IAM policy, SQS also uses SSE to transit sensitive data in the encrypted queue.

SSE protects the message content in Amazon SQS queues using keys managed in the AWS KMS.

When we use SQS with KMS, the data keys that encrypt the message data are also encrypted and stored with the data they protect.

SSE does not encrypt the following:

- Queue metadata (queue name and attributes)
- Message metadata
- Prequeue metrics

Encrypted messages in the queue are sent only when queue encryption is enabled, and it does not encrypt backlogged messages.

Let's have a recap

In Chapter 1, *Introduction to Cloud Security*, we learned about the shared responsibility model of the cloud. We saw that security is always a shared responsibility, where some areas go into the account of the customer and some areas go into the account of the cloud provider.

In IaaS, a customer is responsible for managing security from the compute layer to the application layer, which includes OS, network, storage, application, and so on.

In PaaS, the cloud provider is responsible for managing the security of the platform. The customer is responsible for managing the security for the application they run on this platform.

In PaaS, a customer does not have control of the underlying infrastructure of the platform. However, we can define our custom parameter to run our application. For example, we use MySQL RDS, where we can define custom parameters by defining custom parameter groups. We can also enable encryption for specific or all connections.

In AWS, almost all the services have their own backup policies, to ensure data safety in case of the accidental deletion of data, or in case of other disasters.

In this chapter, we have learned about securing the following different AWS PaaS services:

- **RDS**: In RDS, we can define security starting from VPC level, where we define subnets to reside in the database instance. Apart from this, we also use security groups to manage ingress (inbound) and egress (outbound) policies. Also, we can use SSL encryption to secure the database. AWS RDS also comes with an inbuilt backup facility to take snapshot-based backup. RDS also has a few best practices, such as:
    - Run your RDS under VPC for greater network access control
    - Use IAM policy to grant a specific permission to users to perform actions on databases
    - Use a security group to control and manage the traffic to and from the database
    - Use SSL for connection encryption
    - Use RDS encryption to secure your database instances and snapshots at rest
    - For Oracle database, use Oracle Native Network Encryption and transport data protection

- Use the security features of your DB engine to control who can log into the databases on a DB instance
- **Redshift**: For data warehousing, we have AWS Redshift, which is also PaaS. Here, too, underlying infrastructure is being managed by AWS. However, we have to ensure the security of our cluster. In RDS, when we create clusters inside our VPC, by default, VPC-level security mechanisms such as NACL and security group apply. Apart from this, we use encryption to secure the data in tables. This can be enabled when we are creating the cluster. Also, we use SSL-based encryption to secure data-in-transit. We also use S3-based SSE while loading data from the S3 bucket.
- **DynamoDB**: DynamoDB is a scalable and managed NoSQL database service offered by AWS. Here, we use IAM heavily to ensure the security of DynamoDB services.
- **ElastiCache**: It's a cache service offered by AWS. This is a high-performance, scalable, and cost-effective caching solution, which removes the complexity associated with deploying and managing a distributed cache environment. Similar to Redshift, we also create clusters for ElastiCache. If we are running ElastiCache clusters inside VPC, then again the VPC-level security perimeter comes into the picture. Here, we use the NACL and security groups to ensure security. Apart from this, we use IAM and encryption to ensure the safety of data-in-transit and at rest. For data-in-transit encryption, we have the following:
    - **Encrypted connections**: Here, both the server and client connections are SSL-encrypted
    - **Encrypted replication**: Data traveling between a primary node and replica nodes is encrypted
    - **Server authentication**: Clients can authenticate that they are connecting to the right server
    - **Client authentication**: The server can authenticate the clients using the Redis authentication feature

For data-at-rest encryption in ElastiCache, there are the following limitations:

- Only Redis version 3.2.6-based replication groups are suitable for data-at-rest encryption. They are not suitable for Memcached cluster.
- A replication group running under AWS VPC is suitable for data-at-rest encryption.
- Any node (compute size) is supported.

- Data-at-rest encryption can only be enabled while creating the replication group.
- Data-at-rest encryption, once enabled for replication, cannot be disabled.

- **ECS**: ECS is also offered by AWS as PaaS, which enables you to run your container services on ECS cluster. ECS cluster also gets created inside the VPC, so default VPC security comes into the picture, where we define NACL and security group. Other than NACL and security group, we also use IAM roles and policies to define the accessibility of clusters.
- **SQS**: It's a managed queue service defined by AWS. It's a highly scalable message queuing service. Here too, we use IAM roles to manage the authentication and authorization process. SQS also can be encrypted.

Summary

This chapter instructed us on how to ensure security for PaaS services, such as database and analytics services.

In the next chapter, you will learn how to secure private cloud infrastructures and workloads running on private clouds.

7
Private Cloud Security

In the first chapter, we learned about the different types of cloud, which are private, public, and hybrid.

A **private cloud** is a type of cloud that is deployed for any organization for their internal use. A private cloud is intended to enable the organization to have a self-service, elastic, and scalable model of IT infrastructure and services.

Prior to the private cloud, organizations used to host their applications either on bare metal servers or in a virtualized environment. Bare metal or virtualized environments lacked self-service features; however, scaling and elasticity could be achieved, but with great expenses in terms of human operations.

Making the environment fault tolerant and decoupled was still a challenge. For a development organization, where different technology groups are busy in development operations, it was a very difficult and a time-consuming task to provide the organization and keep track of infrastructure to run their staging and production workloads.

To deploy a private cloud, there are many popular technologies available, such as Apache CloudStack, OpenStack, and Microsoft Azure Stack.

For this chapter, our focus will be on OpenStack. As you might know, OpenStack private cloud combines different open source projects for different services, such as networking, computing, storage, and dashboards.

In this chapter, we will learn how to ensure the security of each service and layer responsible for building the private cloud.

In OpenStack, we basically secure or bridge the security of the public or user domain, management domain, and data domain. In OpenStack, components communicate with each other via APIs using a message queue service called RabbitMQ. OpenStack is the best example of a decoupled IT infrastructure.

In OpenStack, we have the following core components:

- Hypervisor: KVM/ESXi/XenServer/Hyper-V
- Database: MySQL
- Message Queue: RabbitMQ
- Network service: Neutron (in the earlier version, it was nova-network)
- IAM: Keystone
- Image store: Glance
- Block storage: Cinder
- Object storage: Swift
- Compute: Nova
- Dashboard: Horizon

Now, let's see how to enable security for each component.

Securing hypervisor

Hypervisor is a critical component for OpenStack or any private/public cloud environment. One should select a hypervisor very carefully. There are a few parameters that one should consider when selecting a hypervisor, because in any cloud, underlying virtualization technology enterprise-level capabilities are in the realms of scalability, resource efficiency, and uptime.

Let's see the parameters involved in selecting the hypervisor:

- **Skills and expertise of your team**: The more expertise your team has in the project and in technology, the less are the chances of mistakes. It's a very important factor when adopting any technology, this applies for the hypervisor as well. For the hypervisor, you also need to do patch management, configuration, and security management tasks. Having internal skills and expertise increases the availability of your systems, allows segregation of duties, and mitigates problems at any point in time.

- **Maturity of product or project**: One always adopts projects or products that are mature. It helps us to ensure the safety, security, and success of the environment. You need the right skill set to run your project and, for this, availability of skill sets is mandatory. The quality of the community has a direct impact on the timeliness of bug fixes and security updates. Let's take a look at the factors affecting the maturity of the project:
    - Availability of skills sets in the market
    - Active developer and user communities
    - Timeliness and the availability of updates

- **Common criteria**: Common criteria is an internationally standardized software evaluation process, used by governments and commercial companies to ensure software technologies perform as advertised. As per NSTISSP, number 11 mandates that US government agencies only procure software that has been common criteria certified. Apart from this, OpenStack evaluates the hypervisors on different sets of criteria such as audit, RBAC, mandatory access control, object reuse, security management, and storage encryption. Common criteria evaluates how the technology is developed:
    - How is the source code management performed?
    - How are users granted access to build systems?
    - Is the technology cryptographically signed before distribution?

- **Certification and association**: This depicts the production readiness and testing of the hypervisor platform, apart from the regulatory requirement.

- **Hardware concerns**: When selecting the hypervisor, you also need to concentrate on the physical hardware. Apart from this, you also need to focus on the additional features or capabilities the hardware is providing and how these can be utilized with the hypervisor.

- **Other security concerns**: When selecting a hypervisor platform, you should also think of the availability of specific security features. Let's see the list of security features of hypervisors:

	XSM	sVirt	TXT	AppArmor	cgroups	MAC policy
KVM		X	X	X	X	X
Xen	X		X			
ESXi			X			
Hyper-V						

The preceding table shows the security features of a hypervisor. We have also seen the point on which OpenStack lets you choose a suitable hypervisor.

Hypervisors provide one feature called PCI passthrough. This enables the instance to have direct access to resources. However, this leads to the following two security risks:

- **Direct memory access** (**DMA**): DMA allows hardware devices to access arbitrary physical memory addresses in the host computer. Usually, video cards have this capability, but the instance should not be given such access, as it will give full access to the system and other instances running on top of it. The Physical Server vendor uses an **Input Output Memory Management Unit** (**IOMMU**) to manage the DMA.

- **Hardware infection**: This happens when the instance makes some malicious modification of firmware or some other part of a device. As the same machine will be running multiple VMs, it can affect other VMs as well. If this happens, the VM instance can run its code outside of the specified security domain. It's a very significant breach, which can lead to additional exposure such as access to the management network. To solve this hardware infection problem for example, one option could be to re-flash the firmware after use. **Trusted Platform Module** (**TPM**) technology is a solution that is used to unauthorize changes to firmware. However, it is always recommended to disable PCI passthrough, until and unless it is not clearly specified and the associated risk of PCI passthrough is calculated.

Securing KVM

For a KVM hypervisor, we enable security using **compiler hardening**. The current generation compilers come with a variety of compile-time options to improve the security of the resulting binaries.

KVM features include the following:

- **Relocation read-only** (**RELRO**): This hardens the data section of an executable. It also has two types, Full RELRO and Partial RELRO. For QEMU, Full RELRO is the best choice. This will enable the global offset table to be read-only and place various internal data sections before the program data section in the resulting executable.

- **Stack measurement**: This positions values on the stack and verifies their presence to help prevent buffer overflow attacks.

- **Never Execute** (**NX**): This is also known as **Data Execution Prevention** (**DEP**). It ensures that data sections of the executable cannot be executed.

- **Position Independent Executable** (**PIE**): This produces a position-independent executable.

- **Address Space Layout Randomization (ASLR)**: This ensures that the placement of both code and data regions will be randomized. This is also enabled by the kernel, when the executable is built with PIE.

Apart from these, there is another feature to enable security in KVM called **mandatory access control (MAC)**. Compiler hardening makes it very difficult to attack the QEMU process. In case the attacker is successful in the attack, then MAC helps to control it. MAC restricts the privileges on QEMU processes to only what is needed. This is completed using sVirt, SELinux, or AppArmor.

sVirt stands for **secure virtualization**, which is an application of SELinux. It is designed to apply separation control based upon labels and provides isolation between virtual machine processes, devices, data files, and system processes acting upon their behalf. **sVirt** implementation helps to protect hypervisor hosts and virtual machines against the following two primary threats:

- **Hypervisor threat**: When a virtual machine is running with a compromised application, there is a chance that it will infect the underlying physical hardware configuration and it can also expose the network configuration.
- **Virtual machine threat**: On hypervisor, we run multiple virtual machines. If there is a VM running with a compromised application, there is a chance to infect other VMs' metadata, images, and other configurations.

SELinux also helps to manage ACL for users and groups. It helps to manage resources on the basis of permission.

To define the ease of allowing permission to manage Booleans on SELinux, Red Hat has defined the context as follows:

sVirt SELinux Boolean	Description
virt_use_common	This allows serial or parallel communication ports
virt_use_fusefs	This allows reading FUSE mounted files
virt_use_nfs	This allows the use and management of NFS mounted files
virt_use_samba	This allows the use and management of CIFS mounted files
virt_use_sanlock	This allows virtual guests to interact with the sanlock
virt_use_sysfs	This allows the management of device configuration (PCI)
virt_use_usb	This allows the use of USB devices
virt_use_xserver	This allows virtual machines to interact with the GUI-based system

Securing XenServer

XenServer provides a very rich set of features to enable security. It provides you with RBAC, as well as user groups, and users to access the XenServer resources. It also enables you to let your users (management) get authenticated with external authentication services such as LDAP and Active Directory.

XenServer also supports XSM and Flask. **XSM** stands for **Xen Security Model**, which enables administrators and developers to have fine-grained control over the Xen domain.

Xen implements a type of mandatory access control via a security architecture called **Flux Advanced Security Kernel** (**Flask**). Flask is used to separate security enforcement from security policy; it isolates the logical components of security systems.

To protect against complex attacks, security must start at the hardware level and extend to the software stack. In Xen, we have **Trusted Execution Technology** (**TXT**). This ensures that your compute pools remain trusted with hardware-based security.

As we've seen earlier, VMs containing sensitive data can reside on any number of hosts. Virtualized environments create new opportunities for attackers to gain control of the underlying hardware platform. Once the platform is compromised, an attacker might be able to compromise any number of virtual machines running on the platform.

TXT creates a **measured launch environment** (**MLE**) that cryptographically compares critical aspects of the hardware and software environment at startup to determine whether any tampering has taken place.

Securing ESXi

VMware ESXi comes already secured and security hardened, but apart from this, there are a few additional options specified here to further enhance the security:

- **Limit ESXi access**: By default, the ESXi Shell and SSH services are not running and only the root user can log in to the **Direct Console User Interface** (**DCUI**). However, you can enable ESXi or SSH access and can also set timeouts to limit the risk of unauthorized access. Users who can access the ESXi host must have permission to manage the host.

- **Use named users and least privileges**: Most of the tasks can be performed by the root user by default. Instead of allowing administrators to log in to the ESXi host using the root user account, you can apply different host privileges to different named users. You can create a custom role, assign privileges to the role, and associate the role with a named user and an ESXi host object from the vSphere.

Securing compute

We know that OpenStack combines multiple independent projects to set up the cloud environment. For compute, OpenStack uses a project called `nova`.

In OpenStack, all the compute nodes contain configuration files called `nova.conf`, which stores the complete settings, including many sensitive options such as configuration details and service passwords.

There must be strict file-level permissions that are monitored for changes through **file integrity monitoring (FIM)** tools, which will take a hash of the target file in a known good state. It will also periodically take a new hash of the file and compare it to the known good hash. FIM tools will generate an alert if it was found to have been modified unexpectedly.

One can check the permission of files using the `ls- lh` command from the SSH console. This command will display the permissions, owner, and groups that have access to the file, as well as other information such as the last time the file was modified and when it was created.

The `/var/lib/nova` directory contains details about the instances on a given compute host. This directory is also very sensitive; it must have strictly enforced file permissions. One must backup this directory on a regular basis as it contains information and metadata for the instances associated with that host.

Apart from that, we need to check for the current security patches from the OpenStack Security Portal (`https://security.openstack.org`). This is the place where all of the information about security updates and advisories is published.

IAM

For IAM, OpenStack uses the Keystone project. **Keystone** provides the identity, token, catalog, and policy services, which are used specifically by OpenStack services. It is organized as a group of internal services exposed on one or many endpoints. For example, an authentication call validates the user and project credentials with the identity service.

Authentication

Authentication is an integral part of an OpenStack deployment and so we must be careful about the system design.

Authentication is the process of confirming a user's identity, which means that a user is actually who they claim to be. For example, providing a username and a password when logging into a system.

Keystone supports authentication using the username and password, LDAP, and external authentication methods. After successful authentication, the identity service provides the user with an authorization token, which is further used for subsequent service requests. **Transport Layer Security** (**TLS**) provides authentication between services and users using X.509 certificates. The default mode for TLS is server-side only authentication, but we can also use certificates for client authentication.

However, in authentication, there can also be the case where a hacker is trying to access the console by guessing your username and password. If we have not enabled the policy to handle this, it can be disastrous. For this, we can use the Failed Login Policy, which states that a maximum number of attempts are allowed for a failed login; after that, the account is blocked for a certain number of hours and the user will also get a notification about it.

However, the identity service provided in Keystone does not provide a method to limit access to accounts after repeated unsuccessful login attempts. For this, we need to rely on an external authentication system that block out an account after a configured number of failed login attempts. Then, the account might only be unlocked with further side-channel intervention, or on request, or after a certain duration.

We can use detection techniques to the fullest only when we have a prevention method available to save them from damage.

In the detection process, we frequently review the access control logs to identify unauthorized attempts to access accounts.

During the review of access control logs, if we find any hints of a brute force attack (where the user tries to guess the username and password to log in to the system), we can define a strong username and password or block the source of the attack (IP) through firewall rules.

When we define firewall rules on Keystone node, it restricts the connection, which helps to reduce the attack surface.

Apart from this, reviewing access control logs also helps to examine the account activity for unusual logins and suspicious actions, so that we can take corrective actions such as disabling the account.

To increase the level of security, we can also utilize MFA for network access to the privileged user accounts.

Keystone supports external authentication services through the Apache web server that can provide this functionality. Servers can also enforce client-side authentication using certificates.

This will help to get rid of brute force and phishing attacks that may compromise administrator passwords.

Authentication methods – internal and external

Keystone stores user credentials in a database or may use an LDAP-compliant directory server. The Keystone identity database can be kept separate from databases used by other OpenStack services to reduce the risk of a compromise of the stored credentials.

When we use the username and password to authenticate, identity does not apply policies for password strength, expiration, or failed authentication attempts. For this, we need to implement external authentication services.

To integrate an external authentication system or organize an existing directory service to manage users account management, we can use LDAP. LDAP simplifies the integration process.

In OpenStack authentication and authorization, the policy may be delegated to another service. For example, an organization that is going to deploy a private cloud and already has a database of employees and users in an LDAP system.

Using this LDAP as an authentication authority, requests to the Identity service (Keystone) are transferred to the LDAP system, which allows or denies requests based on its policies. After successful authentication, the identity service generates a token for access to the authorized services.

Now, if the LDAP has already defined attributes for the user such as the admin, finance, and HR departments, these must be mapped into roles and groups within identity for use by the various OpenStack services.

We need to define this mapping into Keystone node configuration files stored at `/etc/keystone/keystone.conf`.

Keystone must not be allowed to write to the LDAP used for authentication outside of the OpenStack Scope, as there is a chance to allow a sufficiently privileged Keystone user to make changes to the LDAP directory, which is not desirable from a security point of view.

This can also lead to unauthorized access of other information and resources. So, if we have other authentication providers such as LDAP or Active Directory, then user provisioning always happens at other authentication provider systems.

For external authentication, we have the following methods:

- **MFA**: The MFA service requires the user to provide additional layers of information for authentication such as a one-time password token or X.509 certificate (called MFA token). Once MFA is implemented, the user will have to enter the MFA token after putting the user ID and password in for a successful login.
- **Password policy enforcement**: Once the external authentication service is in place, we can define the strength of the user passwords to conform to the minimum standards for length, diversity of characters, expiration, or failed login attempts.

Keystone also supports TLS-based client authentication. TLS client authentication provides an additional authentication factor, apart from the username and password, which provides greater reliability on user identification. It reduces the risk of unauthorized access when usernames and passwords are compromised. However, TLS-based authentication is not cost effective as we need to have a certificate for each of the clients.

Authorization

Keystone also provides the option of groups and roles. Users belong to groups where a group has a list of roles. All of the OpenStack services, such as Cinder, Glance, nova, and Horizon, reference the roles of the user attempting to access the service. OpenStack policy enforcers always consider the policy rule associated with each resource and use the user's group or role, and their association, to determine and allow or deny the service access.

Before configuring roles, groups, and users, we should document your required access control policies for the OpenStack installation. The policies must be as per the regulatory or legal requirements of the organization.

Additional changes to the access control configuration should be done as per the formal policies. These policies must include the conditions and processes for creating, deleting, disabling, and enabling accounts, and for assigning privileges to the accounts. One needs to review these policies from time to time and ensure that the configuration is in compliance with the approved policies.

For user creation and administration, there must be a user created with the admin role in Keystone for each OpenStack service. This account will provide the service with the authorization to authenticate users.

Nova (compute) and Swift (object storage) can be configured to use the Identity service to store authentication information. For the test environment, we can have *tempAuth*, which records user credentials in a text file, but it is not recommended for the production environment.

The OpenStack administrator must protect sensitive configuration files from unauthorized modification with mandatory access control frameworks such as SELinux or DAC. Also, we need to protect the Keystone configuration files, which are stored at `/etc/keystone/keystone.conf`, and also the X.509 certificates.

It is recommended that cloud admin users must authenticate using the identity service (Keystone) and an external authentication service that supports two-factor authentication. Getting authenticated with two-factor authentication reduces the risk of compromised passwords.

It is also recommended in the NIST guideline called NIST 800-53 IA-2(1). Which defines MFA for network access to privileged accounts, when one factor is provided by a separate device from the system being accessed.

Policy, tokens, and domains

In OpenStack, every service defines the access **policies** for its resources in a policy file, where a resource can be like an API access, it can create and attach Cinder volume, or it can create an instance. The policy rules are defined in JSON format in a file called `policy.json`.

Only administrators can modify the service-based `policy.json` file, to control the access to the various resources. However, one has to also ensure that any changes to the access control policies do not unintentionally breach or create an option to breach the security of any resource. Any changes made to `policy.json` are applied immediately and it does not need any service restart.

After a user is authenticated, a **token** is generated for authorization and access to an OpenStack environment. A token can have a variable lifespan, but the default value is 1 hour. It is also recommended to lower the lifespan of the token to a certain level so that within the specified timeframe the internal service can complete the task. If the token expires before task completion, the system can be unresponsive.

Keystone also supports token revocation. For this, it uses an API to revoke a token and to list the revoked tokens.

In OpenStack Newton release, there are four supported token types: UUID, PKI, PKIZ, and fernet. After the OpenStack Ocata release, there are two supported token types: UUID and fernet. We'll see all of these token types in detail here:

- **UUID**: These tokens are persistent tokens. UUID tokens are 32 bytes in length, which must be persisted in the backend. They are stored in the Keystone backend, along with the metadata for authentication. All of the clients must pass their UUID token to the Keystone (identity service) in order to validate it.
- **PKI and PKIZ**: These are signed documents that contain the authentication content, as well as the service catalog. The difference between the PKI and PKIZ is that PKIZ tokens are compressed to help mitigate the size issues of PKI (sometimes PKI tokens becomes very long). Both of these tokens have become obsolete after the Ocata release. The length of PKI and PKIZ tokens typically exceeds 1,600 bytes. The Identity service uses public and private key pairs and certificates in order to create and validate these tokens.

- **Fernet**: These tokens are the default supported token provider for OpenStack Pike Release. It is a secure messaging format explicitly designed for use in API tokens. They are nonpersistent, lightweight (fall in the range of 180 to 240 bytes), and reduce the operational overhead. Authentication and authorization metadata is neatly bundled into a message-packed payload, which is then encrypted and signed in as a fernet token.

In the OpenStack, the **Keystone Service** domain is a high-level container for projects, users, and groups. Domains are used to centrally manage all Keystone-based identity components. Compute, storage, and other resources can be logically grouped into multiple projects, which can further be grouped under a master account.

Users of different domains can be represented in different authentication backends and have different attributes that must be mapped to a single set of roles and privileges in the policy definitions to access the various service resources.

Domain-specific authentication drivers allow the identity service to be configured for multiple domains, using domain-specific configuration files stored at `keystone.conf`.

Federated identity

Federated identity enables you to establish trusts between identity providers and the cloud environment (OpenStack Cloud).

It gives you secured access to cloud resources using your existing identity. You do not need to remember multiple credentials to access your applications.

Now, the question is, what is the reason for using federated identity? This is answered as follows:

- It enables your security team to manage all of the users (cloud or noncloud) from a single identity application
- It enables you to set up different identity providers on the basis of the application that somewhere creates an additional workload for the security team and leads the security risk as well
- It gives ease of life to users by proving them a single credential for all of the apps so that they can save the time they spend in the forgot password page

Federated identity enables you to have a single sign on mechanism. We can implement it using SAML 2.0. To do this, you need to run the identity service provider under Apache.

Horizon – OpenStack dashboard service

Horizon provides a dashboard for OpenStack, where the user can login and self-provision their infrastructure resources. Here, the admin has the right to define the limit on the resources.

Let's see the first screen when you type the URL of your dashboard:

Horizon is designed on the Django framework, which is basically a Python-based web framework that enables rapid development in a clean and realistic way.

OpenStack dashboard itself comes with the option to enable security for different services.

Horizon comes with the default security setting for the dashboard, where you can see all of the services and define the restrictions.

As we read earlier that OpenStack provides RBAC and a multidomain environment, the user will login using the user ID, password, and their domain:

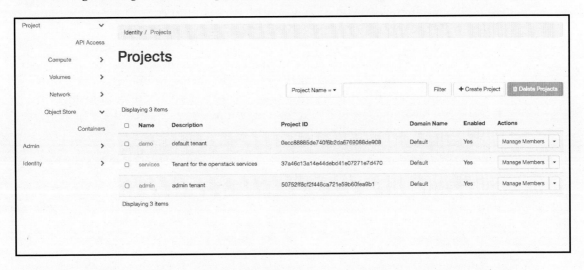

In the preceding screenshot, you can see there are three projects created in a default domain. We can also create additional domains and create projects inside the domains using CLI:

```
openstack domain create --description "MyTestDomain" --enable MyTestDomain
```

There are many other options available for different services, such as in the Project's section the project admin can control and manage all of the resources including virtual machine, images, storage, Elastic IPs, and so on. Under the Project's section, you can manage and compute the following resources:

- You can get a report of all of the utilized and available compute resources.
- You will have an option to view, launch, create a snapshot, stop, pause, or reboot instances.
- For images, you can view all of the images and snapshots created by project users. Apart from this, you can also see any images that are publicly available.
- You will also have options to create, edit, and delete the available images. You can also launch instances using images and snapshots that are available.
- For volumes you can perform the create, edit, view, and delete actions. You can perform the same set of actions for backup and volume snapshots.

- Here, you will find one other section called a consistency group. Let me describe what exactly is a consistency group. This group lets volume stand together or stop together. It enables you to take snapshots of multiple volumes at the same point-in-time to ensure data consistency. This support is available for block storage.
- From your project dashboard you can manage your networking stuff too, such as viewing network topology, management of private and public networks, routers, security groups and floating IPs (floating IPs are not assigned to an instance by default, you have to acquire it and then assign it. Once you acquire a floating IP, you become the owner of the IP).

Let's see what the resources are that we can manage at the project level from the dashboard:

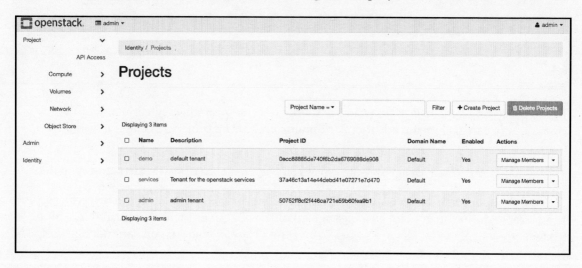

In the preceding screenshot, we can see that we have the following resources at project level that can be managed from the dashboard. This is the API endpoint of all of the services:

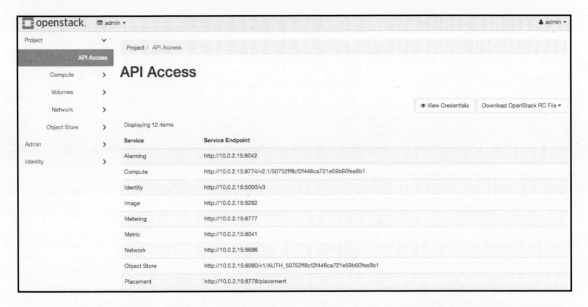

To access these API, you can download the RC file, which is the shell script that looks like this:

```
#!/usr/bin/env bash
# To use an OpenStack cloud you need to authenticate against the Identity
# service named keystone, which returns a **Token** and **Service
Catalog**.
# The catalog contains the endpoints for all services the user/tenant has
# access to - such as Compute, Image Service, Identity, Object Storage,
Block
# Storage, and Networking (code-named nova, glance, keystone, swift,
# cinder, and neutron).
#
# *NOTE*: Using the 3 *Identity API* does not necessarily mean any other
# OpenStack API is version 3. For example, your cloud provider may
implement
# Image API v1.1, Block Storage API v2, and Compute API v2.0. OS_AUTH_URL
is
# only for the Identity API served through keystone.
export OS_AUTH_URL=http://10.0.2.15:5000/v3
# With the addition of Keystone we have standardized on the term
**project**
# as the entity that owns the resources.
```

```
export OS_PROJECT_ID=50752ff8cf2f446ca721e59b60fea9b1
export OS_PROJECT_NAME="admin"
export OS_USER_DOMAIN_NAME="Default"
if [ -z "$OS_USER_DOMAIN_NAME" ]; then unset OS_USER_DOMAIN_NAME; fi
export OS_PROJECT_DOMAIN_ID="default"
if [ -z "$OS_PROJECT_DOMAIN_ID" ]; then unset OS_PROJECT_DOMAIN_ID; fi
# unset v2.0 items in case set
unset OS_TENANT_ID
unset OS_TENANT_NAME
# In addition to the owning entity (tenant), OpenStack stores the entity
# performing the action as the **user**.
export OS_USERNAME="admin"
# With Keystone you pass the keystone password.
echo "Please enter your OpenStack Password for project $OS_PROJECT_NAME as
user $OS_USERNAME: "
read -sr OS_PASSWORD_INPUT
export OS_PASSWORD=$OS_PASSWORD_INPUT
# If your configuration has multiple regions, we set that information here.
# OS_REGION_NAME is optional and only valid in certain environments.
export OS_REGION_NAME="RegionOne"
# Don't leave a blank variable, unset it if it was empty
if [ -z "$OS_REGION_NAME" ]; then unset OS_REGION_NAME; fi
export OS_INTERFACE=public
export OS_IDENTITY_API_VERSION=3
```

Now, let's see how to ensure the security of the dashboard, as it can be accessible on the internet. We must ensure the security of the dashboard so that bad guys can't take over and bombard it with illegitimate traffic:

- **Cross Site Scripting (XSS)**: The OpenStack dashboard provides options to developers so that they can remove the possibility of cross-site scripting vulnerabilities. This only works when developers have correctly used the feature.

- **Cross Site Request Forgery (CSRF)**: We know that the Horizon dashboard is based on the Django framework. Here, Django has defined its dedicated middleware for CSRF protection. In the Django framework, CSRF middleware and template tag provide easy-to-use protection against CSRF. CSRF type attacks takes place when a malicious website contains a link or a form of button or JavaScript that is defined to perform some malicious action on your website using the credentials of a currently logged in user.

- **Cross-Frame Scripting (XFS or CFS)**: We use frames on HTML pages, this is the area where XFS attacks happen. CFS allows an attacker to load their malicious application inside an HTML `iframe` tag on an HTML page. To stop this, the OpenStack dashboard provides the `DISALLOW_IFRAME_EMBED` tag to control CFS where `iframe` tags are not used.

- **Access over SSL**: To secure the access of the OpenStack dashboard, it is recommended to deploy the horizon on the server running the user SSL signed with CA. It is also recommended to use **HTTP Strict Transport Security (HSTS)**.

 HSTS is a method of improving the security level, which is specified by a web application using the special response header. When a supported browser receives this header, that browser will stop any communication from being sent over HTTP to the specified domain and will transfer all communication over HTTPS.

  HSTS addresses threats like the man-in-the-middle attacks (by redirecting all of the HTTP requests to HTTPS for the specified domain), a web application that is intended to be purely HTTPS but also contains HTTP links, and a situation when an attacker attempts to intercept traffic from a victim user using an invalid certificate.

- **Cookie**: A cookie for horizon must be defined for HTTP only and you must also ensure that you have not configured CSRF or session cookie with a wildcard domain name that starts with dot (for example, `*.xyz.com`).
- **Cross Origin Resource Sharing (CORS)**: You need to configure your web server in a way that it sends restrictive CORS headers with each response and should only allow the dashboard domain and protocol.
- **Frontend caching**: It is not recommended to use frontend-based caching for the OpenStack dashboard, as it serves dynamic content, which is being generated in response to OpenStack API calls. Here, if you have enabled frontend cache, then it will not display the appropriate content; instead, it will display the cached content. Or you can configure front end cache in such a way that it can serve dynamic content as well.
- **Session backend**: Horizon has a default session backend as `django.contrib.sessions.backends.signed_cookies`, which saves user data in signed, unencrypted cookies stored in the browser. The OpenStack dashboard application instances are stateless, so storing cookies on the browser helps to implement session backend scaling. However, here we can utilize the separate cache service such as Memcached. So, while using Memcached, one must ensure that there is no data leakage. Memcached uses the spare RAM to store the most frequently accessed data, which reduces the direct load on the database or the filesystem. It's recommended to use Memcached in place of the local cache, as Memcached is fast and stores the cache's session for longer, it can also be shared over multiple servers.

Cinder – OpenStack block storage

In OpenStack, block storage is provided by the Cinder project. **Cinder** is the project that provides a self-managed block-level storage device. This enables on-demand block storage for an OpenStack compute service called nova.

Cinder creates a software-defined storage by virtualizing underlying storage pools, which can be software-defined storage or traditional hardware. Here, we also utilize software-defined storage such as Solidfire and Ceph.

Nova accesses the block storage using Cinder APIs wherein the backend storage is being accessed on iSCSI, ATA over Ethernet, or a fiber channel.

Now, let's see how to ensure the security of Cinder. Similar to all of the other projects, such as Keystone and nova, Cinder also has its configuration files, which contain all of the critical information. Here, we need to ensure security and safety of the configuration files. So, we need to ensure that the configuration files are given access to `root/cinder`. These configuration files are as follows:

- `/etc/cinder/cinder.conf`
- `/etc/cinder/api-paste.ini`
- `/etc/cinder/policy.json`
- `/etc/cinder/rootwrap.conf`

OpenStack Keystone provides authentication for users and also provides permission to access the OpenStack services. For Cinder, we need to ensure that all of the requests to access Cinder must be authenticated with Keystone. For this, we need to modify the `cinder.conf` and add the default `auth_strategy` as the Keystone.

Now, we also need to ensure that all of the communication between Keystone and Cinder happens on TLS. Actually, there is always a chance of eavesdropping because communication between OpenStack services happens via APIs. So, here we need to enable TLS so that all communication happens between Keystone and Cinder through an encrypted channel.

As with communication between Keystone and Cinder, we also need to ensure that nova and Cinder communicate with each other on a TLS-based channel. A TLS-based communication channel is also applicable for communication between Cinder and Glance (**Glance** is an image-based storage service of OpenStack, which is used to store snapshots of VMs).

Cinder supports the NFS driver, which functions in a different manner compared to other block storage drivers. NFS basically creates file share, which is mounted with VMs to function as a local filesystem. Cinder storage also ensures secure access of these files by managing file permissions. It also controls whether files are getting accessed via the root user or any other project users.

Cinder also supports volume encryption to ensure security of data at rest. It is always recommended to enable volume encryption, which will eliminate the data theft issue caused, which can take place on unencrypted volumes due to physical device theft.

Data wiping from block storage is again very critical once the volume is deleted. So, for this, we need to set the `lvm_type` flag to thin and `volume_clear` to zero. If the volume is encrypted, then zeroing of the volume is not necessary; we just need to securely delete the encryption keys.

Glance – OpenStack image storage

In OpenStack, we have a different storage type called image storage. Glance service provides image storage in OpenStack. Glance stores images and metadata information related to images.

Like other services, Glance also provides REST API to perform activities such as discovering, registering and retrieving images.

Now, let's see how one can score the Glance (image storage):

- We must ensure that Glance configuration files only have ownership of the root user and Glance group. This will help to control unauthorized access and modification or deletion of configuration files. These configuration files are as follows:
  - `/etc/glance/glance-api-paste.ini`
  - `/etc/glance/glance-api.conf`
  - `/etc/glance/glance-cache.conf`
  - `/etc/glance/glance-manage.conf`

- `/etc/glance/glance-registry-paste.ini`
- `/etc/glance/glance-registry.conf`
- `/etc/glance/glance-scrubber.conf`
- `/etc/glance/glance-swift-store.conf`
- `/etc/glance/policy.json`
- `/etc/glance/schema-image.json`
- `etc/glance/schema.json`

- All of the communication with Glance API must be authenticated with Keystone. So, `/etc/glance/glance-api.conf` and `/etc/glance/glance-registry.conf` must have the `auth_strategy` parameter under the **Default** section and it must be set to Keystone.
- We must ensure that all of the communication with Glance must take place over TLS.
- In Glance API v1, we have a feature called `copy_from`, which can lead to a masked port scan by attackers. So, we must ensure that this is restricted. To do this, we need to modify the `copy_from` parameter in `/etc/glance/policy.json` and set it to a specific role such as `role:admin`.

Manila – OpenStack shared file storage

In OpenStack, we have a shared filesystem service called Manila. It works similarly to Cinder (block storage). With Manila, you can create a shared filesystem and perform management activity such as visibility, accessibility, and usage quota.

Manila supports file sharing protocols such as NFS, CIFS, HDFS, and GlusterFS.

The following are the different security mechanisms available in OpenStack for a shared filesystem:

- For authentication and authorization of clients, we can use LDAP, Kerberos, and Windows Active Directory services.
- We must ensure explicit grant access of new file shares. By default, users will not have permission to mount and access the newly created file shares.
- Manila also has an entity called security services, which abstracts the definition of the security domain for a shared file system protocol.

- A shared filesystem also allows us to define security using the following:
  - DNS IP of tenant network
  - Security service IP or hostname
  - Security service domain name
  - Tenant's user or group name
  - Users password

- In any existing security service, a shared network entity provides information about the security and network configuration to the shared filesystem.

In a shared filesystem, the sharing can be private or public. Here, private and public define the level of visibility. As the administrator, you can allow or deny the visibility and accessibility of shares. All these access rules are defined in the `policy.json` file.

Apart from all these, there are a few things we must consider:

- We must assign user ownership of configuration files to the user as root and to the group as Manila. Because like other OpenStack files, configuration files contain all critical parameters and information. These configuration files are as follows:
  - `/etc/manila/manila.conf`
  - `/etc/manila/api-paste.ini`
  - `/etc/manila/policy.json`
  - `/etc/manila/rootwrap.conf`
- After assigning the user ownership of configuration files, we must ensure that all of the calls to Manila must get authenticated with Keystone (identity service).
- Now, ensure that all of the communication between Keystone and Manila services happens on TLS.
- Shared filesystems are meant to get mounted on VMs, so that they can communicate with nova (compute service). Here, we need to ensure that all of the communication between nova and Manila takes place on TLS-based channels.
- Shared filesystems will be accessible on the network protocol. For this, Manila will also have to communicate with the neutron (network service), so here too we need to ensure that the communication channel is TLS enabled.

Neutron – OpenStack network

As we know, OpenStack uses different projects to enable you to deploy to the cloud. The neutron project is responsible for providing network services. It provides tenant facing APIs to define network connectivity and IP addressing for instances.

Neutron enables tenants or users to define the network, manage it, and use the network resources for their services.

OpenStack networking comes with the following components:

- **Neutron server**: This runs on the network node to provide networking APIs and its extensions. Neutron plugins let the neutron server access the database via an **asynchronous message queue (AMQP)**.
- **Plugin agent**: This runs on compute nodes to manage the local vSwitch and also check which agent is running.
- **DHCP agent**: This is used to provide DHCP services for tenants.
- **Neutron L3-agent**: This is used to provide external network access to VMs running inside the tenant network.
- **SDN**: This service interacts with the neutron server, neutron plugin, and plugin agent.

OpenStack neutron has the following networks:

- **Management**: This network is used to manage the internal communication between components
- **Guest**: This network is used for VM data communication within services
- **External**: This network is used to provide Elastic IP to VM
- **API**: This network is used to handle all of the OpenStack API traffic, which can be similar to the external network:

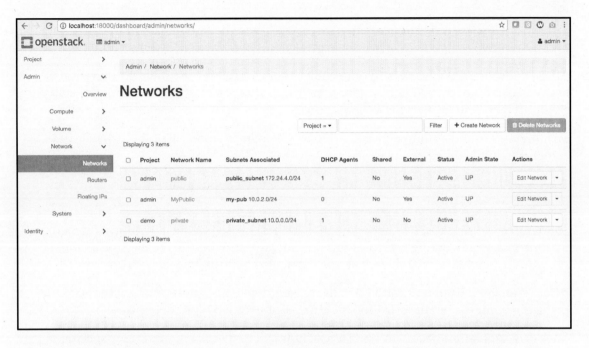

In the preceding screenshot, we can see the networking view of the OpenStack neutron from the admin console of the OpenStack dashboard.

Here, you can define the router, the private and public networks, and the security groups.

Let's see the security best practice for neutron. The following are five services which communicate with neutron at a large scale and these services are mapped with separate security zones:

- **Horizon**: This service always communicates using the public and management network
- **Keystone**: This service communicates using the management network
- **Nova**: Compute (nova) also communicates using the management and guest networks
- **Networking node**: This service communicates using the management, guest, and possibly public network depending upon the neutron-plugin that is in use
- **SDN node**: This service communicates using the management, guest, and possibly public network depending upon the product used

One must need to ensure that all of the communication between OpenStack core services and the OpenStack networking services should be via the isolated management network.

Apart from this, neutron service components use either direct database or message queues to communicate with other networking components, which needs to be secured.

As we know, the OpenStack network enables users for self service and configuration of networks, so it's of utmost importance to do the evaluation of design use cases to enable, create, update, and destroy network resources.

To authenticate and authorize users to access, OpenStack stores all of these details in a configuration file called `policy.json`.

The OpenStack network policy definition defines the network availability, security, and overall network security.

Similar to other services, Keystone (identity service) is used as the authentication method for OpenStack networking services too. Once identity services are enabled, users must provide an authentication token to access the neutron (OpenStack network service).

After receiving the authentication details of users, OpenStack network services authorize the user's request. For authorization, neutron supports two types of policies:

- **Operation-based policy**: This includes all of the access control for specific attributes to perform a specific operation
- **Resource-based policy**: Here, users are authorized to access the specific resources only

The access policy here works on the basis of rules defined to complete the authorization process. The following rules can be defined for OpenStack network access:

- **Rule based on roles**: Here, we have defined a role where only the `network_owner` or the admin can create subnets. So, every time a subnet creation request comes, it will be evaluated on the basis of the role. If the user or request has an admin or `network_owner` role, the subnet creation request will or will not be accepted.
- **Rule based on field**: Here, the authorization request is evaluated on the basis of the field of the resource associated with the request. If it matches, the request will be processed; otherwise, it will fail.
- **Generic rules**: These are based on resource attributes, which are evaluated; again, the attributes come with the user's request.

Let's see a part of the default policy file, which is stored at `/etc/neutron/policy.json`:

```
[root@localhost ~]# cat /etc/neutron/policy.json
{
    "context_is_admin": "role:admin",
    "owner": "tenant_id:%(tenant_id)s",
    "admin_or_owner": "rule:context_is_admin or rule:owner",
    "context_is_advsvc": "role:advsvc",
    "admin_or_network_owner": "rule:context_is_admin or
     tenant_id:%(network:tenant_id)s",
    "admin_owner_or_network_owner": "rule:owner or
     rule:admin_or_network_owner",
    "admin_only": "rule:context_is_admin",
    "regular_user": "",
    "admin_or_data_plane_int": "rule:context_is_admin
     or role:data_plane_integrator",
    "shared": "field:networks:shared=True",
    "shared_subnetpools": "field:subnetpools:shared=True",
    "shared_address_scopes": "field:address_scopes:shared=True",
    "external": "field:networks:router:external=True",
    "default": "rule:admin_or_owner",

    "create_subnet": "rule:admin_or_network_owner",
    "create_subnet:segment_id": "rule:admin_only",
    "create_subnet:service_types": "rule:admin_only",
    "get_subnet": "rule:admin_or_owner or rule:shared",
    "get_subnet:segment_id": "rule:admin_only",
    "update_subnet": "rule:admin_or_network_owner",
    "update_subnet:service_types": "rule:admin_only",
    "delete_subnet": "rule:admin_or_network_owner",

    "create_subnetpool": "",
    "create_subnetpool:shared": "rule:admin_only",
    "create_subnetpool:is_default": "rule:admin_only",
    "get_subnetpool": "rule:admin_or_owner or rule:shared_subnetpools",
    "update_subnetpool": "rule:admin_or_owner",
    "update_subnetpool:is_default": "rule:admin_only",
    "delete_subnetpool": "rule:admin_or_owner",

    "create_address_scope": "",
    "create_address_scope:shared": "rule:admin_only",
    "get_address_scope": "rule:admin_or_owner or
     rule:shared_address_scopes",
    "update_address_scope": "rule:admin_or_owner",
    "update_address_scope:shared": "rule:admin_only",
    "delete_address_scope": "rule:admin_or_owner",
```

```
"create_network": "",
"get_network": "rule:admin_or_owner or rule:shared
 or rule:external or rule:context_is_advsvc",
"get_network:router:external": "rule:regular_user",
"get_network:segments": "rule:admin_only",
"get_network:provider:network_type": "rule:admin_only",
"get_network:provider:physical_network": "rule:admin_only",
"get_network:provider:segmentation_id": "rule:admin_only",
"get_network:queue_id": "rule:admin_only",
"get_network_ip_availabilities": "rule:admin_only",
"get_network_ip_availability": "rule:admin_only",
"create_network:shared": "rule:admin_only",
"create_network:router:external": "rule:admin_only",
"create_network:is_default": "rule:admin_only",
"create_network:segments": "rule:admin_only",
"create_network:provider:network_type": "rule:admin_only",
"create_network:provider:physical_network": "rule:admin_only",
"create_network:provider:segmentation_id": "rule:admin_only",
"update_network": "rule:admin_or_owner",
"update_network:segments": "rule:admin_only",
"update_network:shared": "rule:admin_only",
"update_network:provider:network_type": "rule:admin_only",
"update_network:provider:physical_network": "rule:admin_only",
"update_network:provider:segmentation_id": "rule:admin_only",
"update_network:router:external": "rule:admin_only",
"delete_network": "rule:admin_or_owner",
```

Apart from this, we must ensure that the network configuration files, which are stored at /etc/neutron, are very critical, as small unwanted changes in the configuration can lead to disaster. So, we must ensure that the ownership of these files is set to root:neutron. We can run the following commands to check the status:

```
[root@localhost ~]# stat -L -c "%U %G" /etc/neutron/neutron.conf |
egrep "root neutron"
root neutron
[root@localhost ~]# stat -L -c "%U %G" /etc/neutron/api-paste.ini |
egrep "root neutron"
[root@localhost ~]# stat -L -c "%U %G" /etc/neutron/policy.json | egrep
"root neutron"
root neutron
[root@localhost ~]# stat -L -c "%U %G" /etc/neutron/rootwrap.conf |
egrep "root neutron"
[root@localhost ~]#
```

In the previous example, you can see that my local installed OpenStack has two security loop holes /etc/neutron/api-paste.ini and /etc/neutron/rootwrap.conf that do not have specified ownership to root:neutron. Now, let's see who has the ownership of these files:

```
[root@localhost ~]# stat -L -c "%U %G" /etc/neutron/rootwrap.conf
root root
[root@localhost ~]# stat -L -c "%U %G" /etc/neutron/api-paste.ini
root root
[root@localhost ~]#
```

Here, we can see that both of these files have ownership set to root:root.

- Apart from this, we also need to ensure that we are using Keystone for the request authentication and authorization:

  ```
  [root@localhost ~]# cat /etc/neutron/neutron.conf | grep
  "auth_strategy"
  #auth_strategy = keystone
  auth_strategy=keystone
  ```

- Now, we also need to ensure that there is a secure channel for communication between the Keystone and the neutron.
- We must also enable TLS on the neutron API server. In the neutron.conf file, we should modify use_ssl= false to use_ssl=true.

  ```
  [root@localhost ~]# cat /etc/neutron/neutron.conf | grep
  "use_ssl"
  #use_ssl = false
  ```

- In OpenStack, we also have an option to use flat networking. When we use flat networking, there is a risk of ARP spoofing, which can be the reason for a man-in-the-middle attack. So, we need to define prevent_arp_spoofing=True in the /etc/neutron/plugins/ml2/openvswitch_agent.ini file. This works in cases when we use Open vSwitch as L2 networks for OpenStack resources.

Swift – OpenStack object storage

In the OpenStack project, object storage is provided by Swift, which provides highly available, scalable, distributed, and eventually consistent data storage. It supports the HTTP protocol using APIs and HTTPS to communicate with object storage.

Object storage (Swift) stores data in the hierarchy in which the top layer is the account. Here, the storage provider creates an account for you and you become the owner of this account.

After that, the second layer is the container. The container actually defines the namespace of the object. Namespace helps you to create isolation. For example, you have two objects with the same name and both reside in two different containers; here both will have unique identities.

Apart from this, the container also creates ACL to control the object.

At the bottom, we have the object layer where we store our objects such as documents and images. We can also associate metadata with the object.

Object storage has the following additional features, which helps to protect the data:

- Cross origin object sharing
- Object versioning
- A single URL to give short duration object access using the GET method
- Mark objects for deletion on a specified schedule

Object storage also has the **replication process**, which helps you to make data available in case of any drive failure or network outage. During the replication process, all of the objects are compared with the local data to check whether the latest version of the data is stored or not.

For the object replication process, object storage uses the hash list, and for container and accounts it uses the hash list and high water mark. All of these replications are push based.

In the replication process, the replicator is also sure that all of the data that was marked for deletion is deleted. In the backend, when we delete the file from object storage, the tombstone is set to the latest version. Now, the replicator will see the tombstone and remove the data from the system.

Now, let's see the ACL in object storage. In OpenStack, Swift comes with the following two types of ACLs:

- **Container-based ACL**: Here, the rules are defined on the container which is applied on the container and the object stored under the container
- **Account-based ACL**: Here, the rules are defined on the account which is applied to all containers and objects in a particular account

Container ACLs are specified in the metadata called **X-Container-Write** and **X-Container-Read**. Here, X-Container-Write provides you access to write the data into the container, which means it gives you the PUT, DELETE, and POST operations, where X-Container-Read provides you access to read the data from the container, which means here you can perform the GET and Head operation.

In account-based ACL, the **X-Account-Access-Control** header specifies account-level ACLs in a format specific to the authentication system. X-Account-Access-Control headers are only visible to Swift account owners.

There are three levels, so the access can be specified in ACL. The first is the **read/write access**, where users can create a new container, update objects, and delete the container. The second is **read-only**, where users or identities can get a list of containers in the specified account and read everything.

The last one is **admin**, where users or identities can perform any activity, which can be performed by a Swift owner. Admin access grants them Swift-owner privileges.

OpenStack object storage also supports object encryption. But it's an optional feature. It ensures that data at rest is encrypted. As we read in the earlier sections, data at rest encryption removes the risk of unauthorized access and data theft.

Data encryption in Swift is implemented at middleware and it's an internal feature, which is not even exposed using APIs.

When we enable data encryption on object storage the following gets encrypted:

- All of the objects residing in the container
- All of the users' custom metadata

The following are the things that do not get encrypted:

- Container and accounts
- Object names
- Metadata of container and account custom defined
- System metadata

Data at rest encryption in Swift can be achieved by adding two middleware filters to the proxy server WSGI pipeline. After that, we need to add their respective filter configuration sections in the `proxy-server.conf` file:

```
<other middleware> keymaster encryption proxy-logging proxy-server

[filter:keymaster]
use = egg:swift#keymaster
encryption_root_secret = <specify your secret file>

[filter:encryption]
use = egg:swift#encryption
# disable_encryption = False
```

In the preceding configuration section, `encryption_root_secret` is used to store the master key of the encryption, which is further used to decrypt the data. Here, we make sure that the master key value is not changed once defined.

We can generate `encryption_root_secret` using the `openssl` command.

To add some more security, we also use the key management system. By default, KMS does not come with Swift; so, we need to install this package and do the configuration.

KMS is used to store the encryption root secret, which can also be backed with HSM as an additional layer of security.

The key master uses the username and password defined in the `keymaster.conf` file to retrieve the `encryption_root_secret` stored in the external KMS.

Data at rest encryption does not have any impact on operations such as object versioning, container sync, and container reconciliation.

Message queue

Message queue is the backbone of OpenStack. It's used to provide interprocess communication in OpenStack. There are multiple message queuing services such as RabbitMQ and Apache Qpid.

RabbitMQ and Qpid both work on AMQP for interprocess communication. Message queue is used to decouple the architecture.

The best part about message queues in OpenStack is, after permitting queue access, there is no additional authorization check that happens. Services accessible using message queue only validate the token within the actual message payload. Here, one must consider the token expiration time. Because queues can be replayed and they also authorize other services in the infrastructure.

In the OpenStack message, signing is not available. For high availability configuration, one must have complete queue-to-queue authentication and encryption.

Now, let's see the way to secure the message queue or AMQP:

- AMQP services such as RabbitMQ and Qpid both support TLS. So, we must enable TLS-based communication for message queues. It provides protection for messages in transit.
- There are a few configurations that need to be added to enable SSL in RabbitMQ. RabbitMQ Configuration files are available at `/etc/rabbitmq/rabbitmq.config`. We need to add the following configuration in the RabbitMQ config file:

```
[
  {rabbit, [
    {tcp_listeners, [] },
    {ssl_listeners, [{"<IP address or hostname of
     management network interface>", 5671}] },
    {ssl_options, [{cacertfile,"/etc/ssl/cacert.pem"},
                   {certfile,"/etc/ssl/rabbit-server-cert.pem"},
                   {keyfile,"/etc/ssl/rabbit-server-key.pem"},
                   {verify,verify_peer},
                   {fail_if_no_peer_cert,true}]}
  ]}
]
```

- Access controls are also supported for AMQP services (RabbitMQ and Qpid). For internet protocol, **Simple Authentication and Secure Layer (SASL)** is used for data security and authentication. RabbitMQ and Qpid also support SASL for additional security. However, this is not available in OpenStack with RabbitMQ, so it is recommended to use X.509 certificates for the client to ensure secure authentication over TLS.

- In OpenStack, projects have multiple services which create and consume the messages. The AMQP process must be isolated from each other and other processes as well. Here, we can use the following to create isolation and security of messages:
    - **Namespace**: It is always recommended to use network namespace on all of the nova-compute hypervisors, which helps to prevent bridging of traffic between the management and guest network
    - **Network policy**: Queues will only be allowed to communicate using the management network
    - **Mandatory access control**: This helps to restrict the process communication

Let's see the sample of queue list in OpenStack:

```
[root@localhost ~]# rabbitmqctl list_queues
Listing queues...
neutron-vo-SecurityGroup-1.0_fanout_3181ea14a98c4b038914ffcd78d27d68 0
neutron-vo-Network-1.0 0
cinder-volume.localhost.localdomain@lvm.localhost.localdomain 0
scheduler.localhost.localdomain 0
scheduler 0
cinder-scheduler.localhost.localdomain 0
q-agent-notifier-security_group-
update_fanout_55b1bbddc0ac4d069d4cda079cbcb163 0
q-agent-notifier-tunnel-delete.localhost.localdomain 0
conductor_fanout_8439f189c8ca4620b9dfa0cefab22afb 0
q-agent-notifier-port-delete 0
q-agent-notifier-port-update_fanout_741a33daa26f4d9f8d312e7c259e951e 0
q-agent-notifier-port-update.localhost.localdomain 0
q-agent-notifier-tunnel-update.localhost.localdomain 0
metering_agent.localhost.localdomain 0
q-metering-plugin 0
notifications.info 0
dhcp_agent 0
metering_agent_fanout_fa9cbe82f40245f3a3ecd8c59fbea24f 0
cinder-volume_fanout_ad5e35a8d9fa471293300241c54f92ba 0
notifications.sample 1
```

In the aforementioned queue list, we can find multiple services having separate queues.

Database services

In OpenStack, all of the services, such as nova, neutron, Keystone, and Cinder, use the database to store the state and configuration details.

So, it's very critical to ensure security of the database used for OpenStack. Currently, OpenStack supports MySQL and postures SQL database.

In OpenStack, all of the services use a single database to store the configuration and state. There is no such policy defined at the granular level access of the database. This means that all of the services which need database access have been granted access and privileges to the database.

So, the nodes, having access to the database, have full permission to execute any statement such as drop, update, and insert.

Now, in this situation, if any component is compromised, it can lead to a disaster. Now, to get rid of this situation, the following are the few steps one should take:

- Communication with the database is only allowed on the management network.
- Enable TLS-based communication for the database.
- We need to ensure that each service-based account created on the database and the permissions are granted accordingly. This will help in a compliance audit and also when one service node is compromised, you can simply remove it from the database.
- Apart from this, there must be a separate database administrator account to have complete control of the database. All of the service user accounts only have limited permissions to access the database.
- We can also use X.509 certificate-based authentication for the database. This will ensure that all of the communication with the database is encrypted.

In OpenStack, there is a component called the **nova conductor**, which is part of nova-compute and basically works as a proxy when connecting with the database. This ensures data persistence when accessing the database.

The nova-conductor works on RPC, which means it receives requests on RPC and accordingly performs the action. It does not need granular access to the database. Basically, it abstracts direct communication with the database.

The use of the nova-conductor to access the database has the following advantages too:

- Restricts service to execute methods with parameters (such as stored procedure)
- Also restricts large amounts of direct connection to the database

However, it has got one limitation as well, in that it complicates the process of database access.

To secure the OpenStack database, we also utilize the security offered by database engines. Here, we have Postgres and MySQL as databases. Let's see the method to enable security.

As per **OpenWeb Application Security Project (OWASP)**, there are a few recommendations for MySQL security.

 OWASP is a worldwide not-for-profit charitable organization focused on improving the security of the software. The mission of OWASP is to make software security visible, so that organizations and individuals can make informed decisions. The official website of OWASP is https://www.owasp.org.

- Restricting file access and ACL, the major configuration files of MySQL are stored at /etc/my.conf. So, here we need to give ownership of this file to root:root:

```
# chown -R root:root /etc/mysql/
# chmod 0644 /etc/mysql/my.cnf
```

- MySQL data is getting stored at /var/lib/mysql by default. However, this should not be owned by an administrator; instead, it should be owned by the MySQL user, who is not allowed to do anything on the Unix system.
- MySQL records all of the events that are relevant to the database into a log file. So here log file access can only be granted to the root and MySQL user.
- For MySQL, we can also use ACL to define a more granular level of permission. It provides mechanisms for setting up user-level permissions of a single filesystem and also provides definition of access restrictions.

- As per OWASP, we can encrypt the network traffic to communicate with MySQL. The following are the ways to encrypt the database traffic:
  - **OpenSSL**: To use open SSL, we need to make some configuration changes in the MySQL configuration file on the basis of the certificate file:

    ```
    [mysqld]
    ssl-ca=$DIR/cacert.pem
    ssl-cert=$DIR/server-cert.pem
    ssl-key=$DIR/server-key.pem
    ```

  - **OpenSSH**: To use OpenSSH tunneling, we do not need to make any changes in the MySQL configuration file. Here, SSH tunnel is transparent to MySQL.
  - **OpenVPN**: Here, we create tunnels between two parties to ensure secure and encrypted communication.

Similar to MySQL **OWASP**, we have the following recommendations for Postgres hardening:

- Access privileges, as per OWASP, we must create two users for each database, where one has full control and the other has limited access.
- Remove public schema, by default, Postgres creates a public schema to store all of the information about the database, procedures, and tables. Every user can access and view this schema. So, it is recommended to remove this public schema, create a new private schema, and modify the search_path for users in the private schema.
- By default, the Postgres database prevents all of the users from accessing the filesystem and system routines; only superusers are allowed to do that.
- Apart from this, we can enable encrypted connection to the database. For this, we need to add ssl=true into the Postgres configuration file called Postgres.conf.

You can also isolate communication between the service and the database. It is recommended that you use an isolated management network for the database for to and fro communication. This can be enabled by restricting the address for MySQL and Postgres in their configuration files. For MySQL, we need to modify the /etc/my.cnf file and add the following entry:

```
bind-address <ip address or hostname of management network interface>
```

For PostgreSQL, we need to modify `postgresql.conf` and add the following entry:

```
listen_addresses = <ip address or hostname of management network interface>
```

Data privacy and security for tenants

OpenStack also provides multitenancy, which means you can have multiple tenants in an OpenStack Cloud. Each tenant has their own set of resources as per their requirement. All of these tenants have their own separate identities in the cloud. So here, data privacy and security is of the utmost importance.

Now, let's understand data privacy concerns for a multitenancy environment and its mitigation:

- The first concern is related to data privacy, that is, data residency. It says data privacy and isolation is a crucial point, which works as a barrier in the way of cloud adoption. There are many OpenStack services, which record tenant data and metadata. Tenant data includes objects stored in object storage, data stored on ephemeral storage, data stored on block storage, snapshots, public keys, and so on. Metadata includes details such as name, IP, compute information, and size of storage. Here, being a cloud operator, one must take care of all data privacy issues.

- The second concern is that of data disposal. This states that all of the data stored in storage media must be disposed of in such a way that the data can not be retrieved. There must be a sanitization process for disposal of data which is purging, erasing, or cryptographic erasing. For disposal of data, there is a NIST recommendation for cloud operation, which states that the cloud operator must do the following:
    - Track and verify the sanitization process
    - Verify that all of the devices are sanitized before being plugged into the cloud infrastructure
    - Destroy devices whose data cannot be sanitized completely

- Memory scrubbing of an instance is also done to ensure data privacy. It always goes into the hypervisor part, where it uses best efforts to scrub the memory of the instances that are deleted. XenServer defines dedicated memory ranges to instances, which scrub the memory data in case of VM deletion. KVM does this using Linux page management.

- Data stored on a persistent volume is also a matter of concern for data privacy. Here, it is always encouraged to use encryption for Cinder volume data. So here, destruction of data becomes easy as you just need to delete the encryption key. However, it becomes really very complex to destroy the data if an encryption mechanism is not used.
- Images stored in Glance are also a concern for data privacy. By default, Glance does not delete images immediately after performing the delete operation. Internally, it marks it for deletion and deletes it from storage at a specific time. So, it's highly recommended to disable this feature.
- In OpenStack, project nova compute also provides an option of soft delete, which states the instance that needs to be deleted must be in a soft delete state for a defined time period. The soft delete option basically enables one to restore the VM if it is in the soft delete state. It must be disabled in nova-compute configuration files.
- In OpenStack, nova-compute data is also stored on ephemeral disk. Here, to ensure data privacy and security, we can enable encryption. Also, for data destruction, we can simply delete the encryption keys.

Security for instances

In the earlier sections, we studied about different OpenStack components and how to implement security at different levels.

Now, we will see how to ensure security for instances running in OpenStack.

In OpenStack, we have the scheduler function, which helps us to decide which instances will be allocated to which node. This scheduler in OpenStack is known as nova-scheduler, it's basically a component of nova-compute. The nova-scheduler works on a set of filters to choose the right node for the instance. The nova-scheduler allocates the host to the instances on the basis of the following points:

- Resource allocated to image, the nova-scheduler basically checks the free resource in terms of RAM, CPU, and storage (IO) and then validates the instance requirement to allocate the right host.
- Image, normally in the cloud environment, we define a tag for hypervisor hosts to allocate on the basis of OS images. In OpenStack too, we use this facility such as image OS and size of the image to allocate the right node for the instances.

- Sometimes, node allocation also depends on the network and IP requirement of the instances. We can validate this condition in case of HA deployment, where we always prefer to have two different subnets in different availability zones. Here, no two instances can be deployed on the same host. It always goes for unique host and unique IP CIDR.

This scheduling process of node section, for instance, helps the cloud administrator to effectively implement security and compliance for the organization or tenant.

After applying the scheduler, we also need to focus on the images which we used to create the instance. For the administrator, it becomes very challenging to choose only the images that are coming from trusted sources.

Image creation and hardening also helps us to secure the instances in OpenStack. Normally, it's recommended to use images from trusted sources after the instance is created using the images we have downloaded. After that, we can use configuration management tools to do the hardening of instances.

In OpenStack, most of the hypervisors support live migration of images between host nodes. However, there are many risks associated with this process, such as **Denial Of Service (DoS)**, data manipulation, and chances of data expose. This is because, during live migration of VM in OpenStack, in-memory data and disks are transmitted in plain text format.

To eliminate these risks, we can either disable the live migration option after modifying nova configuration files or enable encrypted live migration.

Apart from the monitoring and alert management process, it also helps to boost the security of instance in OpenStack. For this, we can use tools such as Zabbix, Nagios, and Zenoss. For log analytics and dashboard, we can use **ELK** Stack, which consists of **Elasticsearch, Logstash, and Kibana**.

The last point is about patch management. For the instances running on OpenStack, we also need to deploy patches from time to time after the patch release. Here too, we need to first test the patch in the staging and testing environment stage before rolling out to production. Here, we can use configuration management tools such as Ansible, Chef, and Puppet.

Quick recap

In this chapter, we have learned about different aspects of security in OpenStack. We know that OpenStack consists of multiple independent projects to enable the users to have a self-provisioned, managed, and self-serviced infrastructure.

In OpenStack, we have the following key services:

- **Nova**: This project provides compute resources to instances.
- **Glance**: This project gives image storage where snapshots, ISO images, and templates are stored, which are used to create instances.
- **Cinder**: This project is responsible for providing block storage, which is used to store persistent files or you can say that Cinder volumes are used as root volume and additional data volume for instances.
- **Swift**: For objects storage in OpenStack, we have Swift, which is used to store utility and static content such as image, DOCs, and PDF.
- **Manila**: This project provides shared file storage in OpenStack, which works on NFS protocol.
- **Neutron**: This project provides networking services in OpenStack.
- **Keystone**: For identity and access management we have the Keystone service, which manages the authentication and authorization process in OpenStack.
- **Message queue**: Most of the OpenStack components communicate with each other using message queue. RabbitMQ is the most popular message queue application.
- **Database**: OpenStack configuration files are stored in a relational database. The most commonly used databases are MySQL and Postgres.

To secure the OpenStack environment, we must ensure this since the planning stage of OpenStack deployment. At first, we have to think about the hypervisor selection and security of the hypervisor.

For the hypervisor selection, we should focus on the following criteria:

- What is the expertise level of the team for hypervisor technology?
- What is the user base and community size for the hypervisor project?
- How frequently are updates available for the hypervisor?
- How fast is the resolution of reported incidents?
- What are the encryption methods supported by hypervisor?
- Does hypervisor support RBAC?

Apart from this, we also need to understand the process and other security options available for hypervisor.

To ensure security of Horizon (OpenStack dashboard service), we must ensure that we have disabled options which can lead to the following points:

- XSS
- CSRF
- XFS or CFS

Apart from this, we also ensure that horizon is running on the CA signed SSL certificate and we can also use HSTS.

We also have to ensure that all of the configuration file accesses are authorized to specific users only.

For nova compute, all of the configuration files are stored at `/etc/nova/`, which contains all the information about nova compute. We must ensure that this folder only has access to the root users and nova group.

Apart from this, we also need to ensure that all of the communication between nova and other components is happening on a secured channel.

IAM in OpenStack is provided by Keystone. Keystone provides identity, token, and policies for services. For authentication, Keystone supports user ID and password, LDAP-based authentication, and external authentication using tokens. TLS-based authentication is supported for services and users using X.509 certificates.

Keystone also has the concept of group and roles. On the basis of groups and roles, it authorizes users to access the OpenStack services or resource. The domain section of Keystone also helps to centrally manage all of its components. Here, all the OpenStack resources (such as compute, storage, and network) can be grouped into multiple tenants, which can further be controlled by the master account.

Each service in OpenStack has a specific set of access policies for its resources defined in the Policy file called `policy.json`. Keystone also supports MFA and federated authentication for users and services. One can use an SAML-based identity provider to integrate with Keystone for federated authentication.

In OpenStack, each component has its own configuration file, which must be kept secure by providing access to the root user and specific project group. For example, Cinder configuration files are stored in `/etc/cinder/`. So here, it must only be accessible to the user root and group Cinder.

Then, for storage such as Cinder and Swift, we must enable data at rest encryption and also ensure that all of the communication between internal component APIs is taking place using a TLS-based encrypted channel.

For object storage, we can use CORS and the object versioning feature.

For neutron, we can ensure that all of the communication between different service components of OpenStack takes place on separate isolated networks.

All of the requests to access neutron networking services must get authenticated and authorized by Keystone Identity services.

For the database, which stores all of the configuration details of OpenStack services, it must be secured. Here, it is recommended to follow **OWASP guidelines**. Apart from this, we can also enable encryption for the database and also ensure that all of the communication to the database takes place on a TLS-based channel on the management network only.

For tenant data security in OpenStack, we must take care of all the data privacy concerns such as data disposal and data residency.

For instance security, we also ensure that all of the images used to create instances are taken from a secure and trusted source. Apart from this, we also need to ensure that the instance is security hardened and that the required patches are being applied from time to time.

We must have a monitoring and logging solution to monitor and record all of the events, API calls, and also be able to generate alerts.

Summary

This chapter was all about securing your private cloud at the compute level, the network level, and the storage and application levels.

Next up, we will learn in detail about automation and the role of automation in securing cloud infrastructure.

8
Automating Cloud Security

In Chapter 2, *Understanding the World of Cloud Automation*, we learned about the concept of automation and the DevOps process and tools. Now, in this chapter we will see how to use DevOps tools to automate the security for our infrastructure.

In the AWS public cloud, we have DevOps tools such as CloudFormation, Elastic Beanstalk, and OpsWorks, which help us to convert Infrastructure as Code. Apart from this, we have CodePipeline and CodeDeploy to enable the complete **continuous integration and continuous delivery (CI/CD)** process.

For configuration management, we have Chef, Puppet, and Ansible to automate the configuration management process. In this chapter, we will deep dive into all these tools and technologies.

Earlier, we determined that DevOps is a process or culture, which we need to adhere to in order to ensure the fast, reliable, scalable, and secure delivery of infrastructures and applications.

Like other software development life cycles, here too we have the DevOps life cycle. To complete this life cycle, we have different tools and methods available, which are as follows:

- **Infrastructure as Code**: In this section, we use tools to create the infrastructure template, which can be deployed, configured, and managed like software code. In AWS, we have CloudFormation for this, which helps to create Infrastructure as Code; then we deploy this template using AWS OpsWorks (configuration management tools using Chef and Puppet). Then, we have the patch management process for VMs using the AWS system manager. Security and policies can be implemented using AWS Config.

- **CI/CD**: This is a very important process for DevOps, where we automate the complete process of building, testing, and deploying applications. In AWS, we have a service called **AWS CodeBuild**, which helps to compile the source code, test it, and generate the application package. Once the package is ready, we have another service called **AWS CodeDeploy**, which helps to deploy the code on the infrastructure. And to complete the CI/CD process, we have AWS CodePipeline, which helps us to rapidly deploy the changes made in an application on the servers automatically.

- **Monitoring and management**: Monitoring is also a critical process in DevOps. Here, we monitor the infrastructure and application in real time. We record all the logs and analyze them, almost in real time, to identify the risk or issue associated with any operation. For this, on AWS we have CloudWatch, which helps to monitor the infrastructure and application. For logging on AWS, we use CloudTrail, which records all the API-level events and stores them to an S3 bucket. We also use AWS X-ray to analyze the application builds and production platform to identity an issue and help in troubleshooting for the root cause of that issue.

- **Version control**: In the DevOps process, we also have a version control system, such as GitHub, Bitbucket, or AWS CodeCommit, where we manage the versions of application or code. Its central repository stores all the code and it transfers only changes that get deployed on the infrastructure.

Infrastructure as Code

In Chapter 2, *Understanding the World of Cloud Automation*, we have already seen that Infrastructure as Code involves creating a template for all the required infrastructure, which can be deployed at any point of time. To create a template of the infrastructure, we use JSON or YAML. In AWS, we have CloudFormation, which helps to create the infrastructure template, which can be deployed at any point of time in AWS after making minimal or no changes.

Minimal changes, such as changes in compute size and region-specific details, are required before the deployment of the template when we create a template for a specific region.

When we put our JSON template in the CloudFormation template, it automatically draws a logical diagram, as follows:

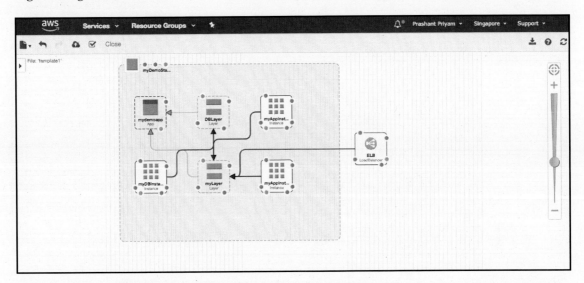

We also learned about AWS OpsWorks in an earlier section. It helps us to create the layered infrastructure and deploy applications on top of it.

In this section, we will see how to deploy a PHP sample application using CloudFormation and OpsWorks.

Let's outline the case as follows:

- **Requirement**: Automatic deployment of PHP applications, where you have two EC2 instances that will run PHP applications and will be load balanced using an ELB. For the database, we have the MySQL database, which is also running on an EC2 instance.
- **Plan for deployment**: We need to create one OpsWorks stack, which will have two layers. One layer is the application layer and the other is the database layer. In the application layer, we need to create two EC2 instances, which will be further introduced to the load balancer. In the database layer, we have one EC2 instance, which will run the MySQL database. In the CloudFormation template, we need to define the stack, instance detail, and other dependencies.

- **Output**: After successful deployment of the template, we should be able to access the application using the ELB URL, which will look like this:

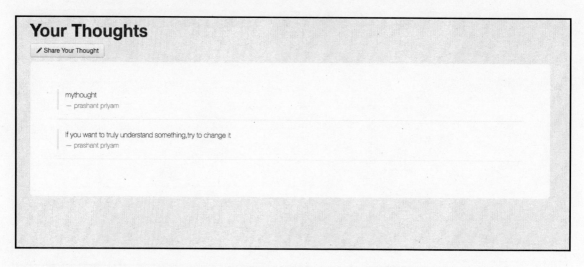

Now, we will start the code section. For this, I have used the AWS Console. To use CloudFormation, log in to the AWS Console and click on **Services**, and then in the search box, type `CloudFormation` and click on it:

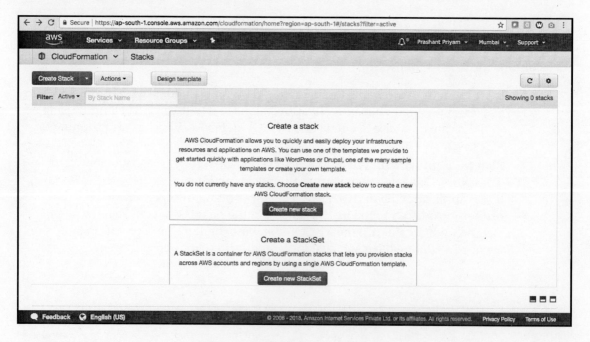

Here, we will not create a stack, but instead will click on the **Design template**. This will open the design template page. Now, click on the **Template** tab at the bottom of the page. This is the section where we write our code and by clicking on the top-right button, we will check whether the template is valid or not. If there is an error, it will show on the pane in the right-hand side:

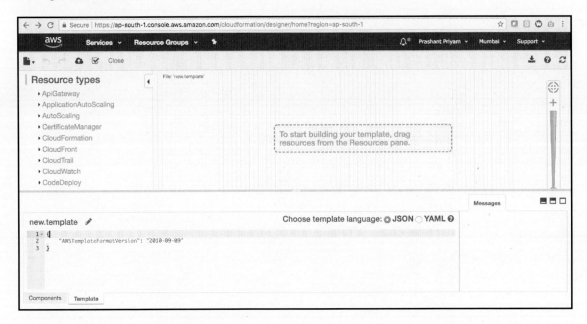

Now, let's see the CloudFormation code to deploy the infrastructure specified in the requirement mentioned earlier. We have already seen examples of the CloudFormation template and its description in an earlier chapter. Here, the CloudFormation code will be a bit longer, so go through it patiently:

```
{
    "AWSTemplateFormatVersion": "2010-09-09",
    "Parameters": {
        "ServiceRole": {
            "Default": "aws-opsworks-service-role",
            "Description": "myOpsworksServcieRole",
            "Type": "String",
            "MinLength": "1",
            "MaxLength": "64",
            "ConstraintDescription": "contains letter and
             alpha numeric character"
        },
        "InstanceRole": {
```

```json
            "Default": "aws-opsworks-ec2-role",
            "Description": "Instance role for Opsworks",
            "Type": "String",
            "MinLength": "1",
            "MaxLength": "64",
            "ConstraintDescription": "contains letter
             and alpha numeric character"
        },
        "AppName": {
            "Default": "mydemoapp",
            "Description": "Name of the Application",
            "Type": "String",
            "MinLength": "1",
            "MaxLength": "64",
            "ConstraintDescription": "contains letter
             and alpha neumeric character."
        },
        "MysqlRootPassword": {
            "Description": "MysqlRootPassword",
            "NoEcho": "true",
            "Type": "String"
        }
    },
    "Resources": {
        "myDemoStack": {
            "Type": "AWS::OpsWorks::Stack",
            "Properties": {
                "Name": {
                    "Ref": "AWS::StackName"
                },
                "ServiceRoleArn": {
                    "Fn::Join": [
                        "",
                        [
                            "arn:aws:iam::",
                            {
                                "Ref": "AWS::AccountId"
                            },
                            ":role/",
                            {
                                "Ref": "ServiceRole"
                            }
                        ]
                    ]
                },
                "DefaultInstanceProfileArn": {
                    "Fn::Join": [
                        "",
```

```json
                    [
                        "arn:aws:iam::",
                        {
                            "Ref": "AWS::AccountId"
                        },
                        ":instance-profile/",
                        {
                            "Ref": "InstanceRole"
                        }
                    ]
                ]
            },
            "ConfigurationManager": {
                "Name": "Chef",
                "Version": "11.10"
            },
            "DefaultOs": "Amazon Linux 2017.09",
            "UseCustomCookbooks": "true",
            "CustomCookbooksSource": {
                "Type": "git",
                "Url": "git://github.com/amazonwebservices/
                opsworks-example-cookbooks.git"
            }
        },
        "Metadata": {
            "AWS::CloudFormation::Designer": {
                "id": "6cbc631f-81d7-4261-867d-a5a49af8e2ef"
            }
        }
    }
},
"myLayer": {
    "Type": "AWS::OpsWorks::Layer",
    "DependsOn": "mydemoapp",
    "Properties": {
        "StackId": {
            "Ref": "myDemoStack"
        },
        "Type": "php-app",
        "Shortname": "php-app",
        "EnableAutoHealing": "true",
        "AutoAssignElasticIps": "false",
        "AutoAssignPublicIps": "true",
        "Name": "MyPHPApp",
        "CustomRecipes": {
            "Configure": [
                "phpapp::appsetup"
            ]
        }
```

```
            },
        "Metadata": {
            "AWS::CloudFormation::Designer": {
                "id": "5669c25d-ed1f-4a36-8cd8-d8e023b10d13"
            }
        }
    },
    "DBLayer": {
        "Type": "AWS::OpsWorks::Layer",
        "DependsOn": "mydemoapp",
        "Properties": {
            "StackId": {
                "Ref": "myDemoStack"
            },
            "Type": "db-master",
            "Shortname": "db-layer",
            "EnableAutoHealing": "true",
            "AutoAssignElasticIps": "false",
            "AutoAssignPublicIps": "true",
            "Name": "MyMySQL",
            "CustomRecipes": {
                "Setup": [
                    "phpapp::dbsetup"
                ]
            },
            "Attributes": {
                "MysqlRootPassword": {
                    "Ref": "MysqlRootPassword"
                },
                "MysqlRootPasswordUbiquitous": "true"
            },
            "VolumeConfigurations": [
                {
                    "MountPoint": "/vol/mysql",
                    "NumberOfDisks": 1,
                    "Size": 20
                }
            ]
        },
        "Metadata": {
            "AWS::CloudFormation::Designer": {
                "id": "edbd7ee2-36ab-4680-bd75-e8b59090066f"
            }
        }
    },
    "ELBAttachment": {
        "Type": "AWS::OpsWorks::ElasticLoadBalancerAttachment",
        "Properties": {
```

```json
                "ElasticLoadBalancerName": {
                    "Ref": "ELB"
                },
                "LayerId": {
                    "Ref": "myLayer"
                }
            },
            "Metadata": {
                "AWS::CloudFormation::Designer": {
                    "id": "68a38b65-512e-4071-8aff-22dafb5a5a98"
                }
            }
        },
        "ELB": {
            "Type": "AWS::ElasticLoadBalancing::LoadBalancer",
            "Properties": {
                "AvailabilityZones": {
                    "Fn::GetAZs": ""
                },
                "Listeners": [
                    {
                        "LoadBalancerPort": "80",
                        "InstancePort": "80",
                        "Protocol": "HTTP",
                        "InstanceProtocol": "HTTP"
                    }
                ],
                "HealthCheck": {
                    "Target": "HTTP:80/",
                    "HealthyThreshold": "2",
                    "UnhealthyThreshold": "10",
                    "Interval": "30",
                    "Timeout": "5"
                }
            },
            "Metadata": {
                "AWS::CloudFormation::Designer": {
                    "id": "40ab7475-af57-4eb5-a9b9-f63926c70df4"
                }
            }
        },
        "myAppInstance1": {
            "Type": "AWS::OpsWorks::Instance",
            "Properties": {
                "StackId": {
                    "Ref": "myDemoStack"
                },
                "LayerIds": [
```

```
                    {
                        "Ref": "myLayer"
                    }
                ],
                "InstanceType": "c3.large"
            },
            "Metadata": {
                "AWS::CloudFormation::Designer": {
                    "id": "4d048ffb-e98f-403f-a36d-3cb4cd7b3a0b"
                }
            }
        },
        "myAppInstance2": {
            "Type": "AWS::OpsWorks::Instance",
            "Properties": {
                "StackId": {
                    "Ref": "myDemoStack"
                },
                "LayerIds": [
                    {
                        "Ref": "myLayer"
                    }
                ],
                "InstanceType": "c3.large"
            },
            "Metadata": {
                "AWS::CloudFormation::Designer": {
                    "id": "dcbe016a-ca6e-4274-a0da-17bfebb30c19"
                }
            }
        },
        "myDBInstance": {
            "Type": "AWS::OpsWorks::Instance",
            "Properties": {
                "StackId": {
                    "Ref": "myDemoStack"
                },
                "LayerIds": [
                    {
                        "Ref": "DBLayer"
                    }
                ],
                "InstanceType": "c3.large"
            },
            "Metadata": {
                "AWS::CloudFormation::Designer": {
                    "id": "0927b5fb-d874-48aa-a1b8-519bc199bccb"
                }
```

```json
                }
            },
            "mydemoapp": {
                "Type": "AWS::OpsWorks::App",
                "Properties": {
                    "StackId": {
                        "Ref": "myDemoStack"
                    },
                    "Type": "php",
                    "Name": {
                        "Ref": "AppName"
                    },
                    "AppSource": {
                        "Type": "git",
                        "Url": "git://github.com/amazonwebservices/
                         opsworks-demo-php-simple-app.git",
                        "Revision": "version2"
                    },
                    "Attributes": {
                        "DocumentRoot": "web"
                    }
                },
                "Metadata": {
                    "AWS::CloudFormation::Designer": {
                        "id": "1faf9f43-5a8b-472d-8a6b-789ba6c4fc63"
                    }
                }
            }
        }
    },
    "Metadata": {
        "AWS::CloudFormation::Designer": {
            "40ab7475-af57-4eb5-a9b9-f63926c70df4": {
                "size": {
                    "width": 60,
                    "height": 60
                },
                "position": {
                    "x": 190,
                    "y": 50
                },
                "z": 1,
                "embeds": []
            },
            "6cbc631f-81d7-4261-867d-a5a49af8e2ef": {
                "size": {
                    "width": 420,
                    "height": 330
                },
```

```
        "position": {
            "x": -260,
            "y": -80
        },
        "z": 1,
        "embeds": [
            "1faf9f43-5a8b-472d-8a6b-789ba6c4fc63",
            "edbd7ee2-36ab-4680-bd75-e8b59090066f",
            "0927b5fb-d874-48aa-a1b8-519bc199bccb",
            "5669c25d-ed1f-4a36-8cd8-d8e023b10d13",
            "dcbe016a-ca6e-4274-a0da-17bfebb30c19",
            "4d048ffb-e98f-403f-a36d-3cb4cd7b3a0b"
        ]
    },
    "1faf9f43-5a8b-472d-8a6b-789ba6c4fc63": {
        "size": {
            "width": 60,
            "height": 60
        },
        "position": {
            "x": -230,
            "y": -20
        },
        "z": 2,
        "parent": "6cbc631f-81d7-4261-867d-a5a49af8e2ef",
        "embeds": [],
        "iscontainedinside": [
            "6cbc631f-81d7-4261-867d-a5a49af8e2ef",
            "6cbc631f-81d7-4261-867d-a5a49af8e2ef"
        ]
    },
    "edbd7ee2-36ab-4680-bd75-e8b59090066f": {
        "size": {
            "width": 60,
            "height": 60
        },
        "position": {
            "x": -110,
            "y": -20
        },
        "z": 2,
        "parent": "6cbc631f-81d7-4261-867d-a5a49af8e2ef",
        "embeds": [],
        "iscontainedinside": [
            "6cbc631f-81d7-4261-867d-a5a49af8e2ef",
            "6cbc631f-81d7-4261-867d-a5a49af8e2ef"
        ],
        "dependson": [
```

```
                "1faf9f43-5a8b-472d-8a6b-789ba6c4fc63"
            ]
        },
        "0927b5fb-d874-48aa-a1b8-519bc199bccb": {
            "size": {
                "width": 60,
                "height": 60
            },
            "position": {
                "x": -230,
                "y": 100
            },
            "z": 2,
            "parent": "6cbc631f-81d7-4261-867d-a5a49af8e2ef",
            "embeds": [],
            "isassociatedwith": [
                "edbd7ee2-36ab-4680-bd75-e8b59090066f"
            ],
            "iscontainedinside": [
                "6cbc631f-81d7-4261-867d-a5a49af8e2ef",
                "6cbc631f-81d7-4261-867d-a5a49af8e2ef"
            ]
        },
        "5669c25d-ed1f-4a36-8cd8-d8e023b10d13": {
            "size": {
                "width": 60,
                "height": 60
            },
            "position": {
                "x": -110,
                "y": 100
            },
            "z": 2,
            "parent": "6cbc631f-81d7-4261-867d-a5a49af8e2ef",
            "embeds": [],
            "iscontainedinside": [
                "6cbc631f-81d7-4261-867d-a5a49af8e2ef",
                "6cbc631f-81d7-4261-867d-a5a49af8e2ef"
            ],
            "dependson": [
                "1faf9f43-5a8b-472d-8a6b-789ba6c4fc63"
            ]
        },
        "dcbe016a-ca6e-4274-a0da-17bfebb30c19": {
            "size": {
                "width": 60,
                "height": 60
            },
```

```
            "position": {
                "x": 10,
                "y": -20
            },
            "z": 2,
            "parent": "6cbc631f-81d7-4261-867d-a5a49af8e2ef",
            "embeds": [],
            "isassociatedwith": [
                "5669c25d-ed1f-4a36-8cd8-d8e023b10d13"
            ],
            "iscontainedinside": [
                "6cbc631f-81d7-4261-867d-a5a49af8e2ef",
                "6cbc631f-81d7-4261-867d-a5a49af8e2ef"
            ]
        },
        "4d048ffb-e98f-403f-a36d-3cb4cd7b3a0b": {
            "size": {
                "width": 60,
                "height": 60
            },
            "position": {
                "x": 10,
                "y": 100
            },
            "z": 2,
            "parent": "6cbc631f-81d7-4261-867d-a5a49af8e2ef",
            "embeds": [],
            "isassociatedwith": [
                "5669c25d-ed1f-4a36-8cd8-d8e023b10d13"
            ],
            "iscontainedinside": [
                "6cbc631f-81d7-4261-867d-a5a49af8e2ef",
                "6cbc631f-81d7-4261-867d-a5a49af8e2ef"
            ]
        },
        "68a38b65-512e-4071-8aff-22dafb5a5a98": {
            "source": {
                "id": "40ab7475-af57-4eb5-a9b9-f63926c70df4"
            },
            "target": {
                "id": "5669c25d-ed1f-4a36-8cd8-d8e023b10d13"
            },
            "z": 2
        }
    }
  }
 }
}
```

In the preceding code, we used OpsWorks to create a stack and layers, then deploy applications, which are stored at `https://github.com/aws-samples/opsworks-demo-php-simple-app`. We defined parameters, which include the service role for OpsWorks, the instance role that needs to be associated with the instance, and application and database components. After that, we defined resources for OpsWorks such as a stack, which has a set of parameters for the instance type, the default OS, and Chef version. The code also contains layer details for the application layer, the database layer, the instances that will be created, and also the ELB. Let's see how to deploy this JSON code using CloudFormation.

First, we insert the code into the **Template** section of CloudFormation:

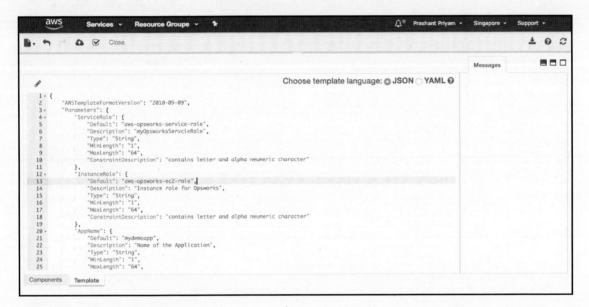

After that, we need to check whether it is valid by clicking on the tick mark button in the top-right corner.

Once it is checked, let's save it to the S3 bucket by clicking on the top-left-most button and then clicking on **Save**. Choose **S3**, specify a name, and then click on **Save**.

Here, we save it because if we come across an error, we can open the code from the S3 bucket and make a modification.

After saving the code, we should keep a record of the URL, which will look like this: `https://s3.ap-south-1.amazonaws.com/cf-templates-1biww5g46xgk1-ap-south-1/2018055W6i-newversiondayaq2f630d`.

Now, we have checked the code validity and saved it on the S3 bucket. Let's click on the cloud icon on top to deploy the code.

After clicking on **Deploy**, you will get another screen where you need to select **Specify an Amazon S3 template URL** and paste the S3 URL recorded earlier while saving the code to S3:

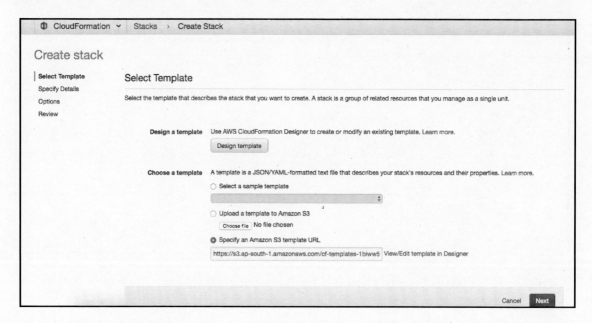

Now, click on **Next** and here you need to specify the details, such as **Stack name** and MySQL password:

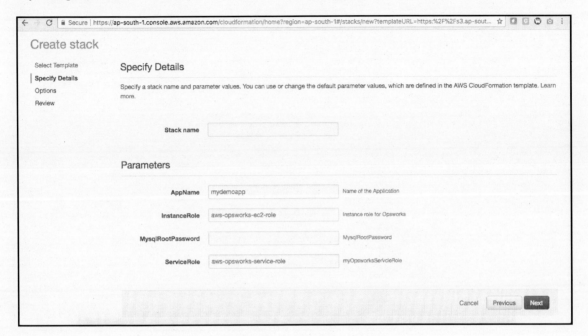

Then, click on **Next** and on the next screen you need to specify the **IAM Role** (which is optional) for CloudFormation and **Monitoring Time** under **Rollback Triggers**:

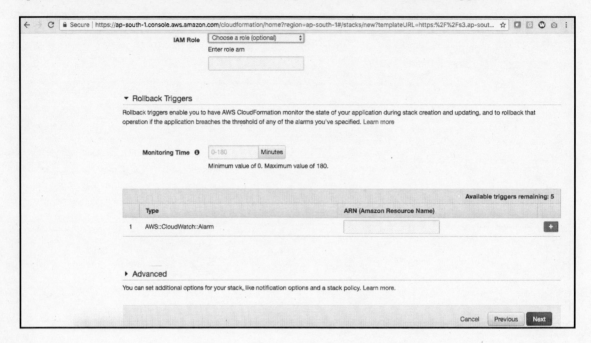

Now, click on the **Advanced** tab to specify details about the rollback policy, **Termination Protection**, SNS topics for notification, and any **Stack policy** if you have one for this deployment:

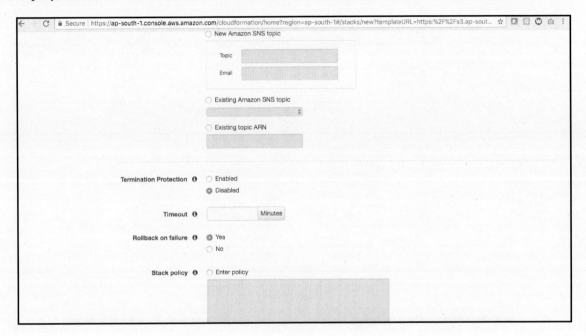

Then, click on **Next** and here you will get a summary of all the inputs; now, click on **Deploy**. It will start deploying and you can see the details by clicking on the stack in CloudFormation:

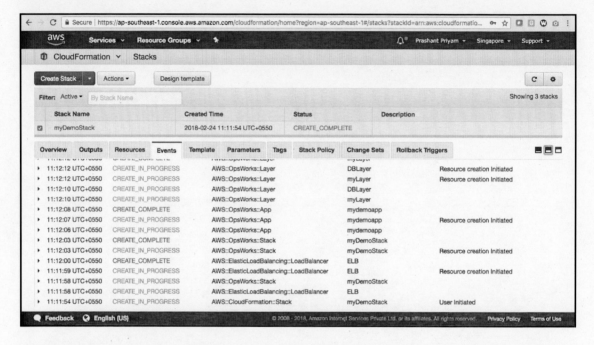

Here in the **Events** section, you can see that the stack deployed is user initiated and then it creates the load balancer, OpsWorks stack, and defined resources. After completing the deployment, you can see the status is **CREATE_COMPLETE**.

Now, let's check whether everything has been created in OpsWorks or not.

For this, we will have to open the OpsWorks service in the AWS Management Console and click on **Stack**, and then click on **Instances**:

In the preceding screenshot, we have PHP-app instances called `php-app1`. In the following screenshot, we have database instances:

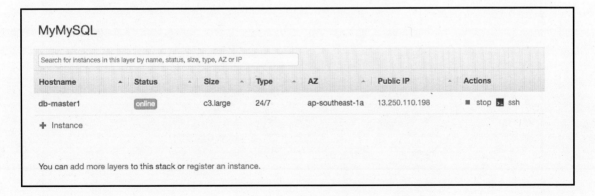

Now, click on **Apps.** Here, we have details of the apps that were created with the source code taken from Git (as specified in the template):

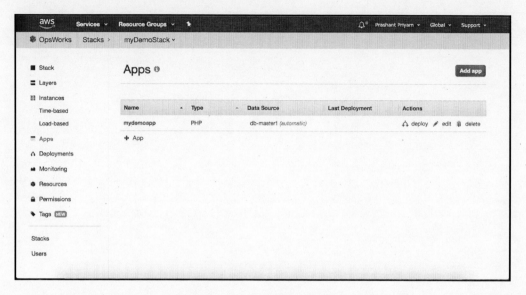

Now, we can say that all the components have been created as per our requirement. Now, let's check whether the load balancer URL is redirecting us to the deployed web application or not:

Here, we have the load balancer URL on top of the **MyPHPApp** section. Now, click on the ELB URL:

Here, the ELB URL is redirecting us on the application. Now, let's test the database connectivity of the application after adding a value in the textbox section and by clicking on the **Share Your Thought** button:

Here, we can see that all the text that we entered in first screen is available. This means that the application is communicating with the database layer.

Let's check the monitoring section and see the resource consumption. For this, click on
Monitoring:

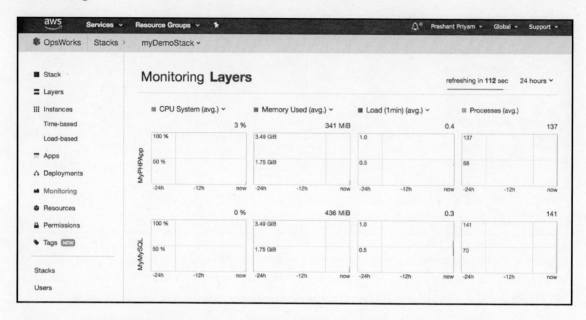

Here too, we have monitoring details in terms of RAM, CPU, load, and process for all the
instances we have deployed.

In this section, we have seen a case where we used CloudFormation and OpsWorks to
deploy the infrastructure, and then deployed one PHP application. Nowhere have we
disclosed any credentials of the VM and database, as everything is done automatically as
defined in code.

If we had to deploy it manually, it would have been a time-consuming process, which is
error prone and less secure. For this, we would have to create two instances for the
application tier and one instance for the database tier. After that we would have to install
the required package for the application and database. Once the application and database
VM are created, we would have to create an ELB and map the application servers to the
ELB.

In the next section, we will establish the complete CodePipeline.

CI/CD

In the CI/CD process, we define a pipeline, which helps to automate the application delivery process. It initiates automatic build and deploys the code on EC2 instances. Using AWS CodePipeline, we automate the build, test, and deployment processes whenever there is a change made in the code.

In this section, we will look at an example to implement AWS CodePipeline, where we will use S3 as the code repository, use CodePipeline to create the pipeline, and AWS CodeDeploy to deploy the application on autoscaling group instances.

The first step of this process will be to create an autoscaling group. For this, log in to the AWS Console and click on **EC2** services. Under the EC2 console, click on the autoscaling group and then click on **Create Auto Scaling group**.

Now, choose new **Launch Configuration**, click on the **Next Step**, and choose an AMI (here we opted for **Amazon Linux AMI**). Click on **Next** and choose **Compute**. Now, click on **Configure Details**, specify the name of the configuration details, and go to the **Advanced** section. In the **Advanced** section, click on **User data** and specify the **User data** as follows:

```
#!/bin/bash

yum -y update

yum install -y ruby

cd /home/ec2-user

#curl -O https://{region based bucket-name for code
deploy}.s3.amazonaws.com/latest/install
# You can get details of region based bucket detail from
https://docs.aws.amazon.com/codedeploy/latest/userguide/resource-kit.html#r
esource-kit-bucket-names
curl -O https://aws-codedeploy-ap-south-1.s3.amazonaws.com/latest/install

chmod +x ./install

./install auto
```

Here, we need to specify IAM roles for the EC2 instances so that the EC2 instances can access S3 bucket stored objects.

For this, go to the IAM service and create an IAM role for the EC2 instances, which should look like this:

```
{
    "Version": "2012-10-17",
    "Statement": [
        {
            "Action": [
                "s3:Get*",
                "s3:List*"
            ],
            "Effect": "Allow",
            "Resource": "*"
        }
    ]
}
```

After specifying the IAM roles, click on **Add Storage** and specify the storage size for your EC2 instances. Now, click on **Configure Security Group**, specify the name of the security group, or add an existing security group. Now, click on **Review** and then click on **Launch Configuration**. Here, it will prompt you to select EC2 access keys. Specify or create new keys, and click on **Create Launch Configuration**.

After creation the launch configuration, it will take you to the autoscaling group console. Here, you need to specify the name of the autoscaling group, VPC, and subnet. Now, it will prompt you to create a scaling policy where you define the group size, scale in, and scale out parameters, and configure the notification policy. It will then finally create the autoscaling group.

Now, we have created another IAM role for CodeDeploy. In CodeDeploy roles, you must have permission to manage the autoscaling group, EC2 instances, S3 bucket access, and CodePipeline process.

Now, log in to the AWS Console, search for `codedeploy`, and click on **CodeDeploy**. In the CodeDeploy console, click on **Create application**:

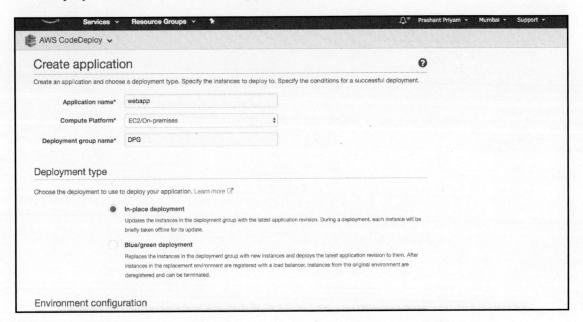

Here, you need to specify the name of your application and deployment group name. Now, we need to configure the environment:

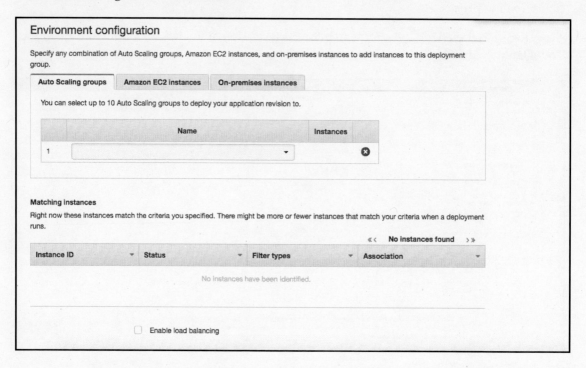

Here, we will specify the name of the autoscaling group, which we created earlier. You can also specify the load balancer if you have one.

After this, we will specify the deployment configuration called one at a time. The deployment configuration has three options: all at once, half at a time, and one at a time.

We can also specify triggers, alarms, and rollback policies. And, finally, we specify the service role and create the application:

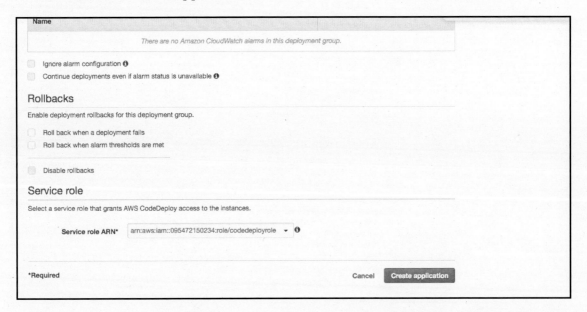

Now, we will create the CodePipeline. To create this, log in to the AWS Console, search for the `codepipeline` service, and then click on **CodePipeline**. In the CodePipeline console, specify the name of the pipeline:

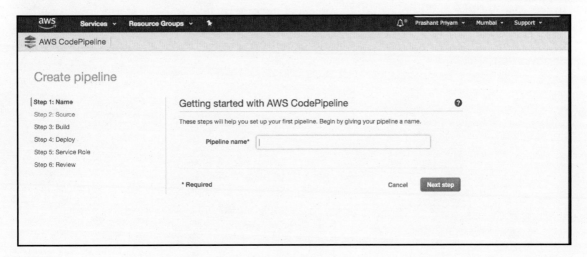

Now, click on **Next step**. On the next screen, it will ask for the source; here, we will choose S3 as the source and specify the object location:

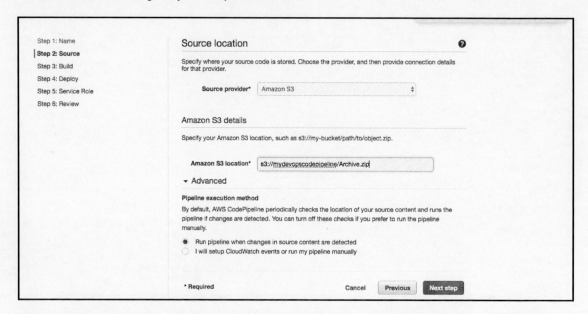

Now, click on **Next step**; it will take us to the **Build** section, where we need to specify the build provider. AWS CodePipeline supports Jenkins and Solano CI as the build provider.

In our case, build is not applicable, so we select none and click on **Next step**. Now, it will ask for the deployment provider. Here, we will choose the **AWS CodeDeploy** option from the other available options, such as **CloudFormation**, **Elastic Beanstalk**, and **No deployment**.

After choosing the **CodeDeploy** option, we need to specify the **Application name** and the **Deployment group**:

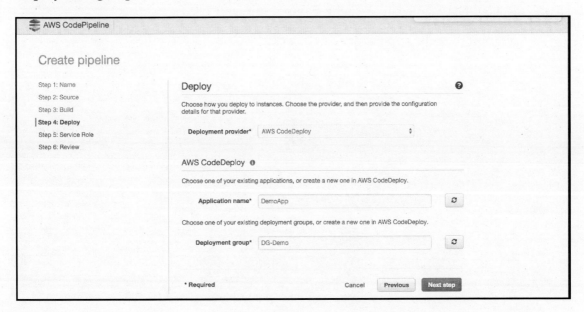

In the next step, we need to specify the CodePipeline role and complete the CodePipeline creation process:

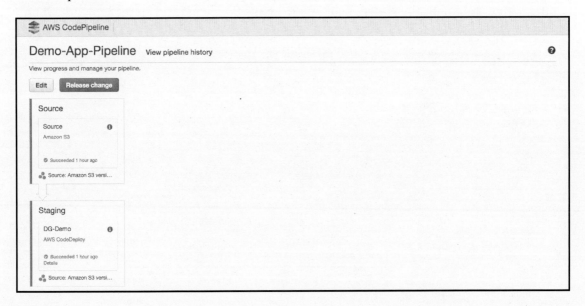

It will take a few minutes to complete the CodePipeline process. Now, to deploy the code instantly, click on **Release change**. It will automatically poll the source and make the deployment on the specified autoscaling group running EC2.

Let's see the output of the application we have deployed:

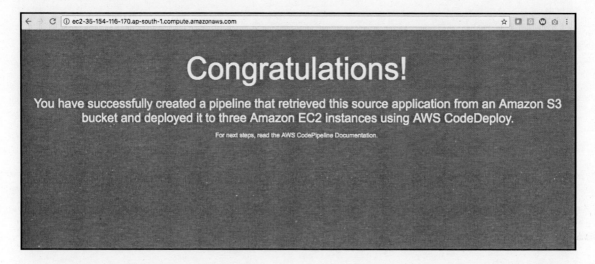

I have made a few changes in the code (modified the HTML file to display the output page content) and updated it in the S3 bucket. After updating the code in the S3 bucket, CodePipeline automatically starts pushing it from the S3 bucket and starts deployment on the autoscaling group:

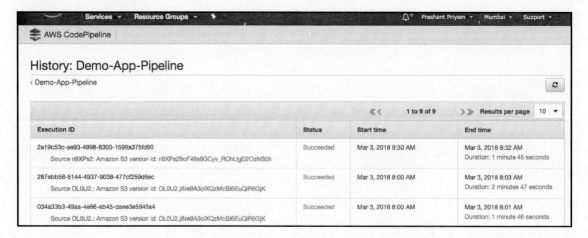

Now, let's access the application URL:

Here, we can see that the modification took place in the EC2 instances as well.

In this section, we have learned to automate the application deployment on the underlying infrastructure without any downtime and manual intervention. Whenever there are changes in the package at source (S3 bucket), CodePipeline will automatically deploy it in the EC2 instances. Automating this process has led to the following:

- **Rapid deployment**: Deploying code manually takes longer and a considerable amount of downtime if anything goes wrong.
- **Secure deployment for the application**: During manual deployment, we share the application code from one system to the other, which is also a security risk. During the complete process, we have seen that we had IAM roles, which control the access and management of resources.
- **Activity logging**: All the activity performed during deployment is logged in CloudTrail and the cloud pipeline history.
- **Version control**: In the S3 bucket, we have all the S3 code versions available. You can see all the versions of the code in the S3 bucket using the S3 console.

Monitoring

Monitoring plays a crucial role in automating security in the cloud environment. For monitoring in AWS, we use CloudWatch. Apart from this, we can also use open source tools, such as Nagios and Zabbix.

CloudWatch helps you define metrics and alerts for your workload running on AWS.

Apart from this, AWS has introduced Amazon Macie under security services, which gives you a very interactive dashboard for your AWS account. Amazon Macie uses machine learning methods to discover, classify, and protect your data:

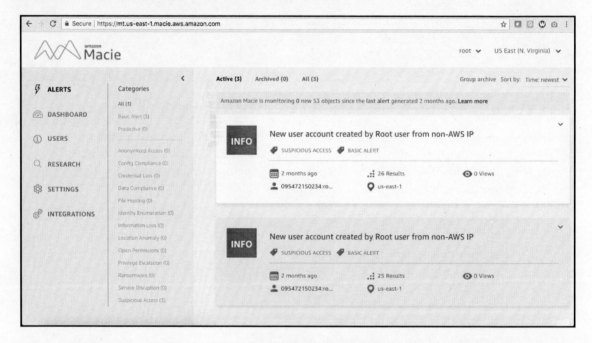

In the preceding screenshot, you can see the alerts recorded by Macie. In the backend, it scans through CloudTrail to generate the alerts and dashboards. It reads all the trails in real time and uses machine learning methods to generate the alerts:

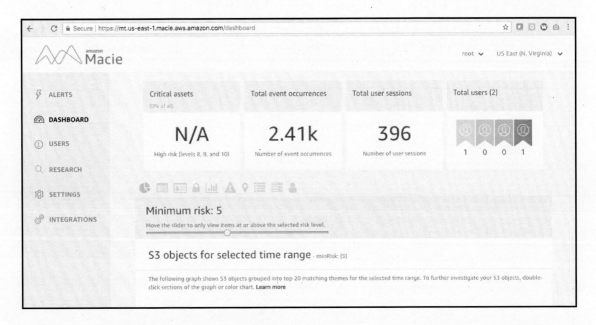

If you go to the **SETTINGS** section of Macie, it will show you the multiple settings that Macie uses to protect your monitored data:

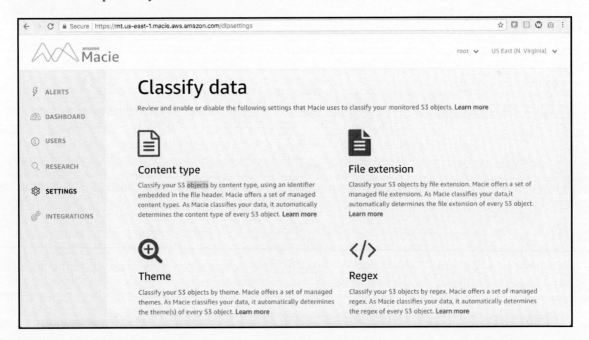

At the bottom, it has one option called **Basic alert**, where you can define the alerts for Macie to inform you about unexpected and potentially unauthorized or malicious activity within your infrastructure:

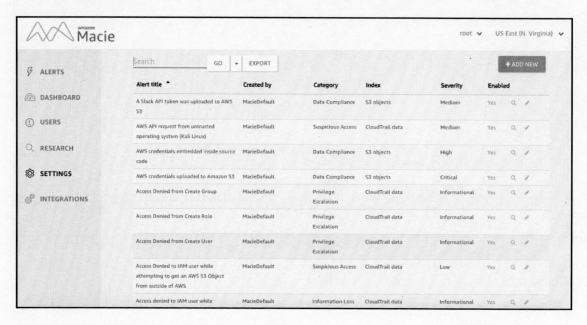

Summary

In this chapter, we looked at an example of automating the application and security deployment on the cloud. In the first section, we deployed a PHP application using CloudFormation, which uses AWS OpsWorks in the backend to configure the infrastructure and deploy applications.

Using CloudFormation, we created a complete Infrastructure as Code, which can be further used to modify the infrastructure with manual activity.

In the second section, we looked at an example where we create a pipeline to automate the code deployment process on the autoscaling group and all the API events are being recorded by CloudTrail. CodePipeline also provides the deployment history while the S3 bucket contains all the versions of the application package.

All resource access is managed by IAM roles. For security and monitoring, we saw Amazon Macie, which gives you a dashboard for all the critical events in your AWS infrastructure.

In the next chapter, we will learn about cloud compliance, and why it is necessary for organizations. We will look at AWS Cloud Compliance, and present a business case to design a solution for compliance, such as ISMS and PCI DSS.

9
Cloud Compliance

Welcome to the last chapter. Here, we will learn about different security compliances for the cloud and also learn how to make a solution compliant with ISMS and PCI DSS.

The following are the topics that we will cover in this chapter:

- Cloud security compliance
- Security compliance—ISMS
- Security compliance—PCI DSS

Cloud security compliance

Before getting into the details of cloud security compliance, let's understand what compliance is. The dictionary definition of **compliance** is meeting with a wish or command.

In the security world, *compliance* is a security blueprint for certain types of data that is defined by a standards public, non-profit organization.

The organization that owns the compliance defines it as a minimum bar of security. The enforcement of the points defined in the blueprint is applied through auditing.

An audit acts as a point-in-time image or snapshot that defines how the organization currently operates. After audit, organizations get recommendations on how to meet the standards defined in the compliance blueprint.

Once the organization meets all the standards defined in the compliance blueprint, it is given a certificate of compliance.

There are many standards organizations (such as NIST, CSA, ISO, PCI DSS, HIPAA, and FedRAMP) across the globe, which own compliances and also provide guidelines to reach the minimum security bar.

Many organizations need to adhere to the following compliances to ensure the security and safety of data:

- **PCI**: This stands for **Payment Card Industry** . PCI is a global organization, which maintains and promotes Payment Card Industry standards for the safety of cardholder data across the globe
- **NIST**: This stands for **National Institute of Standards and Technology**. It provides security recommendations for the IT environment too. Any organization can use the NIST guidelines for data security and become NIST compliant.
- **CSA**: This stands for **Cloud Security Alliance**. It provides the best practices for security assurance for the cloud environment.
- **ISO**: This stands for **International Standard Organization**, which also provides guidelines to ensure quality, security, and safety best practices. These best practices can be used by any organization.
- **HIPAA**: This stands for **Health Insurance Portability and Accountability Act**, which is defined by US law to provide privacy standards to protect all patient records and health-related information.
- **FedRAMP**: This stands for **Federal Risk and Authorization Management Program**. This compliance is specific to the US federal agencies, and is directed by the Office of Management and Budget to ensure security for cloud services.

Apart from the global ones, there are also many national and regional compliances available; for example, in the USA, Asia Pacific, and Europe, we have the following:

- **USA**:
    - **CJIS**: Criminal Justice Information Services
    - **DoD SRG**: DoD data processing
    - **FedRAMP**: Government Data Standards
    - **FERPA**: Educational Privacy Act
    - **FFIEC**: Financial Institutions Regulation
    - **FIPS**: Government security standards
    - **FISMA**: Federal Information Security Management
    - **GxP**: Quality guidelines and regulations
    - **HIPAA**: Protected health information
    - **ITAR**: International arms regulations

- **Asia Pacific:**
  - **FISC (Japan)**: Financial Industry Information Systems
  - **IRAP (Australia)**: Australian security standards
  - **K-ISMS (Korea)**: Korean Information Security
  - **MTCS Tier 3 (Singapore)**: Multi-Tier Cloud Security Standard
  - **My Number Act (Japan)**: Personal Information Protection
- **Europe:**
  - **C5 (Germany)**: Operational security attestation
  - **Cyber Essentials Plus (UK)**: Cyber threat protection
  - **G-Cloud (UK)**: UK government standards
  - **IT-Grundschutz (Germany)**: Baseline protection methodology

In cloud computing, we know that security is a shared-responsibility model, which we have seen in previous chapters. Cloud compliance can also be adhered to in shared responsibility. Here too, cloud providers provide you with the compliance reports for all the available services.

Being consumers, we use only compliant components to deploy applications.

So, we define a solution, including compliant services, and then deploy our application on it. During the design and deployment phases, we must cover all the aspects of security; like AWS, we concentrate on VPC-level security, network ACLs, security groups, logs management, monitoring, VM-level security, storage-level security, and the authentication and authorization process.

Now, to meet the standards set by any compliance, we must do the following:

- Use only the components that are already compliant with the specified compliance
- Once the solution is deployed, it must also be audited to be marked as compliant with the specified compliance

Now, we will take the example of the AWS Inspector (which helps you to check whether your VMs running on AWS comply with specific compliance or not). Here, we will deploy a WordPress application running in two tiers in autoscaling modes and use the AWS Inspector to verify the compliance check using the in-built template.

To use the AWS Inspector, log into the AWS Console, search for `Inspector`, and click on it:

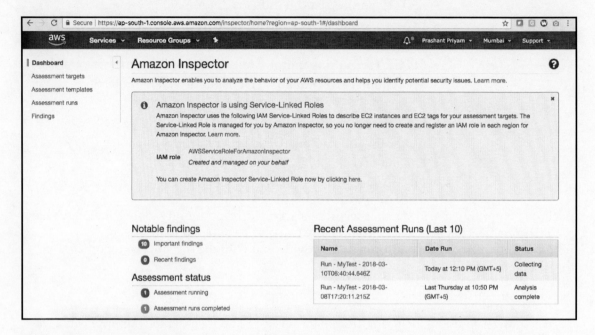

Now, click on **Assessment targets**, and specify the **Name** of the target and the **Tags**. Here, **Key** and **Value** are the same, which you have defined for your instances:

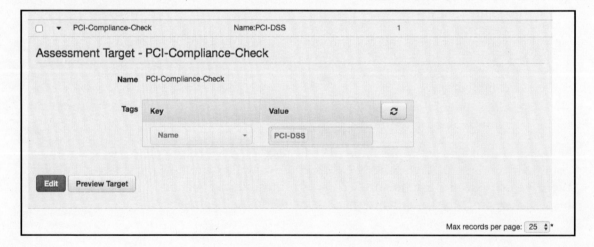

In the preceding screenshot, the **Value** tag is similar to the tag of EC2 instances:

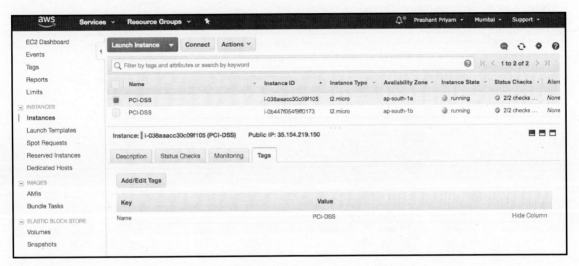

Now, to use the AWS Inspector, there must be an AWS Inspector agent installed on the target instances.

To install, we can use the following user data while creating the instances, or we can install it manually:

```
!#/bin/bash
sudo curl -O https://d1wk0tztpsntt1.cloudfront.net/linux/latest/install

sudo bash install -u false # Ensure automatic update off
```

Now, after creating the Inspector assessment target and installing Inspector agent, we will define the assessment template using the AWS Inspector console:

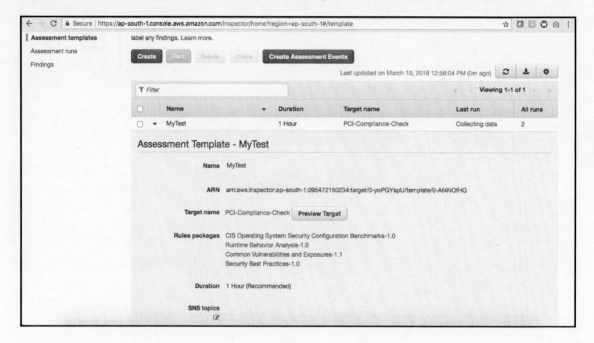

Now, after creating the assessment template, click on **Run**. It will run for one hour and give a list of recommendations:

For WordPress instances, the **Severity** levels are called **High**, **Medium**, **Low**, and **Informational**.

High-severity recommendations need to be fixed urgently to make the infrastructure safe and compliant.

Let's see some examples of category-wise recommendations for the WordPress application infrastructure:

- **High-level severity**: This needs to addressed urgently to mitigate the risk as this will have a direct impact on the application's infrastructure:
    - **Target name**: PCI-Compliance-Check
    - **Template name**: MyTest
    - **Start last**: Thursday at 10:50 PM (GMT+5) (2 days ago)
    - **End last**: Thursday at 11:52 PM (GMT+5) (2 days ago)
    - **Status**: Analysis complete
    - **Rules package**: Common Vulnerabilities and Exposures-1.1
    - **AWS agent ID**: i-03ea82d17dd65a17c
    - **Finding: Instance i-03ea82d17dd65a17c is vulnerable to CVE-2017-3145**

- **Severity**: **High**
- **Description**: A use-after-free flaw leading to denial of service was found in the way BIND internally handled cleanup operations on upstream recursion fetch contexts. A remote attacker could potentially use this flaw to make named, acting as a DNSSEC validating resolver, and exit unexpectedly with an assertion failure via a specially crafted DNS request.
- **Recommendation**: Use your OS's update feature to update package `bind-libs-32:9.9.4-51.amzn2`, `bind-libs-lite-32:9.9.4-51.amzn2`, `bind-license-32:9.9.4-51.amzn2`, `bind-utils-32:9.9.4-51.amzn2`. For more information, see `https://cve.mitre.org/cgi-bin/cvename.cgi?name=CVE-2017-3145`.

- **Medium-level severity**: This needs to be addressed with moderate priority, but do not keep it waiting for too long, as it will have a direct impact on the application's infrastructure:
    - **Run name**: `Run - MyTest - 2018-03-08T17:20:11.215Z`
    - **Target name**: `PCI-Compliance-Check`
    - **Template name**: `MyTest`
    - **Start last**: Thursday at 10:50 PM (GMT+5) (2 days ago)
    - **End last**: Thursday at 11:52 PM (GMT+5) (2 days ago)
    - **Status**: Analysis complete
    - **Rules**: package Common Vulnerabilities and Exposures-1.1
    - **AWS agent ID**: `i-03ea82d17dd65a17c`
    - **Finding: Instance i-03ea82d17dd65a17c is vulnerable to CVE-2018-1049**
    - **Severity**: **Medium**
    - **Description**: In systemd prior to 234 a race condition exists between `.mount` and `.automount` units such that automount requests from kernel may not be serviced by systemd resulting in kernel holding the mountpoint and any processes that try to use said mount will hang. A race condition like this may lead to denial of service, until mount points are unmounted.

- **Recommendation**: Use your OS's update feature to update package `systemd-0:219-42.amzn2.4`, `systemd-libs-0:219-42.amzn2.4`, `systemd-sysv-0:219-42.amzn2.4`. For more information see `https://cve.mitre.org/cgi-bin/cvename.cgi?name=CVE-2018-1049`.

- **Informational-level severity**: Here, the Inspector recommends that you modify the packages, ports, or applications to enhance security. For our WordPress application, we have the following informational recommendations:
  - **Run name**: `Run - MyTest - 2018-03-10T06:40:44.646Z`
  - **Target name**: `PCI-Compliance-Check`
  - **Template name**: `MyTest`
  - **Start**: Today at 12:10 PM (GMT+5) (an hour ago)
  - **End**: Today at 1:12 PM (GMT+5) (7 minutes ago)
  - **Status**: Complete with errors
  - **Rules**: package Runtime Behavior Analysis-1.0
  - **AWS agent ID**: `i-038aaacc30c09f105`
  - **Finding: Instance i-038aaacc30c09f105 is hosting insecure service protocol(s) 80/tcp (http)**
  - **Severity: Informational**
  - **Description**: This rule helps determine whether your EC2 instances are hosting insecure services, such as FTP, Telnet, HTTP, IMAP, POP version 3, SMTP, SNMP versions 1 and 2, rsh, and rlogin.
  - **Recommendation**: We recommend you disable insecure protocols in your assessment target and replace them with secure alternatives, such as in the following:
    - Disable Telnet, rsh, and rlogin and replace them with SSH. Where this is not possible, you should ensure that the insecure service is protected by appropriate network access controls, such as VPC network ACLs and EC2 security groups.
    - Replace FTP with SCP or SFTP where possible. Where this is not possible, you should ensure that the FTP server is protected by appropriate network access controls, such as VPC network ACLs and EC2 security groups.

- Replace HTTP with HTTPS where possible. For more information specific to the web server in question, see `http://nginx.org/en/docs/http/configuring_https_servers.html` and `https://httpd.apache.org/docs/2.4/ssl/ssl_howto.html`.
- Disable IMAP, POP3, and the SMTP services if not required. If required, it's recommended that these email protocols should be used with encrypted protocols, such as TLS.
- Disable SNMP service if it is not required. If required, replace SNMP v1, v2 with more secure SNMP v3, which uses encrypted communication.

The AWS Inspector also lets you download the report when the assessment runs completely using the Inspector Console:

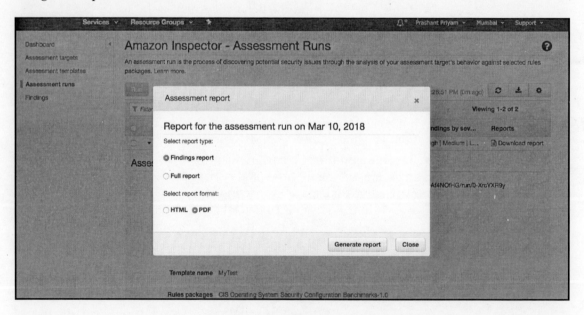

The full report contains all the details regarding the assessment run, including the findings as well.

For WordPress applications, we also have a few parameters where they are passed in the assessment template run test:

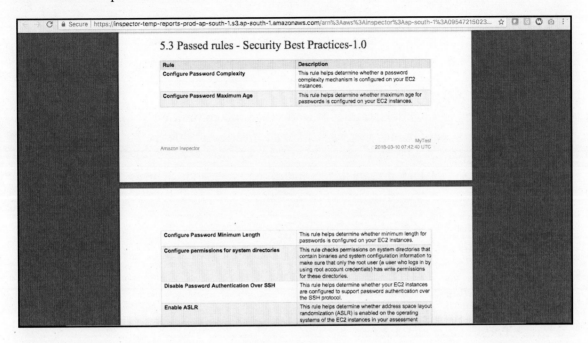

Security compliance – ISMS

ISMS stands for **Information Security Management System**. It is an approach to ensure and manage the security of an organization's information. ISMS applies the risk management process for the people, processes, and IT resources of an organization.

ISMS is defined for small, medium, and enterprise-scale organizations. It is recommended for organizations to have their ISMS in place to ensure the safety and security of data.

For this, there is the ISO 27001 , which defines the process for implementing, operating, managing, monitoring, and improving an organization's ISMS.

To become ISO 27001 compliant, an organization needs to comply with the following clauses:

- Organization context:
  - Focuses on understanding the overall organization context, needs, and interests
  - Defines the ISMS policy scope
- Leadership:
  - Understanding of leadership and commitment
  - Understanding of roles and responsibilities
- Planning:
  - Defining the ISMS objectives and plan to achieve
  - Defining risk management planning
- Support:
  - Understanding the need for resources and competencies
  - Creating awareness among employees about the policies and also defining the communication process
- Operation:
  - Information security and risk planning
- Performance monitoring:
  - Monitoring of information security controls, processes, and management systems
  - Systematically improving things

Apart from these mandatory clauses, there are a few mandatory control areas for IT, which are explained as follows:

- **Information security policy**: This contains a rule that is applicable for users, processes, and IT structures to mandatorily ensure that all data is stored in the digital medium or is being transferred using the digital medium. The information security policy is defined to:
  - Establish a general approach to information security

- Detect and prevent compromises of information security, such as misuse of data, networks, computer systems, and applications
- Protect an organization's reputation as per its ethical and legal responsibilities
- Observe customer rights and define a standard practice for compliance management and the query-handling process

- **Asset management**: This process helps an organization to manage IT systems more effectively, and saves time and money by avoiding unnecessary asset purchases and promoting the harvesting of existing resources. It also helps to minimize the incremental risks and costs of advancing IT portfolio infrastructure projects.
- **Cryptography**: This defines the method to secure confidential data from unauthorized access. It is mandatory for organizations who are going for ISO 27001 certification to ensure the encryption of all critical data at rest or in transit.
- **Physical and environmental security**: This defines the security method to prevent the risk of data theft, loss, or damages for physical or environmental forces, which can also affect organizational operations.
- **Operational security**: This explains how to ensure that all the operations are carried out in a secure fashion in an organization. This includes the following:
    - Operational procedures and responsibilities
    - Protection from virus and malware
    - Backup processes
    - Log management and monitoring
    - Vulnerabilities management
    - Control of operation software
- **Communication security**: This tells us that data transaction is taking place over a secure communication channel. This includes the following:
    - Network security
    - Data transfer security

- **System acquisition, development, and maintenance**: This section defines the security requirements of the information system, including the development, testing, and maintenance processes.

- **Information security incident management**: This includes the steps to be taken to prevent security incidents taking place, and what the steps will be for further improvement.

After going through the clauses and controls of ISO 27001, we have got an idea of what must be taken into consideration to make solutions ISO 27001 compliant.

Now, let's take an example. Suppose we have a **knowledge management portal (KM Portal)**, which is developed with LAMP technology. Here, **LAMP** stands for **Linux, Apache, MySQL, and PHP**. This KM Portal will be used by internal users (that is, the organization's employees only) to store all the important files, business cases, and other important documents. The user base of this application is spread across the globe. Our organization is ISO 27001 compliant, so we need to ensure that our KM Portal application is also ISO 27001 compliant.

Now, let's plan this application deployment on AWS. Let's start planning for component selection, keeping the ISO 27001 controls in mind.

For this solution, we will use the following AWS services, which are already ISO 27001 compliant:

- EC2, EBS, ALB, and autoscaling groups
- VPC, VPN, NACL, security groups, and CloudFront
- S3
- AWS RDS MySQL (multiAz) and ElastiCache (Redis)
- CloudWatch and CloudTrail
- KMS and Route 53
- WAF

The following diagram shows a logical solution design:

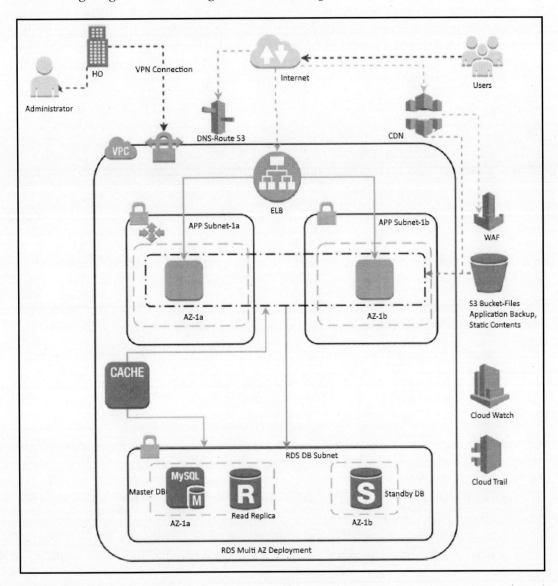

In the preceding solution design, we have considered deploying the solution in a two-tier architecture, where a web server (EC2 instance) is running the DMZ zone. The web server will be running two different availability zones under an application load balancer. Scaling for each web tier is maintained by the autoscaling group. This will scale out once you have aggregated the CPU load on the web servers to more than 70%, and it will scale in once the load on the CPU comes to 30%.

For our database, we have the RDS service, which will also run in a multiAZ environment in a private subnet. To scale out the RDS service, we have an RDS replica. For patch management, RDS instances will access the internet by using the NAT gateway.

Furthermore, to enhance the read-only query and data, we are using ElastiCache.

All the static content of the data will be stored in the S3 bucket. To make this available across the globe with low latency, we have used CloudFront CDN. For Layer 7 security, we have used WAF.

The KM Portal application will be mapped with a public domain, which will be hosted in Route 53.

For management and monitoring purposes, we have a site-to-site VPN connection so that system administrators can control and access resources on the security VPN channel.

Furthermore, AWS KMS-defined certificates will be offloaded to ELB to ensure KM Portal accessibility using the HTTPS protocol.

To ensure the security of data, we will have to consider the following while deploying the solutions:

- VPC must have six subnets, where two subnets will be in the DMZ. For the DMZ subnets, we need to allow only incoming traffic on port 443 and port 22 in the security groups
- For the DB subnet, we must allow only incoming traffic on port 3306 from the web security groups
- Similarly, we need to define incoming and outgoing traffic for ElastiCache
- On the web server, we must enable volume encryption for the security of data at rest
- To access S3-stored objects, we must define an IAM policy for EC2, which will be mapped with each instance
- To provision EC2 instances, we must ensure that all the instances are installed with the AWS Inspector agent

- For the database, we must ensure that backing up is enabled and that encryption is enabled
- For the S3 bucket also, we must enable encryption if the bucket stores any critical data
- We must map the CDN with either S3 as the origin, if you have much static content in the S3 bucket, or you can also map your load balancer as the origin
- Now, coming to WAF, define all the rules against which the traffic will be scanned
- Enable VPC flow logs, S3 access logs, CDN accessibility logs, ELB logs, and store them in the S3 bucket, which is encrypted and only accessible to defined-security users
- Define the CloudWatch dashboard and matrices for all the components for monitoring

Now, deploy the application on our web servers and run the AWS Inspector assessment.

After running the Inspector, you will get the complete audit document and start working on all the critical- and moderate-level severities.

In the testing process, select a group of users, hand over the application to them, and start monitoring the WAF events and CloudTrail events.

Before moving the application to production, it is also recommended to go for **Vulnerability Assessment and Penetration Testing** (**VAPT**). After completing the VAPT process, address all the recommendations.

Now, you will be wondering how we addressed all the recommendations required by ISO 27001.

Let's see all the specified controls one by one:

- To comply with ISMS policy, the application must have IAM roles. If the organization is to have its own identity provider, such as AD, this can also be integrated with the application (if the application allows) as the identity provider. For more security, we can use MFA or two-factor authentication.
- For asset management in AWS, we will not over provision and in case the usage goes high, you have autoscaling to take care of that. So here, this will not affect the application's availability.
- For cryptography, we have enabled encryption at all the levels to ensure data-at-rest security.

- For physical and environmental security, we are using only those AWS services that are already compliant with ISMS. As we know, cloud security is a shared responsibility model. So here, physical and environmental security goes into the account of AWS. AWS provides an ISO 27001 certificate and audit details for all the compliant services.
- We can address operational security as follows:
  - Site-to-site VPN to give encrypted medium to access the resources for management purposes.
  - The backup schedule is defined for both the database and application.
  - CloudTrail and CloudWatch dashboards are defined for log management and monitoring. Apart from that, we are storing logs in an S3 bucket, which is enabled with encryption and has grants to the security person.
  - The AWS Inspector will list all the vulnerabilities of the web servers, and finally, the VAPT process will take care of those vulnerabilities.
- For communication security, we have defined encryption for data in transit as well, as all the web traffic will come via HTTPS. The S3 bucket will also ensure data-in-transit encryption. CloudFront will also access traffic via HTTPS only. The VPN tunnel provides an encrypted communication channel for management purposes. WAF is running on top of CloudFront to scan each and every request, and block if any request does not match the WAF rules.
- For incident management, we need to review the CloudTrail events, CloudWatch logs, and WAF events, and take action accordingly. Any issue related to performance and user experience should be managed by an internal support management system.

Security compliance – PCI DSS

PCI DSS is a security standard that is administered by the PCI Security Standards Council. PCI DSS exists to ensure the security of cardholder data from fraud.

PCI DSS is applicable for all organizations where customer credit card information is stored, processed, and transferred for transaction.

Payment Application Data Security Standard (PA-DSS) was developed and being maintained by the **Payment Card Industry Security Standards Council (PCI SSC)**.

PCI serves all those who deal with and are associated with payment cards. This includes merchants of all sizes, financial institutions, and software developers who create and operate the global infrastructure for processing payments.

For PCI, the following are the two priorities:

- Helping merchants and financial institutions to understand and implement standards for security policies, technologies, and also define ongoing processes that protect their payment systems from breaches and theft of cardholder data
- Helping vendors to understand and implement standards for creating secure payment solutions

Now, the question is, why does anyone need to be PCI DSS compliant? Here, we can say that cardholder data theft affects the PCI globally. Due to theft, the customer loses their trust in merchants or financial institutions, and as a result, their credit can be negatively affected.

Merchants and financial institutions lose their credibility, which results in business loss, and they are also subject to numerous financial liabilities.

Potential liabilities for PCI, if not securing cardholders data, can be:

- Loss of customer confidence, causing customers to go to other merchants
- Diminished sales
- Costs of reissuing new payment cards
- Fraud losses
- Higher subsequent costs of compliance
- Legal costs, settlements, and judgments
- Fines and penalties
- Termination of ability to accept payment cards
- Loss of jobs (CISO, CIO, CEO, and dependent professional positions)
- Going out of business

PCI DSS have a specific set of requirements that it is necessary to meet for the purpose of best security practices:

- Build and maintain a secure network:
    - Install and maintain a firewall configuration to protect cardholder data
    - Do not use vendor-supplied defaults for system passwords and other security parameters

- Protect cardholder data:
    - Protect stored cardholder data
    - Encrypt transmission of cardholder data across open and public networks
- Maintain a vulnerability-management program:
    - Use and regularly update anti-virus software
    - Develop and maintain secure systems and applications
- Implement strong access control measures:
    - Restrict access to cardholder data by businesses on a need-to-know basis
    - Assign a unique ID to each person with computer access
    - Restrict physical access to cardholder data
- Regularly monitor and test networks:
    - Track and monitor all access to network resources and cardholder data
    - Regularly test security systems and processes
- Maintain an information security policy:
    - Maintain a policy that addresses information security

Apart from this, PCI also defines the PTS requirement, where **PTS** stands for **PCI PIN Transaction Security**. The PTS requirement is focused on the characteristics and management of devices used in the protection of cardholder PINs and other payment processing-related activities.

For the PTS, we must follow the industry-tested standards, which are as follows:

- Use only approved PIN entry devices at points of sale
- Use only validated payment software at your points of sale or online shopping cart
- Do not store any sensitive cardholder data in computers or on paper
- Use a firewall in your network and PCs
- Ensure the wireless router is password-protected and uses encryption
- Use strong passwords
- Regularly check PIN entry devices and PCs to make sure no one has installed rogue software or skimming devices
- Educate employees about security and protecting cardholder data
- Follow the PCI DSS

Implementation of PCI DSS starts with scoping. This process includes identifying all system components that are located within or connected to the cardholder data environment, where an environment includes people, processes, and technologies that handle cardholder data or sensitive authentication data.

For assessment, there is a Qualified Security Assessor, which is a data security firm that is qualified by the PCI Council to perform on-site PCI DSS assessments.

The Qualified Security Assessor will:

- Verify all technical information given by a merchant or service provider
- Use independent judgment to confirm that the standard has been met
- Provide support and guidance during the compliance process
- Be on site for the duration of the assessment
- Adhere to the PCI DSS assessment procedures
- Validate the scope of the assessment
- Evaluate compensating controls
- Produce the final Report on Compliance

Now, let's see an example of deploying a solution in a PCI DSS compliant environment.

Scenario: XYZ corporation wants to deploy an in-house-developed application that will be responsible for online transactions and storing customer information, including credit card information. Their application is already developed in accordance with the PCI DSS compliance, but it must be deployed in a PCI DSS-compliant environment, so that they can get a PCI DSS compliance certificate.

Planning: Now, as we have the necessary information about the application and compliance requirements, we must design a solution using only those components that are already compliant with PCI DSS. The solution also must match the other aspect requirements in terms of scalability, performance efficiency, cost, and operational excellence.

The following is the solution design:

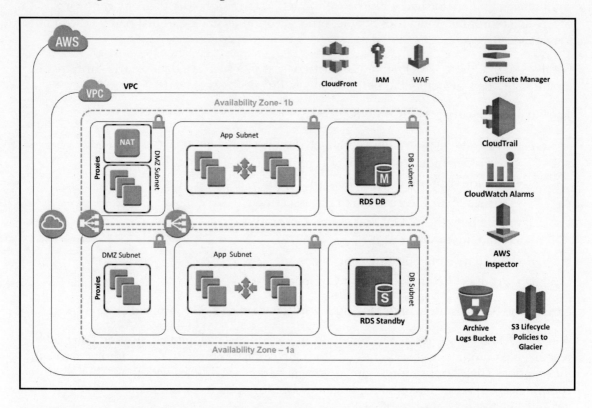

In the preceding design, there is depicted the required set of components and their connectivity inside VPC. There are a few components that are outside the VPC scope, such as IAM, CDN, WAF over CDN, Inspector, Certificate Manager, the S3 bucket, and Glacier, which are kept outside the VPC boundary.

The preceding solution has been designed after evaluating all the requirement inputs regarding the application and compliance requirements. We will discuss a complete solution as to how it matches the PCI DSS compliance and also all the aspects of the standard solution design framework.

Component description: In the preceding solution, we have used the following components:

- **VPC**: It provides you with an isolated logical network boundary. It helps you to create a virtual network, inside which you can create the AWS services. Here, you define subnets, security groups, NACLs, and route tables. VPC also allows you to have complete ownership of your virtual network.

- **AZs**: In the preceding solution design, we have two availability zones. AWS AZs depict two different data centers that are far from each other.
- **Subnets**: We have divided VPC into six subnets, where each availability zone has three subnets:
    - **DMZ**: In DMZ subnets, we are running a proxy server, which is being load balanced by a load balancer (AWS ELB) and a NAT gateway.
    - **Application subnet**: Here, we have an autoscaling group, wherein we have the web servers running the application. The autoscaling group is defined with a scale-in and scale-out policy on the basis of CPU utilization of instances.
    - **DB subnet**: This is running an AWS RDS workload, which is also configured in the multiAZ environment for fault tolerance at the DB level.
- **NACL**: At each level, we have defined the NACL. The NACL is stateless in nature, and here, we have defined rules for inbound and outbound traffic.
- **Security groups**: For each workload, we have defined security groups, which run at the instance level. It's stateful in nature and, here too, we have defined inbound and outbound rules for network traffic.
- **Internet gateway**: This is an AWS networking component that provides internet connectivity to public/DMZ subnets.
- **NAT gateway**: This is also a network component that provides internet connectivity to private subnet instances.
- **RDS**: This stands for **Relational Database Service**, which is a PaaS provided by AWS. Here, RDS is also running in a multizone environment to provide you with a fault-tolerant environment at the DB level. When the master database goes down due to some reason, a standby replica automatically gets promoted to master.
- **CloudFront**: This is a content delivery network that works on the cache concept. CloudFront actually caches all your content from the origin (which can be the S3 bucket or ELB) and stores it to edge locations in specified regions.
- **WAF**: This stands for **Web Application Firewall**, and it provides Layer 7 protection to your application using a defined set of rules for SQL injection, cross-site scripting, common attack patterns, geo-location restriction, and more.
- **IAM**: This stands for **Identity and Access Management**. We use IAM to define rules and policies for accessing AWS resources. In the preceding solution, we have used IAM roles and policies for EC2 instances to access the S3 bucket, logs, and more.

- **Certificate Manager**: This allows you to store your own certificate or generate certificates for your domain, which can be used for data-in-transit security.
- **AWS KMS**: This helps you to store and manage encryption keys, which are used to encrypt your data. It uses HSMs to protect the security of your keys.
- **AWS Inspector**: We use the AWS Inspector to identify the vulnerabilities of EC2 instances. As seen earlier, the AWS Inspector provides you with a complete report after assessment of the basis of severity. To ensure the security of the environment, we must address these points.
- **CloudTrail**: This is responsible for recording all the API events in your AWS account and stores the logs in the S3 bucket.
- **S3**: This is an object storage, which provides you with unlimited scalability and durability of data. We use S3 to store static content of an application, as well as different log files.
- **Glacier**: This is a low-cost, durable, and secure archive storage vault, which we use to transfer logs or data as per the defined S3 lifetime policy.
- **CloudWatch**: We use CloudWatch to monitor our cloud infrastructure, define events, and alert for services, as well as to store logs, such as RDS logs and VPC flow logs.

 All the services we have selected for this solution are PCI compliance certified. For more details about PCI-certified AWS services, you can visit the following URL:
https://aws.amazon.com/compliance/services-in-scope/.

In this chapter, we have learned about the PCI DSS compliance requirements in terms of security.

So now, let's see how we have defined the security in this solution:

- At VPC level:
  - We have created six subnets for the DMZ, application, and database.
  - Each subnet is associated with NACL, which allows incoming traffic on specific ports from valid sources, such as proxy subnet, which is letting in all the traffic coming on port 443 and passing this traffic to the application subnet on port 443. This means all other incoming traffic is blocked by NACL. Similarly, NACL at database only allows application subnet traffic on specific database ports; in our case, 3306.

- Each EC2 instance is associated with security groups. Here, we have defined three security groups for DMZ, application, and database. The DMZ security group allows incoming traffic on port 443 and outgoing traffic on 443 to application security group. Similarly, we had defined security group inbound and outbound policies for the application and database security groups.
- Route tables are very specifically defined as per requirements.
- VPC logs are enabled and are being stored in CloudWatch logs. This gives you a complete insight into network traffic.

- At EC2 instance level:
    - Each component is running in a high availability and scalable environment
    - For data at rest, we have defined encryption on volume, and for data in transit, we have ensured that all communication happens on a security channel
    - All the EC2 instances are configured with specific EC2 roles to consume other AWS services
    - All the application logs are being stored in the S3 bucket

- At RDS level:
    - We have enabled database encryption, and accept only connections from security clients
    - Automatic database backup is defined and scheduled

- At S3:
    - All the buckets are defined with a bucket policy
    - Versioning is enabled
    - Server-side data encryption is also enabled

- At CloudFront:
    - There is use of field-level encryption
    - There is restricted access to objects using a signed URL
    - There is HTTPS-based communication
    - Access logs are defined and stored in the S3 bucket
    - CloudWatch monitoring is enabled

- At WAF:
    - We define rules for cross-site scripting
    - We define rules for SQL injection
    - We block/allow traffic on the basis of geo location
    - There is a condition for string matches
- At Glacier:
    - We define the vault lock policy
    - We enable encryption using AES
- At CloudWatch:
    - A service dashboard is created and permission is given to a specific set of users to modify it
    - We define alerts for all the services

Now, let's review our solution to meet the PCI DSS-specified requirement sets:

- **Build and maintain a secure network**: In the current solution, we have the following services to meet this requirement of PCI:
    - AWS VPC
    - Security groups
    - NACL
- **Do not use vendor-supplied defaults for system passwords and other security parameters**: For this, we have EC2 access keys, which are uniquely defined while creating EC2 instances and these keys also ensure the hardening of EC2 instances using the AWS Inspector.
- **Protect cardholder data**: To protect cardholder data, we have defined data-at-rest and data-in-transit security options in the complete solution using the following:
    - KMS
    - S3 SSE
    - EC2 volume encryption
    - DB encryption
- **Maintain a vulnerability management program**: For this section, we have the AWS Inspector, which helps to identify and address all the vulnerabilities for EC2 instances. For our application, we have WAF and CDN to ensure safe access to the application.

- **Implement strong access control measures**: For this, we are utilizing IAM roles and policies to access the AWS service, which also removes the risk of exposing credentials. We defined IAM roles for EC2 to grant access to S3 buckets. The AWS **Attestation of Compliance (AOC)** ensures the physical security of the infrastructure.
- **Regularly monitor and test networks**: For this, we have defined CloudTrail and CloudWatch. CloudTrail records all the events and stores them in the S3 bucket, while CloudWatch stores VPC flow logs, where you can analyze complete network traffic.
- **Maintain an information security policy**: If XYZ corporation already has predefined security policies, AWS does not need to provide any security policies; the customer needs to define it according to the organization policy.

Apart from this, there are a few things that AWS will take care of, such as hardware decommissioning and storage data erasure. For the PaaS, AWS will take care of security patch deployment and management.

So, all transaction and communication between components happens through secure and encrypted channels that we have defined.

Now, after deploying this solution, we can roll out the application and database back up. It is also recommended to go for VAPT auditing.

If there are any recommendations, we need to address all of them in the current solution and invite the security team to have an audit of PCI DSS.

 To meet any security standard and compliance, we must make sure that the infrastructure as well as the applications are meeting the requirements of the compliance.

In the current case, the XYZ corporation should deploy their application in the preceding suggested infrastructure, as it is ready for PCI-DSS audit.

Quick recap

Compliance is a security blueprint for certain types of data, which is defined by a standards organization that is public and non profit. It provides us with the guidelines on the basis of which we define the security for our infrastructure.

Security compliance ensures the following:

- **Smooth business operation**: In becoming compliant with any security compliance, we ensure that all the recommendations of specific compliances are addressed and that standard processes are adopted. This helps us to run smooth business operations.
- **Reputation management**: Security compliance also defines the standard of the product or service. It helps to build trust among customers. As we have seen, an organization needs to ensure the safety of customers credit card data, but how would the customer know that their data is secure? For this, they need to check whether that portal and organization is PCI certified or not.

There are multiple compliance policies available, which are defined and owned by different regulatory authorities. Each security compliance has its own recommendations for data security, operations, and processes. Every security compliance has its own target audience, such as ISMS being for all small, medium, and enterprise-scale businesses; PCI DSS being for the payment gateway industry or any organization that deals in payment transaction and stores credit card information; and HIPAA being for the health insurance industry.

In this chapter, we also learned about on-premises infrastructures, where we need to make our solution compliant with specific compliance policies as per the nature of the organization and application.

We have also looked in detail at an AWS service called the AWS Inspector, which helps you to do vulnerability assessments for your EC2 instances. After assessment, it provides you with the audit report based on recommendations and risk severity, which is necessary for implementing security hardening of EC2 instances.

In the cloud, as we know, security is a shared responsibility model, so here, compliance is also a shared responsibility. All cloud providers, including AWS, have services certified with against compliance. So, while deploying a solution in AWS, we must select only those components that are certified with specific compliance. As with PCI DSS compliance-based solutions, we should opt for only those AWS services, that are already certified as meeting PCI DSS compliance.

We have also learned about ISMS and its recommendations in terms of security. They are as follows:

- Information security policy
- Asset management
- Cryptography
- Operational security

- Communication security
- System acquisition, development, and maintenance
- Information security incident management

After this, we saw an example where we deployed a solution on AWS, which is ISMS compliant.

After ISMS, we learned about PCI DSS compliance, which is mandatory for the payment gateway industry.

In PCI DSS, we learned about the security recommendations, which must be followed when defining a solution to make PCI DSS compliant.

After that, we also saw an example where we defined a solution for XYZ corporation using AWS, which is PCI DSS compliant. As per the well-architected frameworks, all solutions must be:

- Scalable
- Performance efficient
- Cost effective
- Operationally excellent

Summary

In this chapter, we have learned about security compliance and why security compliance is necessary for any organization. As this is the last chapter of the book, I am sure you have enjoyed reading the book and taken enough away about the different aspects of cloud security automation.

Other Books You May Enjoy

If you enjoyed this book, you may be interested in these other books by Packt:

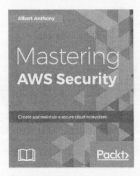

Mastering AWS Security
Albert Anthony

ISBN: 978-1-78829-372-3

- Learn about AWS Identity Management and Access control
- Gain knowledge to create and secure your private network in AWS
- Understand and secure your infrastructure in AWS
- Understand monitoring, logging and auditing in AWS
- Ensure Data Security in AWS
- Learn to secure your applications in AWS
- Explore AWS Security best practices

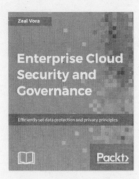

Enterprise Cloud Security and Governance
Zeal Vora

ISBN: 978-1-78829-955-8

- Configure your firewall and Network ACL
- Protect your system against DDOS and application-level attacks
- Explore cryptography and data security for your cloud
- Get to grips with configuration management tools to automate your security tasks
- Perform vulnerability scanning with the help of the standard tools in the industry
- Learn about central log management

Leave a review - let other readers know what you think

Please share your thoughts on this book with others by leaving a review on the site that you bought it from. If you purchased the book from Amazon, please leave us an honest review on this book's Amazon page. This is vital so that other potential readers can see and use your unbiased opinion to make purchasing decisions, we can understand what our customers think about our products, and our authors can see your feedback on the title that they have worked with Packt to create. It will only take a few minutes of your time, but is valuable to other potential customers, our authors, and Packt. Thank you!

Index

G

Glacier
  about 131, 161
  security 162
Glance 221
group 20

H

hardware infection 204
hash-based message authentication codes
  (HMACs) 83
Health Insurance Portability and Accountability Act
  (HIPAA) 284
high availability (HA) 13, 180
Horizon
  about 214, 217
  security 218
HTTP Strict Transport Security (HSTS) 219
hypervisor level 26
hypervisor threat 205
hypervisor
  compute, securing 207
  ESXi, securing 206
  KVM, securing 204
  requisites 202
  securing 202, 204
  XenServer, securing 206

I

Identity and Access Management (IAM)
  about 13, 57, 208, 305
  authentication 208
  authentication methods 209
  authorization 211
  AWS, working 59
  best practices 71
  cross-account access 69
  domains 212
  elements 59
  features 58
  Federated identity 213
  groups 62
  identity federation 70
  policies 67

  policy 212
  roles 63
  temporary credentials 69
  tokens 212
  used, for accessing delegation 69
  users 60
image 190
Information Security Management System (ISMS)
  293, 300
Infrastructure as a Service (IaaS) 9, 173
Infrastructure as Code
  about 35, 40, 245, 246, 249, 259, 262, 264,
  266, 268
  configuration management 42, 45, 47, 50
infrastructure level 19
Input Output Memory Management Unit (IOMMU)
  204
International Standard Organization (ISO) 284
Internet of Things (IoT) 15

J

JavaScript Object Notation (JSON) 36

K

Key Management Service (KMS) 21, 65, 144, 182
Keystone 208
Keystone Service 213
Kinesis 132
knowledge management portal (KM Portal) 296
KVM
  securing 204

M

management 246
mandatory access control (MAC) 205
Manila 222
measured launch environment (MLE) 206
message queue
  about 232, 234
monitoring 246, 278, 280
multi-factor authentication (MFA) 14, 57

N

NACL 102
National Institute of Standards and Technology
    (NIST) 284
natural language processing (NLP) 90
network level 26
network security 99
networking
    best practices 101
Neutron 224
New Relic 15
nova conductor 235

O

object storage 21
Online Certificate Status Protocol (OCSP) 129
OpenStack block storage
    Cinder 220
OpenStack dashboard service
    Horizon 214, 217
OpenStack image storage
    Glance 221
OpenStack network
    API 224
    DHCP agent 224
    external 224
    guest 224
    management 224
    Neutron 224
    neutron L3-agent 224
    neutron server 224
    operation-based policy 226
    plugin agent 224
    resource-based policy 226
    SDN 224
OpenStack object storage
    Swift 229
OpenStack Security Portal
    URL 207
OpenStack shared file storage
    Manila 222
OpenWeb Application Security Project (OWASP)
    236
operating expenditures (OpEx) 7

Orchestration Layer 10
Origin Access Identity (OAI) 128

P

Payment Application Data Security Standard (PA-
    DSS) 300
Payment Card Industry (PCI) 284
Payment Card Industry Data Security Standards
    (PCI DSS)
    about 58, 300
    component 304
Payment Card Industry Security Standards Council
    (PCI SSC) 300
PCI PIN Transaction Security (PTS) 302
persistent 139
personally identifiable information (PII) 90
policies 212
private cloud 201
protected health information (PHI) 90

R

read replica 174
redundant array of independent disk (RAID)
    about 140
    RAID 0 141
    RAID 1 141
Relational Database Service (RDS)
    about 9, 173, 174, 305
    database connections, encrypting with SSL 177,
        179, 180
    database, backing up 181
    database, restoring 181
    IAM, using 176
    monitoring 181
    multi AZ 174
    security 175
    security best practices 180
    security groups, using 175
    Single Availability Zone 174
replication process 230
requisites, DevOps
    CI 33
    collaboration 35
    communication 35

volume gateway 165
storage level 26
Swift 229

T

token
  about 212
  fernet 213
  PKI 212
  PKIZ 212
  UUID 212
Transparent Data Encryption (TDE) 179
Transport Layer Security (TLS) 208
Trusted Execution Technology (TXT) 206
Trusted Platform Module (TPM) 204

U

User Datagram Protocol (UDP) 82
user level 27
users 20

V

version control 246
virtual interfaces (VIFs) 112
virtual machine threat 205
virtual private cloud (VPC)
  about 15, 100
  NACL 102
  security group 105, 107
virtual private gateway (VGW) 101
Virtualization Layer 10
VM level 27
VMware ESXi

options 206
securing 206
volume storage 21
VPN connection
  about 109, 135
  AWS-managed VPN connection 109
  hub 110
  third-party VPN appliance 110
  transit VPC 110
Vulnerability Assessment and Penetration Testing
    (VAPT) 299

W

web application firewall (WAF)
  about 22, 76, 97, 305
  conditions 82
  rules 82
WordPress application infrastructure
  high-level severity 289
  informational-level severity 291
  medium-level severity 290

X

X-Account-Access-Control 231
X-Container-Read 231
X-Container-Write 231
Xen Security Model (XSM) 206
XenServer
  about 206
  securing 206

Y

Yet Another Markup Language (YAML) 36